The Simple Diabetic
Cookbook for Beginners

1600 Days Super Easy, Low-Carb & Affordable Recipes for Adapting to Type 2 Diabetes Newly Diagnosed While Keeping the Food Tasty Incl. 30 Days Meal Plan

D1736578

Ralph B. Goulding

Warning-Disclaimer

The purpose of this book is to educate and entertain. The author or publisher does not guarantee that anyone following the techniques, suggestions, tips, ideas, or strategies will become successful. The author and publisher shall have neither liability or responsibility to anyone with respect to any loss or damage caused, or alleged to be caused, directly or indirectly by the information contained in this book.

Table of Contents

INTRODUCTION

Do you struggle with maintaining a healthy lifestyle? Have you recently been diagnosed with diabetes? Does your fast-paced life make it difficult to stick to a diet plan? Look no further than this cookbook – it's one of the best resources available to you today.

This cookbook is tailored specifically to those who are new to the diabetes meal plan. Being diagnosed with diabetes can be frustrating, as it requires strict dietary control. However, following a well-planned diet can be exhausting and often results in people giving up midway through. This is particularly true for beginners who try to follow the diet plan without proper guidance. Additionally, the fast-paced lifestyle of many people makes it difficult to maintain the necessary precautions.

This book aims to help beginners by providing them with healthy recipes for the diabetes meal plan. The recipes are carefully crafted to ensure that they meet the unique dietary needs and taste preferences of those with diabetes. The book provides a self-explanatory pattern that helps readers adapt to the necessary changes in their diet. The recipes are simple and take into account the availability of ingredients and the level of preparedness of a beginner.

Every recipe includes a nutrient chart to help readers understand the nutritional content of their food. The book is written in plain language, avoiding the use of technical jargon or medical terminology. The recipes are easy to make and are designed to prevent monotony. Most importantly, they are designed to satisfy the reader's taste preferences while following the meal plan.

This book is the result of a team effort by leading nutritionists, food researchers, and market analysts who share a vision for healthy living. The step-by-step plan in the book helps readers understand the recipes in detail. The carefully selected recipes provide flexibility to the program, enabling readers to adapt to the rigidity of the meal plan.

Chapter 1 Things You Need to Know About Diabetes

What is Diabetes?

Diabetes is a complex condition that affects millions of people worldwide. It is a chronic disease that occurs when the body is unable to use glucose (sugar) properly. Glucose is a vital source of energy for the body, and insulin, a hormone produced by the pancreas, helps regulate the amount of glucose in the bloodstream.

When we eat food, it is broken down into glucose, which then enters the bloodstream. Insulin is released by the pancreas, which helps to transport the glucose from the bloodstream into the cells of the body where it is used for energy. However, in people with diabetes, the insulin production and/or its effectiveness is compromised, leading to high levels of glucose in the bloodstream.

Diabetes can lead to a wide range of complications if left untreated, including nerve damage, kidney disease, blindness, and cardiovascular disease. Therefore, it is essential to take care of your diabetes by following a healthy diet, getting regular exercise, taking prescribed medications, and monitoring your blood glucose levels.

Types of diabetes

There are three main types of diabetes which are Type 1 diabetes where the pancreas is unable to produce sufficient insulin, Type 2 diabetes where cells do not respond properly to insulin, and Gestational diabetes where pregnant women with a history of diabetes develop high blood sugar levels.

◊ Type 1 Diabetes. Type 1 diabetes typically affects individuals under the age of 30, especially children and young adults. It is an autoimmune disorder in which the immune system attacks and destroys the beta cells in the pancreas responsible for producing insulin. Common symptoms, such as frequent urination, significant weight loss, and excessive thirst, usually indicate the onset of type 1 diabetes. People with type 1 diabetes are dependent on daily insulin injections to sustain their lives.

◊ Type 2 Diabetes. Type 2 diabetes affects approximately 90% of people with diabetes. Although it generally develops in adults who are over 40 years old, it is increasingly being diagnosed in younger people, including teenagers and children. This type of diabetes occurs when the cells in the body do not effectively respond to the action of insulin, which leads to inadequate absorption of glucose into the cells. This condition is known as insulin resistance. As a result, the insulin-producing cells in the pancreas eventually become exhausted, partly because they work excessively to counteract the body's insulin resistance.

◊ Gestational Diabetes. During pregnancy, some women develop a condition known as gestational diabetes. This happens when hormonal changes during pregnancy cause the body to require more insulin than it can produce or use efficiently. Typically, this affects 3 to 5 percent of pregnant women and usually develops during the second or third trimester, around 24 to 28 weeks. Although gestational diabetes typically goes away after childbirth, women who have had it are at a higher risk of developing type 2 diabetes later in life.

The prevalence of diabetes in the United States

Over 25 million Americans are affected by diabetes, which accounts for more than 8.3 percent of the population. Shockingly, one-third of those individuals are unaware that they have the condition, while another third has prediabetes, a condition that occurs when blood glucose levels are higher than normal but not high enough to be classified as diabetes. If left untreated, prediabetes can progress into diabetes. Losing weight and exercising regularly are effective measures to prevent prediabetes from developing into diabetes, especially for those who are overweight. Medications are also available to prevent the onset of diabetes, and a health-care provider can discuss the options available. The increase in diabetes is largely attributed to the surge in obesity rates caused by diets high in fat and calories and a lack of physical activity. This trend is not only happening in the United States, but also globally. As people become more affluent, their dietary habits change, and they become less active, leading to a surge in diabetes rates. The World Health Organization estimates that the number of people with diabetes worldwide will reach 300 million by 2025. Despite these staggering numbers, diabetes can be managed through a combination of building a healthcare team, balancing food intake with exercise and medication, if necessary, and taking care of mental health.

Risks Associated with Diabetes

Receiving a diabetes diagnosis can be a daunting experience, particularly when it is a first-time diagnosis. Uncontrolled diabetes may result in an increased risk of several health complications such as heart disease, stroke, vision loss, depression, kidney failure, and other issues. The emotional impact of a type 2 diabetes diagnosis can be overwhelming, with changes needed to control blood sugar levels leading to stress and a range of emotions. However, it's important to note that such reactions are normal and expected. During this period, it is critical to pay attention to and acknowledge one's feelings, seek support, and practice self-care. According to a recent study published in Current Diabetes Reports, people with diabetes may have twice the risk of depression, and fluctuations in blood sugar levels can mimic symptoms of anxiety and depression. High blood sugar levels can lead to fatigue and trouble concentrating, while low blood sugar can cause feelings of nervousness and anxiety. It is essential to take a comprehensive approach to one's health, including mental well-being. Speaking to a physician about any concerns and considering the addition of a mental health professional to one's diabetes healthcare team is encouraged. Diabetes can come out of nowhere and can be overwhelming, affecting one's thoughts, emotions, behavior, movement, eating habits, and more. It is a disease that not only impacts the person diagnosed but also those close to them. The dietary and lifestyle changes recommended at diagnosis may leave many individuals feeling inundated, and traditional advice often involves cutting back on certain foods or limiting particular nutrients. The information may feel like diabetes is taking the joy out of food and life. However, with the right tools and knowledge of scientifically proven strategies that make managing blood sugar levels easier, success is attainable.

Chapter 2 Treat Diabetes with Diet

When it comes to managing diabetes, following a healthy-eating plan is essential. A diabetes diet involves consuming nutrient-rich foods in moderate amounts and sticking to regular mealtimes, which can help you utilize insulin produced by your body or taken through medication. This eating plan is naturally low in fat and calories, with fruits, vegetables, and whole grains serving as key components. In fact, it's considered the best eating plan for most people, regardless of whether or not they have diabetes.

Getting nutrition education from a certified diabetes educator who is also a registered dietitian is highly recommended for effective guidance. Medical nutrition therapy (MNT), a diet specifically designed for people with diabetes, can be customized for you. Studies show that MNT can lower hemoglobin A1c levels for people with type 2 diabetes by 0.3 to 2.0 percent, according to the American Diabetes Association.

Remember, there's no one-size-fits-all approach to managing diabetes through diet. Several meal-planning strategies and methods have proven effective. Among the most studied are the Mediterranean diet, the DASH diet, and vegetarian and plant-based foods. These approaches have shown to be beneficial not only in preventing diabetes but also in managing it.

Recommended Foods in Diabetic Diet

Optimize your calorie intake by selecting nutrient-dense foods. Prioritize healthy carbohydrates, fiber-rich options, fish, "good" fats, and high-quality protein to fuel your body with essential nutrients.

◊ Nutritious Carbohydrates. When it comes to carbohydrates, not all are created equal. It's important to focus on consuming healthy carbohydrates, which are beneficial for our overall health. Some examples of healthy carbohydrates include fruits, vegetables, whole grains, legumes such as beans and peas, and low-fat dairy products like milk and cheese. These foods are naturally rich in nutrients, fiber, and other important components that our body needs to function properly. On the other hand, it's important to avoid less healthy carbohydrates, such as those with added fats, sugars, and sodium. These types of foods and drinks can be detrimental to our health, leading to weight gain, high blood pressure, and other health problems. By making a conscious effort to choose healthy carbohydrates and limit unhealthy ones, we can improve our overall health and wellbeing.

◊ High-fiber Foods. Dietary fiber is a crucial component of a healthy diet. It includes all parts of plant foods that your body can't digest or absorb. Consuming fiber can help regulate bowel movements, lower cholesterol levels, and improve blood sugar control. Foods high in fiber include vegetables like broccoli, Brussels sprouts, and artichokes, as well as fruits like raspberries, pears, and apples. Nuts, such as almonds and pistachios, are also good sources of fiber, as are legumes like lentils, chickpeas, and kidney beans. Whole grains like brown rice, quinoa, and oats are another important source of dietary fiber. By incorporating these fiber-rich foods into your diet, you can improve your overall health and reduce your risk of chronic diseases.

◊ Cardio-protective Fish. Eating fish at least twice a week can be beneficial for heart health. Fish like salmon, mackerel, tuna, and sardines are packed with omega-3 fatty acids that can help reduce the risk of heart disease. Omega-3s are a type of unsaturated fat that can help lower levels of triglycerides, reduce inflammation, and prevent the buildup of plaque in the arteries. It's important to avoid fried fish and those that contain high levels of mercury, such as king mackerel. Mercury can accumulate in fish and can be harmful to the nervous system, especially in young children and pregnant women. By incorporating heart-healthy fish into your diet, you can help support your cardiovascular health.

◊ Healthy Fats. Including foods that contain monounsaturated and polyunsaturated fats in your diet can have a positive impact on your cholesterol levels. Avocados, nuts, and oils such as canola, olive, and peanut oils are all good sources of these healthy fats. However, it's important to be mindful of portion sizes and not consume too much, as all fats are high in calories. Replacing saturated and trans fats with these healthier options can help reduce your risk of heart disease and improve your overall health.

◊ Lean protein. Eating high-quality protein is an important part of a diabetic diet. Good sources of protein include eggs, beans, low-fat dairy, and unsweetened yogurt. These foods not only provide essential nutrients but also help keep blood sugar levels stable. Eggs are a great source of protein and can be prepared in many ways, such as boiled or scrambled. Beans are also a good source of protein and can be added to salads, soups or stews. Low-fat dairy products, such as milk and cheese, can provide a good source of protein without added fats. Unsweetened yogurt is another great option for getting high-quality protein and can be enjoyed on its own or mixed with fresh fruit for added flavor.

Foods to Avoid in Diabetic Diet

Consuming certain foods can counteract your efforts to maintain a heart-healthy diet, as diabetes can increase your likelihood of developing clogged and hardened arteries, leading to an increased risk of heart disease and stroke.

◊ Saturated fats. In a diabetic diet, it's important to avoid high-fat dairy products and animal proteins that can increase your risk of heart disease and stroke. These include butter, beef, hot dogs, sausage, and bacon. Coconut and palm kernel oils should also be limited as they are high in saturated fat. Instead, choose lean sources of protein such as poultry, fish, beans, and tofu. Low-fat dairy products like milk and yogurt can be included in moderation. By making these dietary changes, you can lower your risk of heart disease and maintain better control over your blood sugar levels.

◊ Trans fats. Diabetic individuals should be careful to avoid consuming trans fats as they can increase the risk of developing heart disease. Trans fats are often found in processed snacks, baked goods, and stick margarines, as well as in shortening. Therefore, it is important to carefully read food labels and choose products that do not contain trans fats. It is recommended to limit the intake of these unhealthy fats as much as possible to maintain a healthy and balanced diabetic diet.

◊ Cholesterol. People with diabetes are recommended to limit their intake of cholesterol-rich foods to no more than 200 milligrams (mg) per day. Cholesterol sources to avoid include high-fat dairy products, high-fat animal proteins like beef and pork, egg yolks, liver, and other organ meats. It is important to choose leaner protein sources like skinless poultry, fish, beans, and legumes. Additionally, it's essential to watch portion sizes, as even low-cholesterol foods can contribute to high levels if consumed in excess.

◊ Sodium. For people with diabetes, it's important to limit their intake of sodium to prevent complications like high blood pressure and heart disease. The American Diabetes Association recommends aiming for less than 2,300 milligrams (mg) of sodium per day. However, for those with high blood pressure, doctors may suggest an even lower intake. High sodium foods to avoid include processed snacks, canned soups, and frozen meals. Instead, try seasoning your food with herbs and spices, and choose fresh, whole foods that are naturally low in sodium. By reducing your sodium intake, you can improve your overall health and manage your diabetes more effectively.

In a diabetic diet, it's also important to limit or avoid certain foods that can negatively impact blood sugar levels and overall health. These include packaged and fast foods that are high in sugar, baked goods, sweets, chips, and desserts. It's also important to choose whole grain options instead of white bread, sugary cereals, and refined pastas or rice. Processed meat and red meat should be limited or avoided, and low-fat products that have replaced fat with added sugar, such as fat-free yogurt, should also be avoided. It's important to read food labels carefully and choose foods with lower amounts of added sugars, saturated and trans fats, and sodium.

The Outcomes of a Diabetic Meal Plan

A healthy-eating plan is essential for managing diabetes and preventing complications associated with the condition. By following a diabetes diet, you can keep your blood glucose levels under control, reduce your risk of cardiovascular diseases, and lower your chances of developing certain types of cancer. The diet involves consuming generous amounts of fruits, vegetables, and fiber, which help to improve blood glucose control and maintain overall health. It is also recommended to include low-fat dairy products in your diet, as they can reduce the risk of low bone mass in the future.

In addition to managing diabetes, the benefits of a diabetes diet extend beyond blood glucose control. A well-balanced diet can also help with weight management, as it can be tailored to specific weight loss goals. It is important to note that losing weight can significantly improve blood glucose control and reduce the risk of complications associated with diabetes. Following a diabetes diet can also improve overall health, as it provides the body with essential nutrients that support the immune system, bone health, and digestive function.

Fruits and vegetables, which are staples of a diabetes diet, are rich in vitamins, minerals, and fiber. These nutrients help to regulate blood glucose levels, promote healthy digestion, and reduce inflammation. Consuming low-fat dairy products, such as milk and yogurt, can provide the body with calcium and vitamin D, which are essential for strong bones. Additionally, low-fat dairy products are a good source of protein, which helps to maintain muscle mass and promote healthy weight management.

In contrast, a diet high in processed foods, saturated and trans fats, and added sugars can worsen blood glucose control and increase the risk of complications associated with diabetes. Foods to limit or avoid include sugary beverages, baked goods, fried foods, and processed meats. These foods are often high in calories, sodium, and unhealthy fats, which can contribute to weight gain, high blood pressure, and heart disease.

DAYS	BREAKFAST	LUNCH	DINNER	SNACK/DESSERT
1	Apple Millet Porridge	Ham and Egg Calico Salad	Roasted Delicata Squash	Hummus
2	Mini Breakfast Quiches	Broiled Spinach	Roasted Tilapia and Vegetables	Blood Sugar–Friendly Nutty Trail Mix
3	Oatmeal Strawberry Smoothie	Warm Sweet Potato and Black Bean Salad	Roasted Peppers and Eggplant	Caramelized Onion–Shrimp Spread
4	Pumpkin Apple Waffles	Zucchini Sauté	Manhattan Clam Chowder	Chilled Shrimp
5	Sweet Potato Breakfast Bites	Mediterranean Vegetable Salad	Ginger Broccoli	Crab-Filled Mushrooms
6	Cauliflower Scramble	Garlic Roasted Radishes	Stuffed Portobello Mushrooms	Cinnamon Toasted Pumpkin Seeds
7	Simple Grain-Free Biscuits	Herbed Tomato Salad	Curry Roasted Cauliflower	Ground Turkey Lettuce Cups
8	Orange-Berry Pancake Syrup	Lemon-Garlic Mushrooms	Italian Zucchini Boats	Vegetable Kabobs with Mustard Dip
9	Egg-Stuffed Tomatoes	Moroccan Carrot Salad	Lemony Brussels Sprouts with Poppy Seeds	No-Added-Sugar Berries and Cream Yogurt Bowl
10	Three-Berry Dutch Pancake	Broccoli Salad	Farro Bowl	Cucumber Pâté
11	Tomato and Chive Waffles	Strawberry-Blueberry-Orange Salad	Fennel and Chickpeas	Southern Boiled Peanuts
12	Southwestern Egg Casserole	Charred Sesame Broccoli	Lemon Pepper Salmon	Spinach and Artichoke Dip
13	Pumpkin Spice Muffins	Roasted Carrot and Quinoa with Goat Cheese	Soft-Baked Tamari Tofu	Cucumber Roll-Ups
14	Blueberry Coconut Breakfast Cookies	Parmesan Cauliflower Mash	Chickpea-Spinach Curry	Baked Scallops
15	Tofu, Kale, and Mushroom Breakfast Scramble	Rainbow Quinoa Salad	Avocado Slaw	Blackberry Baked Brie
16	Breakfast Hash	Asparagus with Cashews	Stuffed Portobello Mushrooms	Lemon Cream Fruit Dip
17	Seedy Muesli	Couscous Salad	Corn on the Cob	Ginger and Mint Dip with Fruit
18	Quinoa, Teff, and Corn Porridge	Cauliflower "Mashed Potatoes"	Italian Zucchini Boats	Creamy Spinach Dip

DAYS	BREAKFAST	LUNCH	DINNER	SNACK/DESSERT
19	Tropical Fruit 'n Ginger Oatmeal	Thai Broccoli Slaw	Sun-Dried Tomato Brussels Sprouts	Candied Pecans
20	Brussels Sprouts and Egg Scramble	Teriyaki Green Beans	Stuffed Portobellos	Green Goddess White Bean Dip
21	Potato-Bacon Gratin	Mozzarella-Tomato Salad	Mushroom Cassoulets	Creamy Apple-Cinnamon Quesadilla
22	Easy Breakfast Chia Pudding	Spinach and Sweet Pepper Poppers	BBQ Ribs and Broccoli Slaw	Porcupine Meatballs
23	Spinach and Feta Egg Bake	Italian Potato Salad	Roasted Beets, Carrots, and Parsnips	Oatmeal Cookies
24	Polenta Porridge with Berry Swirl	Radish Chips	Haricot Verts, Walnut, and Feta Salad	Fried Apples
25	Stovetop Granola	Shaved Brussels Sprouts and Kale with Poppy Seed Dressing	Garlicky Cabbage and Collard Greens	Grilled Watermelon with Avocado Mousse
26	Shakshuka	Golden Lemony Wax Beans	Pasta Salad–Stuffed Tomatoes	Cherry Almond Cobbler
27	Simple Buckwheat Porridge	Pomegranate "Tabbouleh" with Cauliflower	Tofu and Bean Chili	Chewy Barley-Nut Cookies
28	Quinoa Breakfast Bake with Pistachios and Plums	Zucchini Noodles with Lime-Basil Pesto	BLT Potato Salad	Double-Ginger Cookies
29	Corn, Egg and Potato Bake	Tu-No Salad	Stuffed Portobellos	Cinnamon Spiced Baked Apples
30	Breakfast Tacos	Caramelized Onions	Grilled Scallop Kabobs	Banana Pineapple Freeze

Chapter 3 What to Expect in This Cookbook?

In this cookbook, we have compiled a collection of delicious and nutritious recipes that are tailored to help people with diabetes manage their blood sugar levels while enjoying a variety of flavors and textures. Our recipes feature wholesome ingredients that are low in sugar, saturated fat, and sodium, and high in fiber, vitamins, and minerals. Whether you are looking for quick and easy breakfast ideas, satisfying main courses, flavorful side dishes, or indulgent desserts, you will find plenty of options to choose from in this cookbook. We have also included tips on meal planning, portion control, and ingredient substitutions to help you customize our recipes to your specific needs and preferences.

Get Ready to Prepare Your Meal

In our fast-paced lives, it can be challenging to find time to prepare healthy meals daily, leading many of us to rely on processed or outside food high in sugar and carbs. To help combat this issue, we have created a cookbook filled with recipes that can be made in advance and stored for later consumption. This technique, called prepping the meal, allows you to always have a healthy meal on hand and avoid the temptation of fast food. Our recipes are easy to follow and can be enjoyed at home or on the go, even when visiting friends or family. Prepping meals not only helps maintain healthy eating habits but also saves costs by shopping in bulk. Each recipe includes detailed instructions and the exact amounts of ingredients needed, making meal planning and grocery shopping a breeze. Follow our instructions carefully and enjoy the delicious and healthy meals designed for diabetic patients, anytime and anywhere.

Mistakes to Avoid During Meal-Prep

1.Stocking of food:

One of the most common mistakes when prepping food is buying too much and confusing it with preparing in bulk. It is important to be aware of how much food can be stored for later use. Keeping food in bulk will only end up stuffing your refrigerator with stale food. Avoid this confusion and only stock up on what you can realistically consume.

2.Wastage of food:

It is crucial to read your meal plan carefully and try not to indulge in an extended shopping spree. Many people tend to buy in bulk while prepping food, which can result in unnecessary wastage. Planning your meals ahead of time and sticking to your shopping list can help prevent this.

3.Last minute shopping:

Always try to buy ingredients for your meal well in advance. Last minute shopping often leads to missing important details and can cause unnecessary stress. It's important to have all the necessary ingredients on hand before you start cooking.

4.Being in a rush:

Whenever preparing food, ensure that you have enough time in hand. Preparing in advance may sometimes lead to missing important instructions due to haste. Take your time and carefully follow each step to avoid any mistakes or mishaps.

5.Using stocked items:

While prepping your meals, try to use fresh food items to maximize their nutritional value. Although you are preparing to store them for later consumption, using fresh ingredients will ensure that the meals you consume are healthy and delicious. Avoid using stocked items as they may have lost their freshness and nutritional value over time.

Avoiding these common mistakes can ensure that your prepped meals are healthy, delicious, and cost-effective. With careful planning and attention to detail, prepping your meals can help you maintain a healthy and balanced diet, even on your busiest days. By following the recipes in this cookbook, you can enjoy a balanced and satisfying diet that promotes good health and well-being, while still indulging in the occasional treat. We hope you find this cookbook useful and inspiring, and we wish you all the best on your journey to optimal health and wellness!

Chapter 4 Breakfasts

Sweet Potato Breakfast Bites

Prep time: 5 minutes | Cook time: 17 to 18 minutes | Makes 12 bites

1½ cups precooked and cooled sweet potato
½ cup pure maple syrup
1 teaspoon pure vanilla extract
1¼ cups rolled oats
1 cup oat flour
½ teaspoon cinnamon
½ teaspoon pumpkin pie spice

(optional; can substitute another ½ teaspoon cinnamon)
2 teaspoons baking powder
¼ teaspoon sea salt
2–3 tablespoons raisins or sugar-free nondairy chocolate chips (optional)

1. Preheat the oven to 350°F and line a baking sheet with parchment paper. 2. In a medium bowl, mash the sweet potato. Add the syrup and vanilla and stir to combine. Add the oats, oat flour, cinnamon, pumpkin pie spice (if using), baking powder, and salt, and mix until well combined. Add the raisins or chips (if using), and stir to combine. Refrigerate for 5 to 10 minutes. Scoop 1½tablespoon rounds of the mixture onto the parchment, spacing them 1 to 2 inches apart. Bake for 17 to 18 minutes, or until set to the touch. Remove from the oven, and let cool.

Per Serving:
calorie: 215 | fat: 2g | protein: 6g | carbs: 52g | sugars: 19g | fiber: 5g | sodium: 281mg

Cauliflower Scramble

Prep time: 5 minutes | Cook time: 5 minutes | Serves 3

1 package (12–16 ounces) medium or medium-firm tofu
3½–4 cups steamed cauliflower florets, lightly mashed
½ teaspoon onion powder
½ teaspoon garlic powder
½ teaspoon sea salt
¼ teaspoon prepared mustard

½ teaspoon black salt (or another ¼ teaspoon sea salt)
½ tablespoon tahini
2½–3 tablespoons nutritional yeast
2–3 cups chopped spinach or kale

1. In a large nonstick skillet, use your fingers to crumble the tofu, breaking it up well. Place the skillet over medium heat. Add the cauliflower, onion powder, garlic powder, sea salt, mustard, and black salt. Cook for 3 to 4 minutes, then add the tahini and nutritional yeast and stir to combine thoroughly. If the mixture is sticking, add 1 to 2 tablespoons water. Add the spinach or kale during the final minutes of cooking, stirring until just nicely wilted and still bright green. Taste, season as desired, and serve.

Per Serving:
calorie: 196 | fat: 9g | protein: 21g | carbs: 16g | sugars: 3g | fiber: 10g | sodium: 862mg

Tomato and Chive Waffles

Prep time: 15 minutes | Cook time: 40 minutes | Serves 8

2 cups low-fat buttermilk
½ cup crushed tomato
1 medium egg
2 medium egg whites
1 cup gluten-free all-purpose flour

½ cup almond flour
½ cup coconut flour
2 teaspoons baking powder
½ teaspoon baking soda
½ teaspoon dried chives
Nonstick cooking spray

1. Heat a waffle iron. 2. In a medium bowl, whisk the buttermilk, tomato, egg, and egg whites together. 3. In another bowl, whisk the all-purpose flour, almond flour, coconut flour, baking powder, baking soda, and chives together. 4. Add the wet ingredients to the dry ingredients. 5. Lightly spray the waffle iron with cooking spray. 6. Gently pour ¼- to ½-cup portions of batter into the waffle iron. Cook time for waffles will vary depending on the kind of waffle iron you use, but it is usually 5 minutes per waffle. (Note: Once the waffle iron is hot, the cooking process is a bit faster.) Repeat until no batter remains. 7. Enjoy the waffles warm.

Per Serving:
calories: 128 | fat: 5g | protein: 7g | carbs: 18g | sugars: 4g | fiber: 1g | sodium: 167mg

Southwestern Egg Casserole

Prep time: 10 minutes | Cook time: 20 minutes | Serves 12

1 cup water
2½ cups egg substitute
½ cup flour
1 teaspoon baking powder
⅛ teaspoon salt
⅛ teaspoon pepper
2 cups fat-free cottage cheese

1½ cups shredded 75%-less-fat sharp cheddar cheese
¼ cup no-trans-fat tub margarine, melted
2 (4-ounce) cans chopped green chilies

1. Place the steaming rack into the bottom of the inner pot and pour in 1 cup of water. 2. Grease a round springform pan that will fit into the inner pot of the Instant Pot. 3. Combine the egg substitute, flour, baking powder, salt and pepper in a mixing bowl. It will be lumpy. 4. Stir in the cheese, margarine, and green chilies then pour into the springform pan. 5. Place the springform pan onto the steaming rack, close the lid, and secure to the locking position. Be sure the vent is turned to sealing. Set for 20 minutes on Manual at high pressure. 6. Let the pressure release naturally. 7. Carefully remove the springform pan with the handles of the steaming rack and allow to stand 10 minutes before cutting and serving.

Per Serving:
calories: 130 | fat: 4g | protein: 14g | carbs: 9g | sugars: 1g | fiber: 1g | sodium: 450mg

Corn, Egg and Potato Bake

Prep time: 20 minutes | Cook time: 1 hour | Serves 8

4 cups frozen diced hash brown potatoes (from 2-lb bag), thawed
1/2 cup frozen whole-kernel corn (from 1-lb bag), thawed
1/4 cup chopped roasted red bell peppers (from 7-oz jar)
11/2 cups shredded reduced-fat Colby–Monterey Jack cheese (6 oz)

10 eggs or 21/2 cups fat-free egg product
1/2 cup fat-free small-curd cottage cheese
1/2 teaspoon dried oregano leaves
1/4 teaspoon garlic powder
4 medium green onions, chopped (1/4 cup)

1 Heat oven to 350°F. Spray 11x7-inch (2-quart) glass baking dish with cooking spray. In baking dish, layer potatoes, corn, bell peppers and 1 cup of the shredded cheese. 2 In medium bowl, beat eggs, cottage cheese, oregano and garlic powder with whisk until well blended. Slowly pour over potato mixture. Sprinkle with onions and remaining 1/2 cup shredded cheese. 3 Cover and bake 30 minutes. Uncover and bake about 30 minutes longer or until knife inserted in center comes out clean. Let stand 5 to 10 minutes before cutting.

Per Serving:
calories: 240 | fat: 11g | protein: 16g | carbs: 18g | sugars: 2g | fiber: 2g | sodium: 440mg

Breakfast Tacos

Prep time: 5 minutes | Cook time: 10 minutes | Serves 4

For the Taco Filling:
Avocado oil cooking spray
1 medium green bell pepper, chopped
8 large eggs
1/4 cup shredded sharp Cheddar cheese
4 (6-inch) whole-wheat tortillas
1 cup fresh spinach leaves
1/2 cup Pico de Gallo
Scallions, chopped, for garnish (optional)

Avocado slices, for garnish (optional)
For the Pico De Gallo:
1 tomato, diced
1/2 large white onion, diced
2 tablespoons chopped fresh cilantro
1/2 jalapeño pepper, stemmed, seeded, and diced
1 tablespoon freshly squeezed lime juice
1/8 teaspoon salt

To make the taco filling 1. Heat a medium skillet over medium-low heat. When hot, coat the cooking surface with cooking spray and put the pepper in the skillet. Cook for 4 minutes. 2. Meanwhile, whisk the eggs in a medium bowl, then add the cheese and whisk to combine. Pour the eggs and cheese into the skillet with the green peppers and scramble until the eggs are fully cooked, about 5 minutes. 3. Microwave the tortillas very briefly, about 8 seconds. 4. For each serving, top a tortilla with one-quarter of the spinach, eggs, and pico de gallo. Garnish with scallions and avocado slices (if using). To make the pico de gallo 5. In a medium bowl, combine the tomato, onion, cilantro, pepper, lime juice, and salt. Mix well and serve.

Per Serving:
calories: 316 | fat: 16g | protein: 19g | carbs: 24g | sugars: 4g | fiber: 5g | sodium: 554mg

Simple Grain-Free Biscuits

Prep time: 10 minutes | Cook time: 15 minutes | Serves 4

2 tablespoons unsalted butter
Pinch salt
1/4 cup plain low-fat Greek

yogurt
11/2 cups finely ground almond flour

1. Preheat the oven to 375°F. 2. In a medium bowl, microwave the butter just enough to soften, 15 to 20 seconds. 3. Add the salt and yogurt to the butter and mix well. 4. Add the almond flour and mix. The dough will be crumbly at first, so continue to stir and mash it with a fork until there are no lumps and the mixture comes together. 5. Drop 1/4 cup of dough on a baking sheet for each biscuit. Using your clean hand, flatten each biscuit until it is 1 inch thick. 6. Bake for 13 to 15 minutes.

Per Serving:
calories: 182 | fat: 15g | protein: 6g | carbs: 6g | sugars: 2g | fiber: 3g | sodium: 13mg

Orange-Berry Pancake Syrup

Prep time: 5 minutes | Cook time: 0 minutes | Serves 8

2 cups raspberries, fresh or frozen
1/2 cup fresh orange juice

1/4 cup pure maple syrup
Pinch of sea salt

1. In a blender, combine the raspberries, juice, syrup, and salt. Puree until smooth, stopping to scrape down the blender as needed. If the mixture is too thick (particularly if using frozen berries), you may need to scrape down more often or add a tablespoon or two of water to assist with the blending. Once it's smooth, transfer the syrup to a jar or other airtight container and store it in the refrigerator. It keeps for about a week in the fridge.

Per Serving:
calorie: 65 | fat: 0.4g | protein: 1g | carbs: 16g | sugars: 10g | fiber: 4g | sodium: 38mg

Cheesy Scrambled Eggs

Prep time: 2 minutes | Cook time: 9 minutes | Serves 2

1 teaspoon unsalted butter
2 large eggs
2 tablespoons milk
2 tablespoons shredded Cheddar

cheese
Salt and freshly ground black pepper, to taste

1. Preheat the air fryer to 300°F (149°C). Place the butter in a baking pan and cook for 1 to 2 minutes, until melted. 2. In a small bowl, whisk together the eggs, milk, and cheese. Season with salt and black pepper. Transfer the mixture to the pan. 3. Cook for 3 minutes. Stir the eggs and push them toward the center of the pan. 4. Cook for another 2 minutes, then stir again. Cook for another 2 minutes, until the eggs are just cooked. Serve warm.

Per Serving:
calories: 122 | fat: 9g | protein: 9g | carbs: 1g | sugars: 1g | fiber: 0g | sodium: 357mg

Greek Frittata with Peppers, Kale, and Feta

Prep time: 5 minutes | Cook time: 45 minutes | Serves 6

8 large eggs
½ cup plain 2 percent Greek yogurt
Fine sea salt
Freshly ground black pepper
2 cups firmly packed finely shredded kale or baby kale leaves
One 12-ounce jar roasted red peppers, drained and cut into ¼ by 2-inch strips

2 green onions, white and green parts, thinly sliced
1 tablespoon chopped fresh dill
⅓ cup crumbled feta cheese
6 cups loosely packed mixed baby greens
¾ cup cherry or grape tomatoes, halved
2 tablespoons extra-virgin olive oil

1. Pour 1½ cups water into the Instant Pot. Lightly butter a 7-cup round heatproof glass dish or coat with nonstick cooking spray. 2. In a bowl, whisk together the eggs, yogurt, ¼ teaspoon salt, and ¼ teaspoon pepper until well blended, then stir in the kale, roasted peppers, green onions, dill, and feta cheese. 3. Pour the egg mixture into the prepared dish and cover tightly with aluminum foil. Place the dish on a long-handled silicone steam rack, then, holding the handles of the steam rack, lower it into the Instant Pot. (If you don't have the long-handled rack, use the wire metal steam rack and a homemade sling) 4. Secure the lid and set the Pressure Release to Sealing. Select the Pressure Cook or Manual setting and set the cooking time for 30 minutes at high pressure. (The pot will take about 15 minutes to come up to pressure before the cooking program begins.) 5. When the cooking program ends, let the pressure release naturally for 10 minutes, then move the Pressure Release to Venting to release any remaining steam. Open the pot and let the frittata sit for a minute or two, until it deflates and settles into its dish. Then, wearing heat-resistant mitts, grasp the handles of the steam rack and lift it out of the pot. Uncover the dish, taking care not to get burned by the steam or to drip condensation onto the frittata. Let the frittata sit for 10 minutes, giving it time to reabsorb any liquid and set up. 6. In a medium bowl, toss together the mixed greens, tomatoes, and olive oil. Taste and adjust the seasoning with salt and pepper, if needed. 7. Cut the frittata into six wedges and serve warm, with the salad alongside.

Per Serving:

calories: 227 | fat: 13g | protein: 18g | carbs: 8g | sugars: 2g | fiber: 1g | sodium: 153mg

Easy Breakfast Chia Pudding

Prep time: 5 minutes | Cook time: 0 minutes | Serves 4

4 cups unsweetened almond milk or skim milk
¾ cup chia seeds

1 teaspoon ground cinnamon
Pinch sea salt

1. Stir together the milk, chia seeds, cinnamon, and salt in a medium bowl. 2. Cover the bowl with plastic wrap and chill in the refrigerator until the pudding is thick, about 1 hour. 3. Sweeten with your favorite sweetener and fruit.

Per Serving:

calories: 129 | fat: 3g | protein: 10g | carbs: 16g | sugars: 12g | fiber: 3g | sodium: 131mg

Tropical Fruit 'n Ginger Oatmeal

Prep time: 15 minutes | Cook time: 25 to 30 minutes | Serves 4

2¼ cups water
¾ cup steel-cut oats
2 teaspoons finely chopped gingerroot
⅛ teaspoon salt
½ medium banana, mashed
1 container (6 oz) vanilla low-

fat yogurt
1 medium mango, pitted, peeled and chopped (1 cup)
½ cup sliced fresh strawberries
2 tablespoons shredded coconut, toasted
2 tablespoons chopped walnuts

1 In 1 1/2-quart saucepan, heat water to boiling. Stir in oats, gingerroot and salt. Reduce heat; simmer gently uncovered 25 to 30 minutes, without stirring, until oats are tender yet slightly chewy; stir in banana. Divide oatmeal evenly among 4 bowls. 2 Top each serving with yogurt, mango, strawberries, coconut and walnuts. Serve immediately.

Per Serving:

calories: 200 | fat: 6g | protein: 5g | carbs: 31g | sugars: 16g | fiber: 4g | sodium: 110mg

Oatmeal Strawberry Smoothie

Prep time: 5 minutes | Cook time: 0 minutes | Serves 2

2 tablespoons instant oats
1 cup frozen strawberries

3 cups skim milk
½ teaspoon pure vanilla extract

1. Put the oats, strawberries, milk, and vanilla in a blender and blend until smooth. 2. Pour into two glasses and serve.

Per Serving:

calories: 179 | fat: 1g | protein: 14g | carbs: 27g | sugars: 18g | fiber: 3g | sodium: 156mg

Pumpkin Apple Waffles

Prep time: 10 minutes | Cook time: 20 minutes | Serves 6

2¼ cups whole-wheat pastry flour
2 tablespoons granulated sweetener
1 tablespoon baking powder
1 teaspoon ground cinnamon

1 teaspoon ground nutmeg
4 eggs
1¼ cups pure pumpkin purée
1 apple, peeled, cored, and finely chopped
Melted coconut oil, for cooking

1. In a large bowl, stir together the flour, sweetener, baking powder, cinnamon, and nutmeg. 2. In a small bowl, whisk together the eggs and pumpkin. 3. Add the wet ingredients to the dry and whisk until smooth. 4. Stir the apple into the batter. 5. Cook the waffles according to the waffle maker manufacturer's directions, brushing your waffle iron with melted coconut oil, until all the batter is gone. 6. Serve.

Per Serving:

calories: 241 | fat: 4g | protein: 10g | carbs: 44g | sugars: 7g | fiber: 7g | sodium: 46mg

Seedy Muesli

Prep time: 5 minutes | Cook time: 0 minutes | Makes 6 cups

2 cups gluten-free rolled oats
1 cup roasted, slivered almonds
¾ cup raw sunflower seeds
½ cup raw pumpkin seeds
½ cup pistachios
½ cup apricots, sliced
¼ cup hemp seeds
¼ cup ground flaxseed
¼ cup toasted sesame seeds

1. In a medium bowl, combine the oats, almonds, sunflower seeds, pumpkin seeds, pistachios, apricots, hemp seeds, flaxseed, and sesame seeds. 2. Store the mixture in an airtight container at room temperature for up to 6 months.

Per Serving:

1 cup: calories: 494 | fat: 36g | protein: 23g | carbs: 38g | sugars: 5g | fiber: 14g | sodium: 9mg

Quinoa, Teff, and Corn Porridge

Prep time: 5 minutes | Cook time: 35 minutes | Serves 8

1 cup teff
1 cup stone-ground corn grits
1 cup quinoa
¼ teaspoon whole cloves
1 tablespoon sunflower seed oil
5 cups water
2 cups roughly chopped fresh fruit
2 cups unsalted crushed nuts

1. In an electric pressure cooker, combine the teff, grits, quinoa, and cloves. 2. Add the oil and water, mixing together with a fork. 3. Close and lock the lid, and set the pressure valve to sealing. 4. Select the Porridge setting, and cook for 20 minutes. 5. Once cooking is complete, allow the pressure to release naturally. Carefully remove the lid. 6. Serve each portion with ¼ cup fresh fruit and ¼ cup nuts of your choice.

Per Serving:

calories: 476 | fat: 21g | protein: 14g | carbs: 60g | sugars: 1g | fiber: 7g | sodium: 10mg

Scramble

Prep time: 5 minutes | Cook time: 10 minutes | Serves 2

2 tablespoons extra-virgin olive oil
½ red onion, finely chopped
8 ounces mushrooms, sliced
1 cup chopped kale
8 ounces tofu, cut into pieces
2 garlic cloves, minced
Pinch red pepper flakes
½ teaspoon sea salt
⅛ teaspoon freshly ground black pepper

1. In a medium nonstick skillet over medium-high heat, heat the olive oil until it shimmers. 2. Add the onion, mushrooms, and kale. Cook, stirring occasionally, until the vegetables begin to brown, about 5 minutes. 3. Add the tofu. Cook, stirring, until the tofu starts to brown, 3 to 4 minutes more. 4. Add the garlic, red pepper flakes, salt, and pepper. Cook, stirring constantly, for 30 seconds more.

Per Serving:

calories: 234 | fat: 18g | protein: 12g | carbs: 10g | sugars: 4g | fiber: 2g | sodium: 601mg

Spinach and Feta Egg Bake

Prep time: 7 minutes | Cook time: 23 to 25 minutes | Serves 2

Avocado oil spray
⅓ cup diced red onion
1 cup frozen chopped spinach, thawed and drained
4 large eggs
¼ cup heavy (whipping) cream
Sea salt and freshly ground black pepper, to taste
¼ teaspoon cayenne pepper
½ cup crumbled feta cheese
¼ cup shredded Parmesan cheese

1. Spray a deep pan with oil. Put the onion in the pan, and place the pan in the air fryer basket. Set the air fryer to 350°F (177°C) and bake for 7 minutes. 2. Sprinkle the spinach over the onion. 3. In a medium bowl, beat the eggs, heavy cream, salt, black pepper, and cayenne. Pour this mixture over the vegetables. 4. Top with the feta and Parmesan cheese. Bake for 16 to 18 minutes, until the eggs are set and lightly brown.

Per Serving:

calories: 366 | fat: 26g | protein: 25g | carbs: 8g | fiber: 3g | sodium: 520mg

Breakfast Hash

Prep time: 10 minutes | Cook time: 30 minutes | Serves 6

Oil, for spraying
3 medium russet potatoes, diced
½ yellow onion, diced
1 green bell pepper, seeded and diced
2 tablespoons olive oil
2 teaspoons granulated garlic
1 teaspoon salt
½ teaspoon freshly ground black pepper

1. Line the air fryer basket with parchment and spray lightly with oil. 2. In a large bowl, mix together the potatoes, onion, bell pepper, and olive oil. 3. Add the garlic, salt, and black pepper and stir until evenly coated. 4. Transfer the mixture to the prepared basket. 5. Air fry at 400°F (204°C) for 20 to 30 minutes, shaking or stirring every 10 minutes, until browned and crispy. If you spray the potatoes with a little oil each time you stir, they will get even crispier.

Per Serving:

calories: 133 | fat: 5g | protein: 3g | carbs: 21g | fiber: 2g | sodium: 395mg

Cherry, Chocolate, and Almond Shake

Prep time: 5 minutes | Cook time: 0 minutes | Serves 2

10 ounces frozen cherries
2 tablespoons cocoa powder
2 tablespoons almond butter
2 tablespoons hemp seeds
8 ounces unsweetened almond milk

1. Combine the cherries, cocoa, almond butter, hemp seeds, and almond milk in a blender and blend on high speed until smooth. Use a spatula to scrape down the sides as needed. Serve immediately.

Per Serving:

calories: 243 | fat: 16g | protein: 8g | carbs: 24g | sugars: 13g | fiber: 7g | sodium: 85mg

Two-Cheese Grits

Prep time: 10 minutes | Cook time: 10 to 12 minutes | Serves 4

⅔ cup instant grits	3 ounces (85 g) cream cheese,
1 teaspoon salt	at room temperature
1 teaspoon freshly ground black	1 tablespoon butter, melted
pepper	1 cup shredded mild Cheddar
¾ cup milk, whole or 2%	cheese
1 large egg, beaten	1 to 2 tablespoons oil

1. In a large bowl, combine the grits, salt, and pepper. Stir in the milk, egg, cream cheese, and butter until blended. Stir in the Cheddar cheese. 2. Preheat the air fryer to 400°F (204°C). Spritz a baking pan with oil. 3. Pour the grits mixture into the prepared pan and place it in the air fryer basket. 4. Cook for 5 minutes. Stir the mixture and cook for 5 minutes more for soupy grits or 7 minutes more for firmer grits.

Per Serving:

calories: 302 | fat: 18g | protein: 13g | carbs: 21g | sugars: 4g | fiber: 1g | sodium: 621mg

Apple Millet Porridge

Prep time: 3 minutes | Cook time: 12 minutes | Serves 2

1 cup millet, rinsed and drained	1 tablespoon honey
2½ cups plant-based milk,	1 apple, cored and cut into bite-
divided	size pieces
2 teaspoons ground cinnamon	¼ cup chopped walnuts, toasted
Pinch kosher salt	

1. In a small saucepan, combine the millet, 2 cups of milk, the cinnamon, and salt and place over medium heat. Cook, stirring until the millet puffs up and is fully cooked, 10 to 12 minutes. 2. Remove the millet from the heat and slowly add the remaining ½ cup of milk along with the honey. Adjust the seasonings as desired. 3. Divide the millet between two bowls and top each with half of the apple and walnuts. 4. Store any leftovers in an airtight container in the refrigerator for up to 5 days.

Per Serving:

calories: 580 | fat: 16g | protein: 21g | carbs: 88g | sugars: 17g | fiber: 14g | sodium: 153mg

Egg-Stuffed Tomatoes

Prep time: 20 minutes | Cook time: 15 minutes | Serves 4

1 teaspoon extra-virgin olive oil	¼ cup shredded low-fat
4 large tomatoes	Swiss cheese
¼ teaspoon sea salt, plus more	4 large eggs
for seasoning	1 tablespoon chopped fresh
1 cup shredded kale	parsley
2 tablespoons heavy (whipping)	Freshly ground black pepper
cream	

1. Preheat the oven to 375°F. 2. Lightly grease an 8-by-8-inch baking dish with the olive oil and set it aside. 3. Cut the tops off the tomatoes and carefully scoop out the insides, leaving the outer shells intact. 4. Sprinkle the insides of the tomatoes with ¼ teaspoon of salt and set them cut-side down on paper towels for 30 minutes. 5. Place the tomatoes in the baking dish, hollow-side up, and evenly divide the kale between them. 6. Divide the cream and cheese between the tomatoes. Carefully crack an egg on top of the cheese in each tomato. 7. Bake the tomatoes until the eggs are set, about 15 minutes. 8. Serve the stuffed tomatoes topped with parsley and seasoned lightly with salt and pepper.

Per Serving:

calories: 154 | fat: 9g | protein: 10g | carbs: 8g | sugars: 5g | fiber: 2g | sodium: 244mg

Three-Berry Dutch Pancake

Prep time: 10 minutes | Cook time: 12 to 16 minutes | Serves 4

2 egg whites	1 tablespoon unsalted butter,
1 egg	melted
½ cup whole-wheat pastry flour	1 cup sliced fresh strawberries
½ cup 2% milk	½ cup fresh blueberries
1 teaspoon pure vanilla extract	½ cup fresh raspberries

1. In a medium bowl, use an eggbeater or hand mixer to quickly mix the egg whites, egg, pastry flour, milk, and vanilla until well combined. 2. Use a pastry brush to grease the bottom of a baking pan with the melted butter. Immediately pour in the batter and put the basket back in the fryer. Bake at 330°F (166°C) for 12 to 16 minutes, or until the pancake is puffed and golden brown. 3. Remove the pan from the air fryer; the pancake will fall. Top with the strawberries, blueberries, and raspberries. Serve immediately.

Per Serving:

calories: 151 | fat: 5g | protein: 7g | carbs: 20g | sugars: 6g | fiber: 4g | sodium: 59mg

Tofu, Kale, and Mushroom Breakfast Greek Yogurt Cinnamon Pancakes

Prep time: 5 minutes | Cook time: 20 minutes | Serves 4

1 cup 2 percent plain Greek	1 tablespoon granulated
yogurt	sweetener
3 eggs	1 teaspoon baking powder
1½ teaspoons pure vanilla	1 teaspoon ground cinnamon
extract	Pinch ground cloves
1 cup rolled oats	Nonstick cooking spray

1. Place the yogurt, eggs, and vanilla in a blender and pulse to combine. 2. Add the oats, sweetener, baking powder, cinnamon, and cloves to the blender and blend until the batter is smooth. 3. Place a large nonstick skillet over medium heat and lightly coat it with cooking spray. 4. Spoon ¼ cup of batter per pancake, 4 at a time, into the skillet. Cook the pancakes until the bottoms are firm and golden, about 4 minutes. 5. Flip the pancakes over and cook the other side until they are cooked through, about 3 minutes. 6. Remove the pancakes to a plate and repeat with the remaining batter. 7. Serve with fresh fruit.

Per Serving:

calories: 34 | fat: 7g | protein: 14g | carbs: 34g | sugars: 7g | fiber: 5g | sodium: 92mg

Pumpkin Spice Muffins

Prep time: 10 minutes | Cook time: 15 minutes | Serves 6

1 cup blanched finely ground almond flour	¼ cup pure pumpkin purée
½ cup granular erythritol	½ teaspoon ground cinnamon
½ teaspoon baking powder	¼ teaspoon ground nutmeg
¼ cup unsalted butter, softened	1 teaspoon vanilla extract
	2 large eggs

1. In a large bowl, mix almond flour, erythritol, baking powder, butter, pumpkin purée, cinnamon, nutmeg, and vanilla. 2. Gently stir in eggs. 3. Evenly pour the batter into six silicone muffin cups. Place muffin cups into the air fryer basket, working in batches if necessary. 4. Adjust the temperature to 300ºF (149ºC) and bake for 15 minutes. 5. When completely cooked, a toothpick inserted in center will come out mostly clean. Serve warm.

Per Serving:
calories: 261 | fat: 19g | protein: 8g | carbs: 16g | sugars: 11g | fiber: 3g | sodium: 34mg

Blueberry Coconut Breakfast Cookies

Prep time: 10 minutes | Cook time: 15 minutes | Serves 4

4 tablespoons unsalted butter, at room temperature	1 teaspoon vanilla extract
2 medium bananas	⅔ cup coconut flour
4 large eggs	¼ teaspoon salt
½ cup unsweetened applesauce	1 cup fresh or frozen blueberries

1. Preheat the oven to 375ºF. 2. In a medium bowl, mash the butter and bananas together with a fork until combined. The bananas can be a little chunky. 3. Add the eggs, applesauce, and vanilla to the bananas and mix well. 4. Stir in the coconut flour and salt. 5. Gently fold in the blueberries. 6. Drop about 2 tablespoons of dough on a baking sheet for each cookie and flatten it a bit with the back of a spoon. Bake for about 13 minutes, or until firm to the touch.

Per Serving:
calories: 263 | fat: 15g | protein: 8g | carbs: 24g | sugars: 14g | fiber: 4g | sodium: 225mg

Potato-Bacon Gratin

Prep time: 20 minutes | Cook time: 40 minutes | Serves 8

1 tablespoon olive oil	slices, divided
6-ounces bag fresh spinach	5-ounces reduced-fat grated
1 clove garlic, minced	Swiss cheddar, divided
4 large potatoes, peeled or unpeeled, divided	1 cup lower-sodium, lower-fat chicken broth
6-ounces Canadian bacon	

1. Set the Instant Pot to Sauté and pour in the olive oil. Cook the spinach and garlic in olive oil just until spinach is wilted (5 minutes or less). Turn off the instant pot. 2. Cut potatoes into thin slices about ¼" thick. 3. In a springform pan that will fit into the inner pot of your Instant Pot, spray it with nonstick spray then layer ⅓ the potatoes, half the bacon, ⅓ the cheese, and half the wilted spinach. 4. Repeat layers ending with potatoes. Reserve ⅓ cheese for later. 5.

Pour chicken broth over all. 6. Wipe the bottom of your Instant Pot to soak up any remaining oil, then add in 2 cups of water and the steaming rack. Place the springform pan on top. 7. Close the lid and secure to the locking position. Be sure the vent is turned to sealing. Set for 35 minutes on Manual at high pressure. 8. Perform a quick release. 9. Top with the remaining cheese, then allow to stand 10 minutes before removing from the Instant Pot, cutting and serving.

Per Serving:
calories: 220 | fat: 7g | protein: 14g | carbs: 28g | sugars: 2g | fiber: 3g | sodium: 415mg

Mini Breakfast Quiches

Prep time: 10 minutes | Cook time: 20 minutes | Serves 6

4 ounces diced green chilies	½ teaspoon cumin
¼ cup diced pimiento	1 bunch fresh cilantro or Italian
1 small eggplant, cubed	parsley, finely chopped
3 cups precooked brown rice	1 cup shredded reduced-fat
½ cup egg whites	cheddar cheese, divided
⅓ cup fat-free milk	

1. Preheat the oven to 400 degrees. Spray a 12-cup muffin tin with nonstick cooking spray. 2. In a large mixing bowl, combine all the ingredients except ½ cup of the cheese. 3. Add a dash of salt and pepper, if desired. 4. Spoon the mixture evenly into muffin cups, and sprinkle with the remaining cheese. Bake for 12–15 minutes or until set. Carefully remove the quiches from the pan, arrange on a platter, and serve.

Per Serving:
calories: 189 | fat: 3g | protein: 11g | carbs: 31g | sugars: 6g | fiber: 5g | sodium: 214mg

Brussels Sprouts and Egg Scramble

Prep time: 5 minutes | Cook time: 20 minutes | Serves 4

Avocado oil cooking spray	lengthwise
4 slices low-sodium turkey bacon	8 large eggs
20 Brussels sprouts, halved	¼ cup crumbled feta, for garnish

1. Heat a large skillet over medium heat. When hot, coat the cooking surface with cooking spray and cook the bacon to your liking. 2. Carefully remove the bacon from the pan and set it on a plate lined with a paper towel to drain and cool. 3. Place the Brussels sprouts in the skillet cut-side down, and cook for 3 minutes. 4. Reduce the heat to medium-low. Flip the Brussels sprouts, move them to one side of the skillet, and cover. Cook for another 3 minutes. 5. Uncover. Cook the eggs to over-medium alongside the Brussels sprouts, or to your liking. 6. Crumble the bacon once it has cooled. 7. Divide the Brussels sprouts into 4 portions and top each portion with one-quarter of the crumbled bacon and 2 eggs. Add 1 tablespoon of feta to each portion.

Per Serving:
calories: 314 | fat: 22g | protein: 20g | carbs: 10g | sugars: 3g | fiber: 4g | sodium: 373mg

Simple Buckwheat Porridge

Prep time: 5 minutes | Cook time: 40 minutes | Serves 4

2 cups raw buckwheat groats
3 cups water
Pinch sea salt

1 cup unsweetened almond
milk

1. Put the buckwheat groats, water, and salt in a medium saucepan over medium-high heat. 2. Bring the mixture to a boil, then reduce the heat to low. 3. Cook until most of the water is absorbed, about 20 minutes. Stir in the milk and cook until very soft, about 15 minutes. 4. Serve the porridge with your favorite toppings such as chopped nuts, sliced banana, or fresh berries.

Per Serving:

calories: 314 | fat: 3g | protein: 10g | carbs: 67g | sugars: 5g | fiber: 9g | sodium: 52mg

Quinoa Breakfast Bake with Pistachios and Plums

Prep time: 10 minutes | Cook time: 1 hour | Serves 2

Extra-virgin olive oil cooking
spray
⅓ cup dry quinoa, thoroughly
rinsed
1 teaspoon vanilla extract
1 teaspoon cinnamon
½ teaspoon nutmeg

Stevia, for sweetening
2 large egg whites
1 cup nonfat milk
2 plums, chopped, divided
4 tablespoons chopped unsalted
pistachios, divided

1. Preheat the oven to 350°F. 2. Spray two mini loaf pans with cooking spray. Set aside. 3. In a medium bowl, stir together the quinoa, vanilla, cinnamon, nutmeg, and stevia until the quinoa is coated with the spices. 4. Pour half of the quinoa mixture into each loaf pan. 5. In the same medium bowl, beat the egg whites and thoroughly whisk in the milk. 6. Evenly scatter half of the plums and 2 tablespoons of pistachios in each pan. 7. Pour half of the egg mixture over each loaf. Stir lightly to partially submerge the plums. 8. Place the pans in the preheated oven. Bake for 1 hour, or until the loaves are set, with only a small amount of liquid remaining. 9. Remove from the pans and enjoy hot!

Per Serving:

calories: 295 | fat: 9g | protein: 16g | carbs: 38g | sugars: 14g | fiber: 5g | sodium: 122mg

Plum Smoothie

Prep time: 5 minutes | Cook time: 0 minutes | Serves 2

4 ripe plums, pitted
1 cup skim milk
6 ounces 2 percent plain Greek

yogurt
4 ice cubes
¼ teaspoon ground nutmeg

1. Put the plums, milk, yogurt, ice, and nutmeg in a blender and blend until smooth. 2. Pour into two glasses and serve.

Per Serving:

calories: 144 | fat: 1g | protein: 14g | carbs: 20g | sugars: 17g | fiber: 2g | sodium: 82mg

Spinach, Artichoke, and Goat Cheese Breakfast Bake

Prep time: 10 minutes | Cook time: 35 minutes | Serves 8

Nonstick cooking spray
1 (10-ounce) package frozen
spinach, thawed and drained
1 (14-ounce) can artichoke
hearts, drained
¼ cup finely chopped red bell
pepper
2 garlic cloves, minced

8 eggs, lightly beaten
¼ cup unsweetened plain
almond milk
½ teaspoon salt
½ teaspoon freshly ground
black pepper
½ cup crumbled goat cheese

1. Preheat the oven to 375°F. Spray an 8-by-8-inch baking dish with nonstick cooking spray. 2. In a large mixing bowl, combine the spinach, artichoke hearts, bell pepper, garlic, eggs, almond milk, salt, and pepper. Stir well to combine. 3. Transfer the mixture to the baking dish. Sprinkle with the goat cheese. 4. Bake for 35 minutes until the eggs are set. Serve warm.

Per Serving:

calories: 104 | fat: 5 | protein: 9g | carbs: 6g | sugars: 1g | fiber: 2g | sodium: 488mg

Stovetop Granola

Prep time: 10 minutes | Cook time: 10 minutes | Makes 4½ cups

1½ cups grains (rolled oats, rye
flakes, or any flaked grain)
¼ cup vegetable, grapeseed, or
extra-virgin olive oil
¼ cup honey or maple syrup
1 tablespoon spice (cinnamon,
chai spices, turmeric, ginger, or
cloves)
1 tablespoon citrus zest (orange,
lemon, lime, or grapefruit)
(optional)

1¼ cups roasted, chopped
nuts (almonds, walnuts, or
pistachios)
¾ cup seeds (sunflower,
pumpkin, sesame, hemp, ground
chia, or ground flaxseed)
½ cup dried fruit (golden
raisins, apricots, raisins, dates,
figs, or cranberries)
Kosher salt

1. Heat a large dry skillet, preferably cast iron, over medium-high heat. Add the grains and cook, stirring frequently, until golden brown and toasty. Remove the grains from the skillet and transfer them to a small bowl. 2. Reduce the heat to medium, return the skillet to the heat, and add the vegetable oil, honey, and spice. Stir until thoroughly combined and bring to a simmer. 3. Once the mixture begins to bubble, reduce the heat to low and add the citrus zest (if using), toasted grains, nuts, seeds, and dried fruit. Stir and cook for another 2 minutes or until the granola is sticky and you can smell the spices. Adjust the seasonings as desired and add salt to taste. 4. Allow the granola to cool before storing it in an airtight container at room temperature for up to 6 months.

Per Serving:

½ cup: calories: 259 | fat: 13g | protein: 6g | carbs: 35g | sugars: 10g | fiber: 6g | sodium: 4mg

Baked Oatmeal Cups

Prep time: 5 minutes | Cook time: 20 minutes | Makes 15 cups

3 cups rolled oats
½ cup oat flour
3 tablespoons flax meal
1 teaspoon cinnamon
Rounded ⅛ teaspoon sea salt
2 cups sliced overripe banana

⅓ cup brown rice syrup
⅓ cup raisins
2 tablespoons sugar-free nondairy chocolate chips (optional)

1. Line a muffin pan with 15 parchment cupcake liners. Preheat the oven to 350°F. 2. In a large mixing bowl, combine the oats, oat flour, flax meal, cinnamon, and salt. Stir to combine. Mash or puree the banana using a food processor or immersion blender. Add the banana, syrup, raisins, and chips (if using). Stir until thoroughly combined. Using a cookie scoop, place ¼ to ⅓ cup of the batter in each muffin cup. Use a spatula or your fingers to lightly pack in the mixture. (Dampen your fingers to make it easier.) Bake for 20 minutes. Remove and let cool in the pan for about 5 minutes, then transfer to a cooling rack. Enjoy warm or cooled. Store in an airtight container in the fridge.

Per Serving:
calorie: 133 | fat: 2g | protein: 3g | carbs: 27g | sugars: 7g | fiber: 3g | sodium: 37mg

Pizza Eggs

Prep time: 5 minutes | Cook time: 10 minutes | Serves 2

1 cup shredded Mozzarella cheese
7 slices pepperoni, chopped
1 large egg, whisked

¼ teaspoon dried oregano
¼ teaspoon dried parsley
¼ teaspoon garlic powder
¼ teaspoon salt

1. Place Mozzarella in a single layer on the bottom of an ungreased round nonstick baking dish. Scatter pepperoni over cheese, then pour egg evenly around baking dish. 2. Sprinkle with remaining ingredients and place into air fryer basket. Adjust the temperature to 330°F (166°C) and bake for 10 minutes. When cheese is brown and egg is set, dish will be done. 3. Let cool in dish 5 minutes before serving.

Per Serving:
calories: 240 | fat: 18g | protein: 17g | carbs: 2g | net carbs: 2g | fiber: 0g

Grain-Free Coconut and Almond Waffles

Prep time: 5 minutes | Cook time: 10 minutes | Serves 4

⅔ cup (164 g) no-added-sugar applesauce
4 large eggs, beaten
2 tsp (10 ml) pure vanilla extract
2 tsp (10 ml) pure almond extract

1 cup (240 ml) milk of choice
½ cup (56 g) coconut flour
1 cup (96 g) almond flour
1 tbsp (12 g) baking powder
Cooking oil spray, as needed
Almond butter, sliced almonds, and toasted coconut (optional)

1. Preheat the waffle iron per the manufacturer's instructions. 2.

Meanwhile, in a blender, combine the applesauce, eggs, vanilla, almond extract, milk, coconut flour, almond flour, and baking powder. Blend the ingredients for about 20 seconds, until the batter is smooth. 3. If your waffle iron does not have a nonstick surface, spray it lightly with cooking oil spray before proceeding. 4. Pour about 3 tablespoons (45 ml) of the batter into the waffle iron for each waffle (this amount also depends on the size of your waffle iron). Follow the instructions for your waffle iron to cook the waffles. 5. Carefully remove the waffle from the waffle iron and let each waffle cool on a wire rack. Top the waffles with the almond butter, sliced almonds, and toasted coconut (if using).

Per Serving:
calorie: 354 | fat: 22g | protein: 16g | carbs: 24g | sugars: 10g | fiber: 9g | sodium: 141mg

Green Nice Cream Breakfast Bowl

Prep time: 5 minutes | Cook time: 0 minutes | Serves 3

3 cups sliced, frozen, overripe banana
1 cup frozen pineapple chunks
2 cups baby spinach
Flesh of 1 ripe avocado (about ½ cup)
Pinch of sea salt

3–5 tablespoons low-fat nondairy milk
1–2 tablespoons coconut syrup (optional)
½ cup fresh sliced banana
½ cup fresh berries

1. In a blender or food processor, combine the banana, pineapple, spinach, avocado, salt, and 3 tablespoons of the milk. Puree until very smooth. If the mixture is stubborn and not blending, add the additional 2 tablespoons of milk as needed to get the mixture moving. Taste, and add the syrup if desired to sweeten. Spoon the mixture into 3 serving bowls, and top with the banana and berries.

Per Serving:
calorie: 337 | fat: 8g | protein: 5g | carbs: 70g | sugars: 37g | fiber: 12g | sodium: 126mg

Harvest Blackberry Quinoa Bowl

Prep time: 5 minutes | Cook time: 20 minutes | Serves 2

1½ cups water
Pinch kosher salt
¾ cup quinoa, rinsed

1 cup halved blackberries
Ground cinnamon, for garnish

1. In a medium saucepan, bring the water and salt to a boil over high heat, reduce the heat to low, and add the quinoa. 2. Cook until you see the grains are tender and the liquid is absorbed, about 15 minutes. 3. Remove the quinoa from the heat. If you prefer your quinoa to be fluffy, then cover with a lid for a few minutes and allow it to rest. Once the quinoa is rested, use a fork to fluff it up, top it with the blackberries and a sprinkle of cinnamon, and serve. 4. If you like your grains creamier, serve immediately topped with blackberries and cinnamon.

Per Serving:
calories: 266 | fat: 4g | protein: 10g | carbs: 48g | sugars: 4g | fiber: 8g | sodium: 7mg

Very Cherry Overnight Oatmeal in a Jar

Prep time: 30 minutes | Cook time: 0 minutes | Serves 2

½ cup uncooked old-fashioned rolled oats
½ cup nonfat milk
½ cup plain nonfat Greek yogurt
2 tablespoons chia seeds
1 teaspoon liquid stevia
1 teaspoon cinnamon
½ teaspoon vanilla extract
½ cup frozen cherries, divided

1. In a small bowl, mix together the oats, milk, yogurt, chia seeds, stevia, cinnamon, and vanilla. 2. Evenly divide the oat mixture between 2 mason jars or individual containers. Cover tightly and shake until well combined. 3. To each jar, stir in ¼ cup of cherries. 4. Seal the containers and refrigerate overnight. 5. The next day, enjoy chilled or heated.

Per Serving:
calories: 247 | fat: 4g | protein: 13g | carbs: 41g | sugars: 11g | fiber: 7g | sodium: 81mg

Coddled Huevos Rancheros

Prep time: 5 minutes | Cook time: 10 minutes | Serves 2

2 teaspoons unsalted butter
4 large eggs
1 cup drained cooked black beans, or two-thirds 15-ounce can black beans, rinsed and drained
Two 7-inch corn or whole-wheat tortillas, warmed
½ cup chunky tomato salsa (such as Pace brand)
2 cups shredded romaine lettuce
1 tablespoon chopped fresh cilantro
2 tablespoons grated Cotija cheese

1. Pour 1 cup water into the Instant Pot and place a long-handled silicone steam rack into the pot. (If you don't have the long-handled rack, use the wire metal steam rack and a homemade sling) 2. Coat each of four 4-ounce ramekins with ½ teaspoon butter. Crack an egg into each ramekin. Place the ramekins on the steam rack in the pot. 3. Secure the lid and set the Pressure Release to Sealing. Select the Steam setting and set the cooking time for 3 minutes at low pressure. (The pot will take about 5 minutes to come up to pressure before the cooking program begins.) 4. While the eggs are cooking, in a small saucepan over low heat, warm the beans for about 5 minutes, stirring occasionally. Cover the saucepan and remove from the heat. (Alternatively, warm the beans in a covered bowl in a microwave for 1 minute. Leave the beans covered until ready to serve.) 5. When the cooking program ends, let the pressure release naturally for 5 minutes, then move the Pressure Release to Venting to release any remaining steam. Open the pot and, wearing heat-resistant mitts, grasp the handles of the steam rack and carefully lift it out of the pot. 6. Place a warmed tortilla on each plate and spoon ½ cup of the beans onto each tortilla. Run a knife around the inside edge of each ramekin to loosen the egg and unmold two eggs onto the beans on each tortilla. Spoon the salsa over the eggs and top with the lettuce, cilantro, and cheese. Serve right away.

Per Serving:
calorie: 112 | fat: 8g | protein: 8g | carbs: 3g | sugars: 0g | fiber: 0g | sodium: 297mg

Shakshuka

Prep time: 5 minutes | Cook time: 25 minutes | Serves 4

2 tablespoons extra-virgin olive oil
1 onion, diced
2 tablespoons tomato paste
2 red bell peppers, diced
2 tablespoons harissa (optional)
4 garlic cloves, minced
2 teaspoons ground cumin
½ teaspoon ground coriander (optional)
1 teaspoon smoked paprika
2 (14-ounce) cans diced tomatoes
4 large eggs
½ cup plain Greek yogurt
Bread, for dipping (optional)

1. Heat the extra-virgin olive oil in a Dutch oven or large saucepan over medium heat. When it starts to shimmer, add the onion and cook until translucent, about 3 minutes. 2. Add the tomato paste, peppers, harissa (if using), garlic, cumin, coriander (if using), paprika, and tomatoes. Bring to a simmer and cook 10 to 15 minutes, until the peppers are cooked and the sauce is thick. Adjust the seasoning as desired. 3. Make four wells in the mixture with the back of a large spoon and gently break one egg into each well. Cover the saucepan and simmer gently until the egg whites are set but the yolks are still runny, 5 to 8 minutes. 4. Remove the saucepan from the heat and spoon the tomato mixture and one cooked egg into each of four bowls. Top with the Greek yogurt and serve with bread (if using).

Per Serving:
calories: 229 | fat: 13g | protein: 11g | carbs: 20g | sugars: 13g | fiber: 7g | sodium: 127mg

Mini Spinach–Broccoli Quiches

Prep time: 5 minutes | Cook time: 35 minutes | Serves 2

Extra-virgin olive oil cooking spray
1 cup frozen broccoli florets
½ cup frozen spinach
2 large eggs
2 large egg whites
¼ cup unsweetened almond
milk, or nonfat dairy milk
Salt, to season
Freshly ground black pepper, to season
2 tablespoons fresh dill, divided
Shredded nonfat cheese, for garnish (optional)

1. Preheat the oven to 400°F. 2. Spray two (8-ounce) ramekins with cooking spray. 3. In a small microwave-safe dish, mix together the broccoli and spinach. Place in the microwave and thaw on high for 30 seconds. Remove from the microwave and drain off any excess liquid. 4. Fill each ramekin with half of the vegetable mixture. 5. In a medium bowl, beat the eggs and egg whites with the almond milk. Season with salt and pepper. 6. Evenly divide the egg mixture between the ramekins. 7. Top each with 1 tablespoon of dill. Garnish with the shredded cheese (if using). 8. Place the ramekins on a baking sheet. Carefully transfer the sheet to the preheated oven. Bake for about 35 minutes, or until the center is firm and the top is golden brown.

Per Serving:
calories: 151 | fat: 6g | protein: 16g | carbs: 11g | sugars: 3g | fiber: 5g | sodium: 188mg

Chorizo Mexican Breakfast Pizzas

Prep time: 15 minutes | Cook time: 15 minutes | Serves 4

6 oz chorizo sausage, casing removed, crumbled, or 6 oz bulk chorizo sausage
2 (10-inch) whole-grain lower-carb lavash flatbreads or tortillas
1/4 cup chunky-style salsa
1/2 cup black beans with cumin and chili spices (from 15-oz can)

1/2 cup chopped tomatoes
1/2 cup frozen whole-kernel corn, thawed
1/4 cup reduced-fat shredded Cheddar cheese (1 oz)
1 tablespoon chopped fresh cilantro
2 teaspoons crumbed cotija (white Mexican) cheese

1 Heat oven to 425°F. In 8-inch skillet, cook sausage over medium heat 4 to 5 minutes or until brown; drain. 2 On 1 large or 2 small cookie sheets, place flatbreads. Spread each with 2 tablespoons salsa. Top each with half the chorizo, beans, tomatoes, corn and Cheddar cheese. 3 Bake about 8 minutes or until cheese is melted. Sprinkle each with half the cilantro and cotija cheese; cut into wedges. Serve immediately.

Per Serving:

calories: 330 | fat: 2g | protein: 20g | carbs: 19g | sugars: 2g | fiber: 6g | sodium: 1030mg

Veggie-Stuffed Omelet

Prep time: 15 minutes | Cook time: 10 minutes | Serves 1

1 teaspoon olive or canola oil
2 tablespoons chopped red bell pepper
1 tablespoon chopped onion
1/4 cup sliced fresh mushrooms
1 cup loosely packed fresh baby spinach leaves, rinsed

1/2 cup fat-free egg product or 2 eggs, beaten
1 tablespoon water
Pinch salt
Pinch pepper
1 tablespoon shredded reduced-fat Cheddar cheese

1 In 8-inch nonstick skillet, heat oil over medium-high heat. Add bell pepper, onion and mushrooms to oil. Cook 2 minutes, stirring frequently, until onion is tender. Stir in spinach; continue cooking and stirring just until spinach wilts. Transfer vegetables from pan to small bowl. 2 In medium bowl, beat egg product, water, salt and pepper with fork or whisk until well mixed. Reheat same skillet over medium-high heat. Quickly pour egg mixture into pan. While sliding pan back and forth rapidly over heat, quickly stir with spatula to spread eggs continuously over bottom of pan as they thicken. Let stand over heat a few seconds to lightly brown bottom of omelet. Do not overcook; omelet will continue to cook after folding. 3 Place cooked vegetable mixture over half of omelet; top with cheese. With spatula, fold other half of omelet over vegetables. Gently slide out of pan onto plate. Serve immediately.

Per Serving:

calorie: 140 | fat: 5g | protein: 16g | carbs: 6g | sugars: 3g | fiber: 2g | sodium: 470mg

Breakfast Panini

Prep time: 10 minutes | Cook time: 10 minutes | Serves 2

2 eggs, beaten
1/2 teaspoon salt-free seasoning blend
2 tablespoons chopped fresh chives
2 whole wheat thin bagels

2 slices tomato
2 thin slices onion
4 ultra-thin slices reduced-sodium deli ham
2 thin slices reduced-fat Cheddar cheese

1 Spray 8-inch skillet with cooking spray; heat skillet over medium heat. In medium bowl, beat eggs, seasoning and chives with fork or whisk until well mixed. Pour into skillet. As eggs begin to set at bottom and side, gently lift cooked portions with spatula so that thin, uncooked portion can flow to bottom. Avoid constant stirring. Cook 3 to 4 minutes or until eggs are thickened throughout but still moist and creamy; remove from heat. 2 Meanwhile, heat closed contact grill or panini maker 5 minutes. 3 For each panini, divide cooked eggs evenly between bottom halves of bagels. Top each with 1 slice each tomato and onion, 2 ham slices, 1 cheese slice and top half of bagel. Transfer filled panini to heated grill. Close cover, pressing down lightly. Cook 2 to 3 minutes or until browned and cheese is melted. Serve immediately.

Per Serving:

1 Panini: calories: 260 | fat: 7g | protein: 15g | carbs: 32g | sugars: 5g | fiber: 2g | sodium: 410mg

Wild Mushroom Frittata

Prep time: 10 minutes | Cook time: 15 minutes | Serves 4

8 large eggs
1/2 cup skim milk
1/4 teaspoon ground nutmeg
Sea salt
Freshly ground black pepper
2 teaspoons extra-virgin olive oil

2 cups sliced wild mushrooms (cremini, oyster, shiitake, portobello, etc.)
1/2 red onion, chopped
1 teaspoon minced garlic
1/2 cup goat cheese, crumbled

1. Preheat the broiler. 2. In a medium bowl, whisk together the eggs, milk, and nutmeg until well combined. Season the egg mixture lightly with salt and pepper and set it aside. 3. Place an ovenproof skillet over medium heat and add the oil, coating the bottom completely by tilting the pan. 4. Sauté the mushrooms, onion, and garlic until translucent, about 7 minutes. 5. Pour the egg mixture into the skillet and cook until the bottom of the frittata is set, lifting the edges of the cooked egg to allow the uncooked egg to seep under. 6. Place the skillet under the broiler until the top is set, about 1 minute. 7. Sprinkle the goat cheese on the frittata and broil until the cheese is melted, about 1 minute more. 8. Remove from the oven. Cut into 4 wedges to serve.

Per Serving:

calories: 258 | fat: 17g | protein: 19g | carbs: 7g | sugars: 3g | fiber: 1g | sodium: 316mg

Polenta Porridge with Berry Swirl

Prep time: 5 minutes | Cook time: 8 minutes | Serves 4

1 cup frozen raspberries
¼ cup + 1 tablespoon pure maple syrup
2 cups vanilla or plain low-fat nondairy milk
1 cup water
¼ teaspoon nutmeg

Couple pinches of sea salt
1 cup cornmeal
1 cup fresh berries for serving or 1 cup sliced ripe banana (optional)
Sprinkle of coconut sugar for serving (optional)

1. In a blender, combine the raspberries and ¼ cup of the syrup. Blend until pureed. In a saucepan over medium-high heat, bring the milk, water, nutmeg, and salt to a boil. Reduce the heat to medium and slowly whisk in the cornmeal. Stir frequently for about 5 minutes, until the cornmeal comes to a slow bubble and thickens. Add the remaining 1 tablespoon syrup and stir to combine. Remove from the heat. Pour the porridge into bowls, and add the raspberry sauce, swirling it through the porridge with a butter knife or spoon. Serve, topping with the berries or banana (if using) and a sprinkle of coconut sugar (if using).

Per Serving:

calorie: 300 | fat: 2g | protein: 6g | carbs: 65g | sugars: 23g | fiber: 6g | sodium: 207mg

Ginger Blackberry Bliss Smoothie Bowl

Prep time: 5 minutes | Cook time: 0 minutes | Serves 2

½ cup frozen blackberries
1 cup plain Greek yogurt
1 cup baby spinach

½ cup unsweetened almond milk
½ teaspoon peeled and grated fresh ginger
¼ cup chopped pecans

1. In a blender or food processor, combine the blackberries, yogurt, spinach, almond milk, and ginger. Blend until smooth. 2. Spoon the mixture into two bowls. 3. Top each bowl with 2 tablespoons of chopped pecans and serve.

Per Serving:

calories: 211 | fat: 11g | protein: 10g | carbs: 18g | sugars: 13g | fiber: 4g | sodium: 149mg

Chapter 5 Beans and Grains

Baked Vegetable Macaroni Pie

Prep time: 15 minutes | Cook time: 35 minutes | Serves 6

1 (16-ounce) package whole-wheat macaroni
1 small yellow onion, chopped
2 garlic cloves, minced
2 celery stalks, thinly sliced
¼ teaspoon freshly ground black pepper
2 tablespoons chickpea flour

1 cup fat-free milk
2 cups grated reduced-fat sharp Cheddar cheese
2 large zucchini, finely grated and squeezed dry
2 roasted red peppers, chopped into ¼-inch pieces

1. Preheat the oven to 350°F. 2. Bring a large pot of water to a boil. 3. Add the macaroni and cook for 2 to 5 minutes, or until al dente. 4. Drain the macaroni, reserving 1 cup of the pasta water for the cheese sauce. Rinse under cold running water, and transfer to a large bowl. 5. In a large cast iron skillet, warm the pasta water over medium heat. 6. Add the onion, garlic, celery, and pepper. Cook for 3 to 5 minutes, or until the onion is translucent. 7. Add the chickpea flour slowly, mixing often. 8. Stir in the milk and cheese until a thick liquid is formed. It should be about the consistency of a smoothie. 9. Add the pasta to the cheese mixture along with the zucchini and red peppers. Mix thoroughly so the ingredients are evenly dispersed. 10. Cover the skillet tightly with aluminum foil, transfer to the oven, and bake for 15 to 20 minutes, or until the cheese is well melted. 11. Uncover and bake for 5 minutes, or until golden brown.

Per Serving:
calorie: 382 | fat: 4g | protein: 24g | carbs: 67g | sugars: 6g | fiber: 8g | sodium: 373mg

Thai Red Lentils

Prep time: 5 minutes | Cook time: 25 minutes | Serves 4

2 cups dried red lentils
1 can (13½ ounces) lite coconut milk
2 tablespoons red or yellow Thai curry paste
¼–½ teaspoon sea salt (use less

if using more curry paste)
2–2¼ cups water
⅓ cup finely chopped fresh basil
3–4 tablespoons lime juice

1. In a large saucepan over high heat, combine the lentils, coconut milk, curry paste, salt, and 2 cups of the water. Stir and bring to a boil. Reduce the heat to low, cover, and cook for 20 minutes, or until the lentils are fully softened. Add the basil and 3 tablespoons of the lime juice, and stir. Season to taste with more salt and the remaining 1 tablespoon lime juice, if desired. Add the remaining ¼ cup water to thin, if desired.

Per Serving:
calorie: 389 | fat: 8g | protein: 25g | carbs: 58g | sugars: 4g | fiber: 16g | sodium: 441mg

Curried Rice with Pineapple

Prep time: 5 minutes | Cook time: 35 minutes | Serves 8

1 onion, chopped
1½ cups water
1¼ cups low-sodium chicken broth
1 cup uncooked brown basmati rice, soaked in water 20 minutes and drained before cooking
2 red bell peppers, minced

1 teaspoon curry powder
1 teaspoon ground turmeric
1 teaspoon ground ginger
2 garlic cloves, minced
One 8-ounce can pineapple chunks packed in juice, drained
¼ cup sliced almonds, toasted

1. In a medium saucepan, combine the onion, water, and chicken broth. Bring to a boil, and add the rice, peppers, curry powder, turmeric, ginger, and garlic. Cover, placing a paper towel in between the pot and the lid, and reduce the heat. Simmer for 25 minutes. 2. Add the pineapple, and continue to simmer 5–7 minutes more until rice is tender and water is absorbed. Taste and add salt, if desired. Transfer to a serving bowl, and garnish with almonds to serve.

Per Serving:
calorie: 144 | fat: 3g | protein: 4g | carbs: 27g | sugars: 6g | fiber: 3g | sodium: 16mg

Spicy Couscous and Chickpea Salad

Prep time: 20 minutes | Cook time: 10 minutes | Serves 4

Salad
1/2 cup uncooked whole wheat couscous
11/2 cups water
1/4 teaspoon salt
1 can (15 oz) chickpeas (garbanzo beans), drained, rinsed
1 can (14.5 oz) diced tomatoes with green chiles, undrained
1/2 cup frozen shelled edamame

(green soybeans) or lima beans, thawed
2 tablespoons chopped fresh cilantro
Green bell peppers, halved, if desired
Dressing
2 tablespoons olive oil
1 teaspoon ground coriander
1/2 teaspoon ground cumin
1/2 teaspoon ground cinnamon

1. Cook couscous in the water and salt as directed on package. 2. Meanwhile, in medium bowl, mix chickpeas, tomatoes, edamame and cilantro. In small bowl, mix dressing ingredients until well blended. 3. Add cooked couscous to salad; mix well. Pour dressing over salad; stir gently to mix. Spoon salad mixture into halved bell peppers. Serve immediately, or cover and refrigerate until serving time.

Per Serving:
calorie: 370 | fat: 11g | protein: 16g | carbs: 53g | sugars: 6g | fiber: 10g | sodium: 460mg

Eggplant and Lentils with Curried Yogurt

Prep time: 10 minutes | Cook time: 20 minutes | Serves 4

2 large eggplants	divided
4 tablespoons extra-virgin olive oil, divided	¾ cup plain Greek yogurt
Kosher salt	2 teaspoons curry powder
2 cups water	Zest and juice of 1 lime
1 cup brown lentils, rinsed and soaked (optional to soak)	1 onion, thinly sliced
	¼ cup sliced almonds
1 teaspoon ground cumin,	½ teaspoon ground coriander
	¼ cup pomegranate seeds

1. Preheat the oven to 450°F. Line a baking sheet with parchment paper. 2. Use a peeler to peel strips of the skin off of the eggplant lengthwise. Alternate strips, leaving some of the purplish-black skin on the eggplant. It should be reminiscent of a zebra with the white flesh and dark skin. Cut the peeled eggplant width-wise into ½-inch-thick slices. Place them in a medium bowl. 3. Toss the eggplant with 2 tablespoons of extra-virgin olive oil and a pinch of salt. Spread the slices in a single layer on the prepared baking sheet. Roast the eggplant for 20 minutes, until slightly crispy and soft. 4. Meanwhile, in a medium stockpot over medium-high heat, combine the water, lentils, ½ teaspoon of cumin, and a pinch of salt. Bring to a boil, then reduce the heat to low, cover, and simmer for 20 minutes or until the lentils are tender. Set aside. 5. In a small bowl, combine the Greek yogurt with the curry powder, a pinch of lime zest, and 1 tablespoon of lime juice. Taste and adjust the seasonings as desired. Use the additional lime juice if you feel it should have more citrus or a looser consistency. Set aside. 6. Heat the remaining 2 tablespoons of extra-virgin olive oil in a medium skillet over medium-high heat. Sauté the onion until translucent, about 3 minutes. Add the remaining ½ teaspoon of cumin, the sliced almonds, and coriander to the skillet, stirring to combine. 7. Arrange the slices of eggplant on four plates, followed by the lentils, spiced yogurt, sautéed onions, and garnish with pomegranate seeds.

Per Serving:

calorie: 436 | fat: 18g | protein: 19g | carbs: 56g | sugars: 16g | fiber: 16g | sodium: 49mg

Easy Lentil Burgers

Prep time: 10 minutes | Cook time: 20 minutes | Serves 5

1 medium-large clove garlic	2 teaspoons onion powder
2 tablespoons tamari	¼ teaspoon sea salt
2 tablespoons tomato paste	Few pinches freshly ground black pepper
1 tablespoon red wine vinegar	
1½ tablespoons tahini	3 cups cooked brown lentils
2 tablespoons fresh thyme or oregano	1 cup toasted breadcrumbs
	½ cup rolled oats

1. In a food processor, combine the garlic, tamari, tomato paste, vinegar, tahini, thyme or oregano, onion powder, salt, pepper, and 1½ cups of the lentils. Puree until fairly smooth. Add the breadcrumbs, rolled oats, and the remaining 1½ cups of lentils. Pulse a few times. At this stage you're looking for a sticky texture that will hold together when pressed. If the mixture is still a little crumbly, pulse a few more times. 2. Preheat the oven to 400°F. Line a baking sheet with parchment paper. 3. Use an ice cream scoop to scoop the mixture onto the prepared baking sheet, flattening to shape into patties. Bake for about 20 minutes, flipping the burgers halfway through. Alternatively, you can cook the burgers in a nonstick skillet over medium heat for 4 to 5 minutes Per side, or until golden brown.

Per Serving:

calorie: 148 | fat: 2g | protein: 8g | carbs: 24g | sugars: 1g | fiber: 5g | sodium: 369mg

Hoppin' John

Prep time: 15 minutes | Cook time: 50 minutes | Serves 12

1 tablespoon canola oil	2 cups brown rice, rinsed
2 celery stalks, thinly sliced	5 cups store-bought low-sodium vegetable broth, divided
1 small yellow onion, chopped	
1 medium green bell pepper, chopped	2 bay leaves
	1 teaspoon smoked paprika
1 tablespoon tomato paste	1 teaspoon Creole seasoning
2 garlic cloves, minced	1¼ cups frozen black-eyed peas

1. In a Dutch oven, heat the canola oil over medium heat. 2. Add the celery, onion, bell pepper, tomato paste, and garlic and cook, stirring often, for 3 to 5 minutes, or until the vegetables are softened. 3. Add the rice, 4 cups of broth, bay leaves, paprika, and Creole seasoning. 4. Reduce the heat to low, cover, and cook for 30 minutes, or until the rice is tender. 5. Add the black-eyed peas and remaining 1 cup of broth. Mix well, cover, and cook for 12 minutes, or until the peas soften. Discard the bay leaves. 6. Enjoy.

Per Serving:

calorie: 155 | fat: 2g | protein: 4g | carbs: 30g | sugars: 1g | fiber: 2g | sodium: 24mg

Veggies and Kasha with Balsamic Vinaigrette

Prep time: 15 minutes | Cook time: 8 minutes | Serves 4

Salad	seeded, chopped (1¼ cups)
1 cup water	Vinaigrette
½ cup uncooked buckwheat kernels or groats (kasha)	2 tablespoons balsamic or red wine vinegar
4 medium green onions, thinly sliced (¼ cup)	1 tablespoon olive oil
	2 teaspoons sugar
2 medium tomatoes, seeded, coarsely chopped (1½ cups)	½ teaspoon salt
	¼ teaspoon pepper
1 medium unpeeled cucumber,	1 clove garlic, finely chopped

1 In 8-inch skillet, heat water to boiling. Add kasha; cook over medium-high heat 7 to 8 minutes, stirring occasionally, until tender. Drain if necessary. 2 In large bowl, mix kasha and remaining salad ingredients. 3 In tightly covered container, shake vinaigrette ingredients until blended. Pour vinaigrette over kasha mixture; toss. Cover; refrigerate 1 to 2 hours to blend flavors.

Per Serving:

calorie: 120 | fat: 4g | protein: 2g | carbs: 19g | sugars: 6g | fiber: 3g | sodium: 310mg

Colorful Rice Casserole

Prep time: 5 minutes | Cook time: 20 minutes | Serves 12

1 tablespoon extra-virgin olive oil	added chopped tomatoes, undrained
1½ pounds zucchini, thinly sliced	¼ cup chopped parsley
¾ cup chopped scallions	1 teaspoon oregano
2 cups corn kernels (frozen or fresh; if frozen, defrost)	3 cups cooked brown (or white) rice
One 14.5-ounce can no-salt-	⅛ teaspoon freshly ground black pepper

1. In a large skillet, heat the oil. Add the zucchini and scallions, and sauté for 5 minutes. 2. Add the remaining ingredients, cover, reduce heat, and simmer for 10–15 minutes or until the vegetables are heated through. Season with salt, if desired, and pepper. Transfer to a bowl, and serve.

Per Serving:
calorie: 109 | fat: 2g | protein: 3g | carbs: 21g | sugars: 4g | fiber: 3g | sodium: 14mg

Beet Greens and Black Beans

Prep time: 10 minutes | Cook time: 20 minutes | Serves 4

1 tablespoon unsalted non-hydrogenated plant-based butter	ribbons
½ Vidalia onion, thinly sliced	1 bunch dandelion greens, cut into ribbons
½ cup store-bought low-sodium vegetable broth	1 (15-ounce) can no-salt-added black beans
1 bunch beet greens, cut into	Freshly ground black pepper

1. In a medium skillet, melt the butter over low heat. 2. Add the onion, and sauté for 3 to 5 minutes, or until the onion is translucent. 3. Add the broth and greens. Cover the skillet and cook for 7 to 10 minutes, or until the greens are wilted. 4. Add the black beans and cook for 3 to 5 minutes, or until the beans are tender. Season with black pepper.

Per Serving:
calorie: 153 | fat: 3g | protein: 9g | carbs: 25g | sugars: 2g | fiber: 11g | sodium: 312mg

BBQ Bean Burgers

Prep time: 10 minutes | Cook time: 20 minutes | Makes 8 burgers

2 cups sliced carrots	½ tablespoon vegan Worcestershire sauce
1 medium-large clove garlic, quartered	½ tablespoon Dijon mustard
1 can (15 ounces) kidney beans, rinsed and drained	Scant ½ teaspoon sea salt
1 cup cooked, cooled brown rice	¼–½ teaspoon smoked paprika
¼ cup barbecue sauce	1 tablespoon chopped fresh thyme
	1¼ cups rolled oats

1. In a food processor, combine the carrots and garlic. Pulse until minced. Add the beans, rice, barbecue sauce, Worcestershire sauce, mustard, salt, paprika, and thyme. Puree until well combined. Once the mixture is fairly smooth, add the oats and pulse to combine.

Chill the mixture for 30 minutes, if possible. 2. Preheat the oven to 400°F. Line a baking sheet with parchment paper. 3. Use an ice cream scoop to scoop the mixture onto the prepared baking sheet, flattening to shape it into patties. Bake for about 20 minutes, flipping the burgers halfway through. Alternatively, you can cook the burgers in a nonstick skillet over medium heat for 6 to 8 minutes Per side, or until golden brown.

Per Serving:
calorie: 152 | fat: 2g | protein: 6g | carbs: 29g | sugars: 6 | fiber: 5g | sodium: 247mg

Sunshine Burgers

Prep time: 10 minutes | Cook time: 18 to 20 minutes | Makes 10 burgers

2 cups sliced raw carrots	1 teaspoon red wine vinegar or apple cider vinegar
1 large clove garlic, sliced or quartered	1 teaspoon smoked paprika
2 cans (15 ounces each) chickpeas, rinsed and drained	½ teaspoon dried rosemary
¼ cup sliced dry-packed sun-dried tomatoes	½ teaspoon ground cumin
2 tablespoons tahini	½ teaspoon sea salt
	1 cup rolled oats

1. In a food processor, combine the carrots and garlic. Pulse several times to mince. Add the chickpeas, tomatoes, tahini, vinegar, paprika, rosemary, cumin, and salt. Puree until well combined, scraping down the sides of the bowl once or twice. Add the oats, and pulse briefly to combine. Refrigerate the mixture for 30 minutes, if possible. 2. Preheat the oven to 400°F. Line a baking sheet with parchment paper. 3. Use an ice cream scoop to scoop the mixture onto the prepared baking sheet, flattening to shape it into patties. Bake for 18 to 20 minutes, flipping the burgers halfway through. Alternatively, you can cook the burgers in a nonstick skillet over medium heat for 6 to 8 minutes Per side, or until golden brown. Serve.

Per Serving:
calorie: 137 | fat: 4 | protein: 6g | carbs: 21g | sugars: 4g | fiber: 6g | sodium: 278mg

Asian Fried Rice

Prep time: 5 minutes | Cook time: 20 minutes | Serves 4

2 tablespoons peanut oil	½ cup water chestnuts, drained
¼ cup chopped onion	½ cup sliced mushrooms
1 cup sliced carrot	1 tablespoon light soy sauce
1 green bell pepper, diced	2 egg whites
1 tablespoon grated fresh ginger	½ cup sliced scallions
2 cups cooked brown rice, cold	

1. In a large skillet, heat the oil. Sauté the onion, carrot, green pepper, and ginger for 5–6 minutes. 2. Stir in the rice, water chestnuts, mushrooms, and soy sauce, and stir-fry for 8–10 minutes. 3. Stir in the egg whites, and continue to stir-fry for another 3 minutes. Top with the sliced scallions to serve.

Per Serving:
calorie: 223 | fat: 9g | protein: 6g | carbs: 32g | sugars: 5g | fiber: 4g | sodium: 151mg

Southwestern Quinoa Salad

Prep time: 15 minutes | Cook time: 25 minutes | Serves 6

Salad
1 cup uncooked quinoa
1 large onion, chopped (1 cup)
1 1/2 cups reduced-sodium chicken broth
1 cup packed fresh cilantro leaves
1/4 cup raw unsalted hulled pumpkin seeds (pepitas)
2 cloves garlic, sliced
1/8 teaspoon ground cumin
2 tablespoons chopped green

chiles (from 4.5-oz can)
1 tablespoon olive oil
1 can (15 oz) no-salt-added black beans, drained, rinsed
6 medium plum (Roma) tomatoes, chopped (2 cups)
2 tablespoons lime juice
Garnish
1 avocado, pitted, peeled, thinly sliced
4 small cilantro sprigs

1 Rinse quinoa thoroughly by placing in a fine-mesh strainer and holding under cold running water until water runs clear; drain well. 2 Spray 3-quart saucepan with cooking spray. Heat over medium heat. Add onion to pan; cook 6 to 8 minutes, stirring occasionally, until golden brown. Stir in quinoa and chicken broth. Heat to boiling; reduce heat. Cover and simmer 10 to 15 minutes or until all liquid is absorbed; remove from heat. 3 Meanwhile, in small food processor*, place cilantro, pumpkin seeds, garlic and cumin. Cover; process 5 to 10 seconds, using quick on-and-off motions; scrape side. Add chiles and oil. Cover; process, using quick on-and-off motions, until paste forms. 4 To cooked quinoa, add pesto mixture and the remaining salad ingredients. Refrigerate at least 30 minutes to blend flavors. 5 To serve, divide salad evenly among 4 plates; top each serving with 3 or 4 slices avocado and 1 sprig cilantro.

Per Serving:

calorie: 310 | fat: 12g | protein: 13g | carbs: 38g | sugars: 5g | fiber: 9g | sodium: 170mg

Chicken–Wild Rice Salad with Dried Cherries

Prep time: 30 minutes | Cook time: 10 minutes | Serves 5

1 package (6.2 oz) fast-cooking long-grain and wild rice mix
2 cups chopped cooked chicken or turkey
1 medium unpeeled apple, chopped (1 cup)
1 medium green bell pepper, chopped (1 cup)
1 medium stalk celery, chopped

(1/2 cup)
1/2 cup chopped dried apricots
1/3 cup chopped dried cherries
2 tablespoons reduced-sodium soy sauce
2 tablespoons water
2 teaspoons sugar
2 teaspoons cider vinegar
1/3 cup dry-roasted peanuts

1 Cook rice mix as directed on package, omitting butter. On large cookie sheet, spread rice evenly in thin layer. Let stand 10 minutes, stirring occasionally, until cool. 2 Meanwhile, in large bowl, mix chicken, apple, bell pepper, celery, apricots and cherries. In small bowl, mix soy sauce, water, sugar and vinegar until sugar is dissolved. 3 Add rice and soy sauce mixture to apple mixture; toss gently until coated. Add peanuts; toss gently.

Per Serving:

calorie: 380 | fat: 7g | protein: 24g | carbs: 54g | sugars: 21g | fiber: 4g | sodium: 760mg

Chicken and Vegetables with Quinoa

Prep time: 25 minutes | Cook time: 25 minutes | Serves 4

1 1/3 cups uncooked quinoa
2 2/3 cups water
2/3 cup chicken broth
2 cups 1-inch pieces fresh green beans
1/2 cup ready-to-eat baby-cut carrots, cut in half lengthwise
1 tablespoon olive oil
1/2 lb boneless skinless chicken

breasts, cut into bite-size pieces
1/2 cup bite-size strips red bell pepper
1/2 cup sliced fresh mushrooms
1/2 teaspoon dried rosemary leaves
1/4 teaspoon salt
2 cloves garlic, finely chopped

1 Rinse quinoa thoroughly by placing in a fine-mesh strainer and holding under cold running water until water runs clear; drain well. 2 In 2-quart saucepan, heat water to boiling. Add quinoa; return to boiling. Reduce heat to low. Cover; cook 12 to 16 minutes or until liquid is absorbed. 3 Meanwhile, in 12-inch nonstick skillet, heat broth to boiling over high heat. Add green beans and carrots. Reduce heat to medium-high. Cover; cook 5 to 7 minutes or until vegetables are crisp-tender. 4 Stir oil, chicken, bell pepper, mushrooms, rosemary, salt and garlic into vegetables. Cook over medium-high heat 8 to 9 minutes, stirring frequently, until chicken is no longer pink in center. Serve over quinoa.

Per Serving:

calorie: 350 | fat: 9g | protein: 22g | carbs: 46g | sugars: 6g | fiber: 6g | sodium: 380mg

Farmers' Market Barley Risotto

Prep time: 30 minutes | Cook time: 15 minutes | Serves 4

1 tablespoon olive oil
1 medium onion, chopped (1/2 cup)
1 medium bell pepper, coarsely chopped (1 cup)
2 cups chopped fresh mushrooms (4 oz)
1 cup frozen whole-kernel corn
1 cup uncooked medium pearled barley
1/4 cup dry white wine or

chicken broth
2 cups reduced-sodium chicken broth
3 cups water
1 1/2 cups grape tomatoes, cut in half (if large, cut into quarters)
2/3 cup shredded Parmesan cheese
3 tablespoons chopped fresh or 1 teaspoon dried basil leaves
1/2 teaspoon pepper

1 In 4-quart Dutch oven or saucepan, heat oil over medium heat. Cook onion, bell pepper, mushrooms and corn in oil about 5 minutes, stirring frequently, until onion is crisp-tender. Add barley, stirring about 1 minute to coat. 2 Stir in wine and 1/2 cup of the broth. Cook 5 minutes, stirring frequently, until liquid is almost absorbed. Repeat with remaining broth and 3 cups water, adding 1/2 to 3/4 cup of broth or water at a time and stirring frequently, until absorbed. 3 Stir in tomatoes, 1/4 cup of the cheese, the basil and pepper. Cook until thoroughly heated. Sprinkle with remaining 1/4 cup cheese.

Per Serving:

calorie: 370 | fat: 8g | protein: 15g | carbs: 55g | sugars: 6g | fiber: 11g | sodium: 520mg

Pressure-Stewed Chickpeas

Prep time: 10 minutes | Cook time: 25 minutes | Serves 5

3 tablespoons water	Rounded ½ teaspoon sea salt
2 large or 3 small to medium onions, chopped (3–3½ cups)	2 cans (15 ounces each) chickpeas, rinsed and drained
1½ tablespoons smoked paprika	⅔ cup chopped, pitted dates
½ teaspoon ground cumin	1 jar (24 ounces) strained tomatoes
⅛–¼ teaspoon ground allspice	

1. In the instant pot set on the sauté function, combine the water, onions, paprika, cumin, allspice, and salt. Cook for 6 to 7 minutes, stirring occasionally. If the mixture is sticking, add another tablespoon or two of water. Add the chickpeas, dates, and tomatoes, and stir well. Turn off the sauté function, and put on the lid. Manually set to pressure cook on high for 18 minutes. Release the pressure or let the pressure release naturally. Stir, taste, season as desired, and serve.

Per Serving:

calorie: 258 | fat: 4g | protein: 10g | carbs: 50g | sugars: 23g | fiber: 13g | sodium: 742mg

Brown Rice–Stuffed Butternut Squash

Prep time: 30 minutes | Cook time: 50 minutes |

Serves 4

2 small butternut squash (about 2 lb each)	1 bay leaf
4 teaspoons olive oil	2 links (3 oz each) sweet Italian turkey sausage, casings removed
1/4 teaspoon salt	
1/2 teaspoon freshly ground pepper	1 small onion, chopped (1/3 cup)
1/3 cup uncooked brown basmati rice	1 cup sliced cremini mushrooms
11/4 cups reduced-sodium chicken broth	1 cup fresh baby spinach leaves
1 thyme sprig	1 teaspoon chopped fresh or 1/4 teaspoon dried sage leaves

1 Heat oven to 375°F. Cut each squash lengthwise in half; remove seeds and fibers. Drizzle cut sides with 3 teaspoons of the olive oil; sprinkle with salt and pepper. On cookie sheet, place squash, cut side down. Bake 35 to 40 minutes, until squash is tender at thickest portion when pierced with fork. When cool enough to handle, cut off long ends of squash to within 1/2 inch edge of cavities (peel and refrigerate ends for another use). 2 Meanwhile, in 1-quart saucepan, heat remaining 1 teaspoon oil over medium heat. Add rice to oil, stirring well to coat. Stir in chicken broth, thyme and bay leaf. Heat to boiling; reduce heat. Cover and simmer 30 to 35 minutes, until all liquid is absorbed and rice is tender. Remove from heat; discard thyme sprig and bay leaf. 3 In 10-inch nonstick skillet, cook sausage and onion over medium-high heat 8 to 10 minutes, stirring frequently, until sausage is thoroughly cooked. Add mushrooms. Cook 4 minutes or until mushrooms are tender. Stir in cooked rice, spinach and sage; cook about 3 minutes or until spinach is wilted and mixture is hot. Divide sausage-rice mixture between squash halves, pressing down on filling so it forms a slight mound over cavity.

Per Serving:

calorie: 350 | fat: 10g | protein: 14g | carbs: 50g | sugars: 14g | fiber: 5g | sodium: 670mg

BBQ Lentils

Prep time: 10 minutes | Cook time: 55 minutes | Serves 5

2 cups dried green or brown lentils, rinsed	2 teaspoons dried rosemary
3 tablespoons balsamic vinegar	1 teaspoon onion powder
4½ cups water	½ teaspoon garlic powder
½ cup tomato paste	½ teaspoon allspice
2 tablespoons vegan Worcestershire sauce	¼ teaspoon sea salt
	1 tablespoon coconut nectar or pure maple syrup

1. In a large saucepan over medium-high heat, combine the lentils with 2 tablespoons of the vinegar. Cook, stirring, for 5 to 7 minutes to lightly toast the lentils. Once the pan is getting dry, add the water, tomato paste, Worcestershire sauce, rosemary, onion powder, garlic powder, allspice, salt, nectar or syrup, and the remaining 1 tablespoon vinegar, and stir through. Bring to a boil, then reduce the heat to low, cover the pot, and cook for 37 to 40 minutes, or until the lentils are fully tender. Season to taste, and serve.

Per Serving:

calorie: 295 | fat: 1g | protein: 20g | carbs: 54g | sugars: 9g | fiber: 14g | sodium: 399mg

Italian Bean Burgers

Prep time: 10 minutes | Cook time: 20 minutes |

Makes 9 burgers

2 cans (14 or 15 ounces each) chickpeas, drained and rinsed	Scant ½ teaspoon sea salt
1 medium–large clove garlic, cut in half	2 tablespoons chopped fresh oregano
2 tablespoons tomato paste	⅓ cup roughly chopped fresh basil leaves
1½ tablespoons red wine vinegar (can substitute apple cider vinegar)	1 cup rolled oats
	⅓ cup chopped sun-dried tomatoes (not packed in oil)
1 tablespoon tahini	½ cup roughly chopped kalamata or green olives
1 teaspoon Dijon mustard	
½ teaspoon onion powder	

1. In a food processor, combine the chickpeas, garlic, tomato paste, vinegar, tahini, mustard, onion powder, and salt. Puree until fully combined. Add the oregano, basil, and oats, and pulse briefly. (You want to combine the ingredients but retain some of the basil's texture.) Finally, pulse in the sun-dried tomatoes and olives, again maintaining some texture. Transfer the mixture to a bowl and refrigerate, covered, for 30 minutes or longer. 2. Preheat the oven to 400°F. Line a baking sheet with parchment paper. Use an ice cream scoop to scoop the mixture onto the prepared baking sheet, flattening to shape into patties. Bake for about 20 minutes, flipping the burgers halfway through. Alternatively, you can cook the burgers in a nonstick skillet over medium heat for 6 to 8 minutes Per side, or until golden brown. Serve.

Per Serving:

calorie: 148 | fat: 4g | protein: 6g | carbs: 23g | sugars: 4g | fiber: 6g | sodium: 387mg

Rice with Spinach and Feta

Prep time: 10 minutes | Cook time: 15 minutes | Serves 4

¾ cup uncooked brown rice
1½ cups water
1 tablespoon extra-virgin olive oil
1 medium onion, diced
1 cup sliced mushrooms
2 garlic cloves, minced
1 tablespoon lemon juice

½ teaspoon dried oregano
9 cups fresh spinach, stems trimmed, washed, patted dry, and coarsely chopped
⅓ cup crumbled fat-free feta cheese
⅛ teaspoon freshly ground black pepper

1. In a medium saucepan over medium heat, combine the rice and water. Bring to a boil, cover, reduce heat, and simmer for 15 minutes. Transfer to a serving bowl. 2. In a skillet, heat the oil. Sauté the onion, mushrooms, and garlic for 5–7 minutes. Stir in the lemon juice and oregano. Add the spinach, cheese, and pepper, tossing until the spinach is slightly wilted. 3. Toss with rice and serve.

Per Serving:
calorie: 205 | fat: 5g | protein: 7g | carbs: 34g | sugars: 2g | fiber: 4g | sodium: 129mg

Green Chickpea Falafel

Prep time: 10 minutes | Cook time: 11 to 12 minutes | Serves 4

1 bag (14 ounces) green chickpeas, thawed (about 3½ cups)
½ cup fresh flat-leaf parsley leaves
½ cup fresh cilantro leaves
1½ tablespoons freshly squeezed lemon juice

2 medium-large cloves garlic
2 teaspoons ground cumin
½ teaspoon turmeric
1 teaspoon ground coriander
1 teaspoon sea salt
¼–½ teaspoon crushed red-pepper flakes
1 cup rolled oats

1. In a food processor, combine the chickpeas, parsley, cilantro, lemon juice, garlic, cumin, turmeric, coriander, salt, and red-pepper flakes. (Use ¼ teaspoon if you like it mild and ½ teaspoon if you like it spicier.) Process until the mixture breaks down and begins to smooth out. Add the oats and pulse a few times to work them in. Refrigerate for 30 minutes, if possible. 2. Preheat the oven to 400°F. Line a baking sheet with parchment paper. 3. Use a cookie scoop to take small scoops of the mixture, 1 to 1½ tablespoons each. Place falafel balls on the prepared baking sheet. Bake for 11 to 12 minutes, until the falafel balls begin to firm (they will still be tender inside) and turn golden in spots.

Per Serving:
calorie: 253 | fat: 4g | protein: 12g | carbs: 43g | sugars: 5g | fiber: 10g | sodium: 601mg

Coconut-Ginger Rice

Prep time: 10 minutes | Cook time: 20 minutes | Serves 8

2½ cups reduced-sodium chicken broth
⅔ cup reduced-fat (lite) coconut milk (not cream of coconut)
1 tablespoon grated gingerroot
½ teaspoon salt
1⅓ cups uncooked regular

long-grain white rice
1 teaspoon grated lime peel
3 medium green onions, chopped (3 tablespoons)
3 tablespoons flaked coconut, toasted*
Lime slices

1 In 3-quart saucepan, heat broth, coconut milk, gingerroot and salt to boiling over medium-high heat. Stir in rice. Return to boiling. Reduce heat; cover and simmer about 15 minutes or until rice is tender and liquid is absorbed. Remove from heat. 2 Add lime peel and onions; fluff rice mixture lightly with fork to mix. Garnish with coconut and lime slices.

Per Serving:
calorie: 150 | fat: 2g | protein: 3g | carbs: 30g | sugars: 1g | fiber: 0g | sodium: 340mg

Lentil Bolognese

Prep time: 10 minutes | Cook time: 30 minutes | Serves 4

⅓ cup red wine
1 cup diced onion
½ cup minced carrot
1 tablespoon dried oregano leaves
1 teaspoon vegan Worcestershire sauce
¾ teaspoon smoked paprika
½ teaspoon sea salt
¼ teaspoon ground nutmeg
1½ cups cooked brown or green

lentils
¼ cup chopped sun-dried tomatoes
1 can (28 ounces) diced tomatoes (use fire-roasted, if you'd like a spicy kick)
2–3 tablespoons minced dates
1 pound dry pasta
½ cup almond meal (toast until lightly golden if you want extra flavor)

1. In a large pot over high heat, combine the wine, onion, carrot, oregano, Worcestershire sauce, paprika, salt, and nutmeg. Cook for 5 minutes, stirring frequently. Add the lentils, sun-dried tomatoes, diced tomatoes, and dates, and bring to a boil. Reduce the heat to low, cover, and cook for 20 to 25 minutes. 2. While the sauce is simmering, prepare the pasta according to package directions. Once the pasta is almost cooked (still having some "bite," not mushy), drain and return it to the cooking pot. 3. Add the almond meal to the sauce, stir to incorporate, and cook for a couple of minutes. Taste, season as desired, and toss with the pasta before serving.

Per Serving:
calorie: 754 | fat: 11g | protein: 31g | carbs: 132g | sugars: 14g | fiber: 17g | sodium: 622mg

Chapter 6 Beef, Pork, and Lamb

Swiss Steak Casserole

Prep time: 20 minutes | Cook time: 1 hour 45 minutes | Serves 6

3 tablespoons all-purpose flour
1/2 teaspoon salt
1 teaspoon paprika
1/2 teaspoon pepper
1 lb boneless beef round steak, cut into 3/4-inch cubes
2 tablespoons canola oil

2 cups sliced fresh mushrooms
1 cup frozen pearl onions
1 clove garlic, finely chopped
4 cups sliced carrots (8 medium)
1 can (14.5 oz) stewed tomatoes, undrained

1 Heat oven to 350°F. In medium bowl, mix flour, salt, paprika and pepper. Add beef; toss to coat. In 12-inch skillet, heat 1 tablespoon of the oil over medium-high heat. Add beef, reserving remaining flour mixture. Cook beef on all sides. Spoon into ungreased 2 1/2-quart casserole. 2 To same skillet, add remaining 1 tablespoon oil, the mushrooms, onions and garlic. Cook 2 to 3 minutes, stirring constantly, until browned; add to casserole. Stir in carrots, tomatoes and reserved flour mixture until well mixed. 3 Cover casserole. Bake 1 hour 30 minutes to 1 hour 45 minutes or until beef and vegetables are tender.

Per Serving:
calories: 260 | fat: 9g | protein: 25g | carbs: 20g | sugars: 10g | fiber: 4g | sodium: 660mg

Goat Cheese-Stuffed Flank Steak

Prep time: 10 minutes | Cook time: 14 minutes | Serves 6

1 pound (454 g) flank steak
1 tablespoon avocado oil
1/2 teaspoon sea salt
1/2 teaspoon garlic powder
1/4 teaspoon freshly ground

black pepper
2 ounces (57 g) goat cheese, crumbled
1 cup baby spinach, chopped

1. Place the steak in a large zip-top bag or between two pieces of plastic wrap. Using a meat mallet or heavy-bottomed skillet, pound the steak to an even 1/4-inch thickness. 2. Brush both sides of the steak with the avocado oil. 3. Mix the salt, garlic powder, and pepper in a small dish. Sprinkle this mixture over both sides of the steak. 4. Sprinkle the goat cheese over top, and top that with the spinach. 5. Starting at one of the long sides, roll the steak up tightly. Tie the rolled steak with kitchen string at 3-inch intervals. 6. Set the air fryer to 400°F (204°C). Place the steak roll-up in the air fryer basket. Air fry for 7 minutes. Flip the steak and cook for an additional 7 minutes, until an instant-read thermometer reads 120°F (49°C) for medium-rare (adjust the cooking time for your desired doneness).

Per Serving:
calories: 151 | fat: 8g | protein: 18g | carbs: 0g | fiber: 0g | sodium: 281mg

Steak Gyro Platter

Prep time: 30 minutes | Cook time: 8 to 10 minutes | Serves 4

1 pound (454 g) flank steak
1 teaspoon garlic powder
1 teaspoon ground cumin
1/2 teaspoon sea salt
1/2 teaspoon freshly ground black pepper
5 ounces (142 g) shredded romaine lettuce

1/2 cup crumbled feta cheese
1/2 cup peeled and diced cucumber
1/3 cup sliced red onion
1/4 cup seeded and diced tomato
2 tablespoons pitted and sliced black olives
Tzatziki sauce, for serving

1. Pat the steak dry with paper towels. In a small bowl, combine the garlic powder, cumin, salt, and pepper. Sprinkle this mixture all over the steak, and allow the steak to rest at room temperature for 45 minutes. 2. Preheat the air fryer to 400°F (204°C). Place the steak in the air fryer basket and air fry for 4 minutes. Flip the steak and cook 4 to 6 minutes more, until an instant-read thermometer reads 120°F (49°C) at the thickest point for medium-rare (or as desired). Remove the steak from the air fryer and let it rest for 5 minutes. 3. Divide the romaine among plates. Top with the feta, cucumber, red onion, tomato, and olives.

Per Serving:
calories: 229 | fat: 10g | protein: 28g | carbs: 5g | fiber: 2g | sodium: 559mg

Chipotle Chili Pork Chops

Prep time: 5 minutes | Cook time: 20 minutes | Serves 4

Juice and zest of 1 lime
1 tablespoon extra-virgin olive oil
1 tablespoon chipotle chili powder
2 teaspoons minced garlic

1 teaspoon ground cinnamon
Pinch sea salt
4 (5-ounce) pork chops, about 1 inch thick
Lime wedges, for garnish

1. Combine the lime juice and zest, oil, chipotle chili powder, garlic, cinnamon, and salt in a resealable plastic bag. Add the pork chops. Remove as much air as possible and seal the bag. 2. Marinate the chops in the refrigerator for at least 4 hours, and up to 24 hours, turning them several times. 3. Preheat the oven to 400°F and set a rack on a baking sheet. Let the chops rest at room temperature for 15 minutes, then arrange them on the rack and discard the remaining marinade. 4. Roast the chops until cooked through, turning once, about 10 minutes per side. 5. Serve with lime wedges.

Per Serving:
calorie: 224 | fat: 9g | protein: 32g | carbs: 4g | sugars: 0g | fiber: 2g | sodium: 140mg

Coffee-and-Herb-Marinated Steak

Prep time: 10 minutes | Cook time: 10 minutes | Serves 4

¼ cup whole coffee beans	pepper
2 teaspoons minced garlic	2 tablespoons apple cider
2 teaspoons chopped fresh	vinegar
rosemary	2 tablespoons extra-virgin olive
2 teaspoons chopped fresh	oil
thyme	1 pound flank steak, trimmed of
1 teaspoon freshly ground black	visible fat

1. Place the coffee beans, garlic, rosemary, thyme, and black pepper in a coffee grinder or food processor and pulse until coarsely ground. 2. Transfer the coffee mixture to a resealable plastic bag and add the vinegar and oil. Shake to combine. 3. Add the flank steak and squeeze the excess air out of the bag. Seal it. Marinate the steak in the refrigerator for at least 2 hours, occasionally turning the bag over. 4. Preheat the broiler. Line a baking sheet with aluminum foil. 5. Take the steak out of the bowl and discard the marinade. 6. Place the steak on the baking sheet and broil until it is done to your liking, about 5 minutes per side for medium. 7. Let the steak rest for 10 minutes before slicing it thinly on a bias. 8. Serve with a mixed green salad or your favorite side dish.

Per Serving:
calorie: 191 | fat: 9g | protein: 25g | carbs: 1g | sugars: 0g | fiber: 0g | sodium: 127mg

Sage-Parmesan Pork Chops

Prep time: 30 minutes | Cook time: 25 minutes | Serves 2

Extra-virgin olive oil cooking	½ cup soy Parmesan cheese
spray	1½ teaspoons rubbed sage
2 tablespoons coconut flour	½ teaspoon grated lemon zest
¼ teaspoon salt	2 (4-ounce) boneless pork
Pinch freshly ground black	chops
pepper	1 large egg, lightly beaten
¼ cup almond meal	1 tablespoon extra-virgin olive
½ cup finely ground flaxseed	oil
meal	

1. Preheat the oven to 425°F. 2. Lightly coat a medium baking dish with cooking spray. 3. In a shallow dish, mix together the coconut flour, salt, and pepper. 4. In a second shallow dish, stir together the almond meal, flaxseed meal, soy Parmesan cheese, sage, and lemon zest. 5. Gently press one pork chop into the coconut flour mixture to coat. Shake off any excess. Dip into the beaten egg. Press into the almond meal mixture. Gently toss between your hands so any coating that hasn't stuck can fall away. Place the coated chop on a plate. Repeat the process with the remaining pork chop and coating ingredients. 6. In a large skillet set over medium heat, heat the olive oil. 7. Add the coated chops. Cook for about 4 minutes per side, or until browned. Transfer to the prepared baking dish. Place the dish in the preheated oven. Bake for 10 to 15 minutes, or until the juices run clear and an instant-read thermometer inserted into the middle of the pork reads 160°F.

Per Serving:
calorie: 520 | fat: 31g | protein: 45g | carbs: 14g | sugars: 1g | fiber: 6g | sodium: 403mg

Chinese Spareribs

Prep time: 10 minutes | Cook time: 40 minutes | Serves 2

2 tablespoons hoisin sauce	powder
2 tablespoons tomato paste	2 garlic cloves, minced
2 tablespoons water	1 teaspoon freshly squeezed
1 tablespoon rice vinegar	lemon juice
2 teaspoons sesame oil	1 teaspoon grated fresh ginger
2 teaspoons low-sodium soy	½ teaspoon granulated stevia
sauce	1 pound pork spareribs
2 teaspoons Chinese five-spice	

1. In a shallow glass dish, mix together the hoisin sauce, tomato paste, water, rice vinegar, sesame oil, soy sauce, Chinese five-spice powder, garlic, lemon juice, ginger, and stevia. 2. Add the ribs to the marinade. Turn to coat. Cover and refrigerate for 2 hours, or overnight. 3. Preheat the oven to 325°F. 4. Place a rack in the center of the oven. 5. Fill a broiler tray with enough water to cover the bottom. Place the grate over the tray. Arrange the ribs on the grate. Reserve the marinade. 6. Place the broiler pan in the preheated oven. Cook for 40 minutes, turning and brushing with the reserved marinade every 10 minutes. 7. Finish under the broiler for a crispier texture, if desired. Discard any remaining marinade. 8. Serve immediately with lots of napkins and enjoy!

Per Serving:
calorie: 594 | fat: 39g | protein: 45g | carbs: 13g | sugars: 8g | fiber: 1g | sodium: 557mg

Grilled Pork Loin Chops

Prep time: 15 minutes | Cook time: 30 minutes | Serves 2

2 garlic cloves, minced	½ teaspoon ground ginger
3 tablespoons Worcestershire	½ teaspoon onion powder
sauce	¼ teaspoon cinnamon
2 tablespoons water	⅛ teaspoon cayenne pepper
1 tablespoon low-sodium soy	2 (6-ounce) thick-cut boneless
sauce	pork loin chops
2 teaspoons tomato paste	Olive oil, for greasing the grill
1 teaspoon granulated stevia	

1. In a small bowl, mix together the garlic, Worcestershire sauce, water, soy sauce, tomato paste, stevia, ginger, onion powder, cinnamon, and cayenne pepper. Pour half of the marinade into a large plastic sealable bag. Cover and refrigerate the remaining marinade. 2. Add the pork chops to the bag and seal. Refrigerate for 4 to 8 hours, turning occasionally. 3. Preheat the grill to medium. 4. With the olive oil, lightly oil the grill grate. 5. Remove the pork chops from the bag. Discard the marinade in the bag. 6. Place the chops on the preheated grill, basting with the remaining reserved half of the marinade. Grill for 8 to 12 minutes per side, or until the meat is browned, no longer pink inside, and an instant-read thermometer inserted into the thickest part of the chop reads at least 145°F. 7. In a saucepan set over medium heat, pour any remaining reserved marinade. Bring to a boil. Reduce the heat to low. Simmer for about 5 minutes, stirring constantly, until slightly thickened. 8. To serve, plate the chops and spoon the sauce over.

Per Serving:
calorie: 254 | fat: 6g | protein: 39g | carbs: 9g | sugars: 3g | fiber: 1g | sodium: 593mg

Pork Chop Diane

Prep time: 10 minutes | Cook time: 20 minutes | Serves 4

¼ cup low-sodium chicken broth
1 tablespoon freshly squeezed lemon juice
2 teaspoons Worcestershire sauce
2 teaspoons Dijon mustard
4 (5-ounce) boneless pork top

loin chops, about 1 inch thick
Sea salt
Freshly ground black pepper
1 teaspoon extra-virgin olive oil
1 teaspoon lemon zest
1 teaspoon butter
2 teaspoons chopped fresh chives

1. In a small bowl, stir together the chicken broth, lemon juice, Worcestershire sauce, and Dijon mustard and set it aside. 2. Season the pork chops lightly with salt and pepper. 3. Place a large skillet over medium-high heat and add the olive oil. 4. Cook the pork chops, turning once, until they are no longer pink, about 8 minutes per side. 5. Transfer the chops to a plate and set it aside. 6. Pour the broth mixture into the skillet and cook until warmed through and thickened, about 2 minutes. 7. Whisk in the lemon zest, butter, and chives. 8. Serve the chops with a generous spoonful of sauce.

Per Serving:

calorie: 203 | fat: 7g | protein: 32g | carbs: 1g | sugars: 0g | fiber: 0g | sodium: 130mg

5-Ingredient Mexican Lasagna

Prep time: 15 minutes | Cook time: 15 minutes | Serves 4

Nonstick cooking spray
½ (15-ounce) can light red kidney beans, rinsed and drained
4 (6-inch) gluten-free corn tortillas

1½ cups cooked shredded beef, pork, or chicken
1⅓ cups salsa
1⅓ cups shredded Mexican cheese blend

1. Spray a 6-inch springform pan with nonstick spray. Wrap the bottom in foil. 2. In a medium bowl, mash the beans with a fork. 3. Place 1 tortilla in the bottom of the pan. Add about ⅓ of the beans, ½ cup of meat, ⅓ cup of salsa, and ⅓ cup of cheese. Press down. Repeat for 2 more layers. Add the remaining tortilla and press down. Top with the remaining salsa and cheese. There are no beans or meat on the top layer. 4. Tear off a piece of foil big enough to cover the pan, and spray it with nonstick spray. Line the pan with the foil, sprayed-side down. 5. Pour 1 cup of water into the electric pressure cooker. 6. Place the pan on the wire rack and carefully lower it into the pot. Close and lock the lid of the pressure cooker. Set the valve to sealing. 7. Cook on high pressure for 15 minutes. 8. When the cooking is complete, hit Cancel. Allow the pressure to release naturally for 10 minutes, then quick release any remaining pressure. 9. Once the pin drops, unlock and remove the lid. 10. Using the handles of the wire rack, carefully remove the pan from the pot. Let the lasagna sit for 5 minutes. Carefully remove the ring. 11. Slice into quarters and serve.

Per Serving:

calorie: 380 | fat: 18g | protein: 32g | carbs: 22g | sugars: 4g | fiber: 4g | sodium: 594mg

Roasted Beef with Peppercorn Sauce

Prep time: 10 minutes | Cook time:1hour | Serves 4

1½ pounds top rump beef roast
Sea salt
Freshly ground black pepper
3 teaspoons extra-virgin olive oil, divided
3 shallots, minced

2 teaspoons minced garlic
1 tablespoon green peppercorns
2 tablespoons dry sherry
2 tablespoons all-purpose flour
1 cup sodium-free beef broth

1. Heat the oven to 300°F. 2. Season the roast with salt and pepper. 3. Place a large skillet over medium-high heat and add 2 teaspoons of olive oil. 4. Brown the beef on all sides, about 10 minutes in total, and transfer the roast to a baking dish. 5. Roast until desired doneness, about 1½ hours for medium. When the roast has been in the oven for 1 hour, start the sauce. 6. In a medium saucepan over medium-high heat, sauté the shallots in the remaining 1 teaspoon of olive oil until translucent, about 4 minutes. 7. Stir in the garlic and peppercorns, and cook for another minute. Whisk in the sherry to deglaze the pan. 8. Whisk in the flour to form a thick paste, cooking for 1 minute and stirring constantly. 9. Pour in the beef broth and whisk until the sauce is thick and glossy, about 4 minutes. Season the sauce with salt and pepper. 10. Serve the beef with a generous spoonful of sauce.

Per Serving:

calorie: 272 | fat: 10g | protein: 40g | carbs: g | sugars: 0g | fiber: 0g | sodium: 331mg

Steaks with Walnut-Blue Cheese Butter

Prep time: 30 minutes | Cook time: 10 minutes | Serves 6

½ cup unsalted butter, at room temperature
½ cup crumbled blue cheese
2 tablespoons finely chopped walnuts
1 tablespoon minced fresh rosemary

1 teaspoon minced garlic
¼ teaspoon cayenne pepper
Sea salt and freshly ground black pepper, to taste
1½ pounds (680 g) New York strip steaks, at room temperature

1. In a medium bowl, combine the butter, blue cheese, walnuts, rosemary, garlic, and cayenne pepper and salt and black pepper to taste. Use clean hands to ensure that everything is well combined. Place the mixture on a sheet of parchment paper and form it into a log. Wrap it tightly in plastic wrap. Refrigerate for at least 2 hours or freeze for 30 minutes. 2. Season the steaks generously with salt and pepper. 3. Place the air fryer basket or grill pan in the air fryer. Set the air fryer to 400ºF (204ºC) and let it preheat for 5 minutes. 4. Place the steaks in the basket in a single layer and air fry for 5 minutes. Flip the steaks, and cook for 5 minutes more, until an instant-read thermometer reads 120ºF (49ºC) for medium-rare (or as desired). 5. Transfer the steaks to a plate. Cut the butter into pieces and place the desired amount on top of the steaks. Tent a piece of aluminum foil over the steaks and allow to sit for 10 minutes before serving. 6. Store any remaining butter in a sealed container in the refrigerator for up to 2 weeks.

Per Serving:

calories: 283 | fat: 18g | protein: 30g | carbs: 1g | net carbs: 1g | fiber: 0g

Herb-Crusted Lamb Chops

Prep time: 10 minutes | Cook time: 5 minutes | Serves 2

1 large egg
2 cloves garlic, minced
¼ cup pork dust
¼ cup powdered Parmesan cheese
1 tablespoon chopped fresh oregano leaves
1 tablespoon chopped fresh rosemary leaves
1 teaspoon chopped fresh thyme

leaves
½ teaspoon ground black pepper
4 (1-inch-thick) lamb chops
For Garnish/Serving (Optional):
Sprigs of fresh oregano
Sprigs of fresh rosemary
Sprigs of fresh thyme
Lavender flowers
Lemon slices

1. Spray the air fryer basket with avocado oil. Preheat the air fryer to 400ºF (204ºC). 2. Beat the egg in a shallow bowl, add the garlic, and stir well to combine. In another shallow bowl, mix together the pork dust, Parmesan, herbs, and pepper. 3. One at a time, dip the lamb chops into the egg mixture, shake off the excess egg, and then dredge them in the Parmesan mixture. Use your hands to coat the chops well in the Parmesan mixture and form a nice crust on all sides; if necessary, dip the chops again in both the egg and the Parmesan mixture. 4. Place the lamb chops in the air fryer basket, leaving space between them, and air fry for 5 minutes, or until the internal temperature reaches 145ºF (63ºC) for medium doneness. Allow to rest for 10 minutes before serving. 5. Garnish with sprigs of oregano, rosemary, and thyme, and lavender flowers, if desired. Serve with lemon slices, if desired. 6. Best served fresh. Store leftovers in an airtight container in the fridge for up to 4 days. Serve chilled over a salad, or reheat in a 350ºF (177ºC) air fryer for 3 minutes, or until heated through.

Per Serving:
calories: 510 | fat: 42g | protein: 30g | carbs: 3g | fiber: 1g | sodium: 380mg

Orange-Marinated Pork Tenderloin

Prep time: 10 minutes | Cook time: 30 minutes | Serves 4

¼ cup freshly squeezed orange juice
2 teaspoons orange zest
2 teaspoons minced garlic
1 teaspoon low-sodium soy sauce

1 teaspoon grated fresh ginger
1 teaspoon honey
1½ pounds pork tenderloin roast, trimmed of fat
1 tablespoon extra-virgin olive oil

1. In a small bowl, whisk together the orange juice, zest, garlic, soy sauce, ginger, and honey. 2. Pour the marinade into a resealable plastic bag and add the pork tenderloin. 3. Remove as much air as possible and seal the bag. Marinate the pork in the refrigerator, turning the bag a few times, for 2 hours. 4. Preheat the oven to 400°F. 5. Remove the tenderloin from the marinade and discard the marinade. 6. Place a large ovenproof skillet over medium-high heat and add the oil. 7. Sear the pork tenderloin on all sides, about 5 minutes in total. 8. Transfer the skillet to the oven and roast the pork until just cooked through, about 25 minutes. 9. Let the meat stand for 10 minutes before serving.

Per Serving:
calorie: 232 | fat: 7g | protein: 36g | carbs: 4g | sugars: 3g | fiber: 0g | sodium: 131mg

Spice-Infused Roast Beef

Prep time: 5 minutes | Cook time: 1 hour 30 minutes | Serves 8

¾ cup grated onion, divided
1 tablespoon caraway seeds
1 teaspoon ground coriander
1 teaspoon ground ginger
2-pound lean boneless chuck roast

1 tablespoon extra-virgin olive oil
⅓ cup red wine vinegar
1 cup unsweetened apple juice
1 bunch fresh parsley, minced

1. Preheat the oven to 325 degrees. 2. In a small bowl, combine ¼ cup of the onion, caraway seeds, coriander, and ginger, and rub into the roast. 3. In a medium saucepan over medium heat, sauté the remaining ½ cup of onion in olive oil. Place the roast in a roasting pan, and add the sautéed onion. 4. Add the vinegar, apple juice, parsley, and ½ cup water to the roasting pan. Bake the roast uncovered at 325 degrees for 1–1½ hours, basting frequently. Transfer the roast to a platter, and slice.

Per Serving:
calorie: 194 | fat: 8g | protein: 24g | carbs: 6g | sugars: 4g | fiber: 1g | sodium: 105mg

Open-Faced Pulled Pork

Prep time: 15 minutes | Cook time: 1 hour 35minutes | Serves 2

2 tablespoons hoisin sauce
2 tablespoons tomato paste
2 tablespoons rice vinegar
1 tablespoon minced fresh ginger
2 teaspoons minced garlic

1 teaspoon chile-garlic sauce
¾ pound pork shoulder, trimmed of any visible fat, cut into 2-inch-square cubes
4 large romaine lettuce leaves

1. Preheat the oven to 300°F. 2. In a medium ovenproof pot with a tight-fitting lid, stir together the hoisin sauce, tomato paste, rice vinegar, ginger, garlic, and chile-garlic sauce. 3. Add the pork. Toss to coat. 4. Place the pot over medium heat. Bring to a simmer. Cover and carefully transfer the ovenproof pot to the preheated oven. Cook for 90 minutes. 5. Check the meat for doneness by inserting a fork into one of the chunks. If it goes in easily and the pork falls apart, the meat is done. If not, cook for another 30 minutes or so, until the meat passes the fork test. 6. Using a coarse strainer, strain the cooked pork into a fat separator. Shred the meat. Set aside. If you don't have a fat separator, remove the meat from the sauce and set aside. Let the sauce cool until any fat has risen to the top. With a spoon, remove as much fat as possible or use paper towels to blot it off. 7. In a small saucepan set over high heat, pour the defatted sauce. Bring to a boil, stirring frequently to prevent scorching. Cook for 2 to 3 minutes, or until thickened. 8. Add the shredded meat. Toss to coat with the sauce. Cook for 1 minute to reheat the meat. 9. Spoon equal amounts of pork into the romaine lettuce leaves and enjoy!

Per Serving:
calorie: 289 | fat: 11g | protein: 33g | carbs: 13g | sugars: 7g | fiber: 1g | sodium: 391mg

Homey Pot Roast

1 pound boneless beef chuck roast
2 tablespoons Creole seasoning
2 cups store-bought low-sodium chicken broth, divided
1 large portobello mushroom, cut into 2-inch pieces
1 small onion, roughly chopped
3 celery stalks, roughly chopped
4 medium tomatoes, chopped
2 garlic cloves, minced
1 medium green pepper, roughly chopped
8 ounces steamer potatoes, skin on, halved
6 small parsnips, peeled and halved
2 large carrots, peeled and cut into 2-inch pieces
3 bay leaves
Freshly ground black pepper
Pinch cayenne pepper
Pinch smoked paprika

1. Preheat the oven to 325°F. 2. Massage the roast all over with the Creole seasoning. 3. In a Dutch oven, bring ½ cup of broth to a simmer over medium heat. 4. Add the beef and cook on all sides, turning to avoid burning the meat, no more than about 2½ minutes per side, or until browned. Remove the beef from the pot and set aside. 5. Add the mushroom, onion, celery, tomatoes, garlic, and green pepper to pot, adding up to ½ cup of broth if needed to prevent blackening of the vegetables. 6. Reduce the heat to medium-low and cook, stirring continuously, for 5 to 7 minutes, or until the vegetables have softened. 7. Return the beef to the pot. Add the potatoes, parsnips, carrots, bay leaves, and remaining 1 cup of broth. 8. Season with the black pepper, cayenne, and paprika. 9. Cover the pot, transfer to the oven, and bake for 2 hours, or until the beef is juicy and falls apart easily. Discard the bay leaves. 10. Serve.

Per Serving:
calorie: 237 | fat: 5g | protein: 20g | carbs: 29g | sugars: 8g | fiber: 7g | sodium: 329mg

Zesty Swiss Steak

Prep time: 35 minutes | Cook time: 35 minutes | Serves 6

3–4 tablespoons flour
½ teaspoon salt
¼ teaspoon pepper
1½ teaspoons dry mustard
1½–2 pounds round steak, trimmed of fat
1 tablespoon canola oil
1 cup sliced onions
1 pound carrots, sliced
14½-ounce can whole tomatoes
⅓ cup water
1 tablespoon brown sugar
1½ tablespoons Worcestershire sauce

1. Combine flour, salt, pepper, and dry mustard. 2. Cut steak in serving pieces. Dredge in flour mixture. 3. Set the Instant Pot to Sauté and add in the oil. Brown the steak pieces on both sides in the oil. Press Cancel. 4. Add onions and carrots into the Instant Pot. 5. Combine the tomatoes, water, brown sugar, and Worcestershire sauce. Pour into the Instant Pot. 6. Secure the lid and make sure the vent is set to sealing. Press Manual and set the time for 35 minutes. 7. When cook time is up, let the pressure release naturally for 15 minutes, then perform a quick release.

Per Serving:
calories: 236 | fat: 8g | protein: 23g | carbs: 18g | sugars: 9g | fiber: 3g | sodium: 426mg

Steak with Bell Pepper

¼ cup avocado oil
¼ cup freshly squeezed lime juice
2 teaspoons minced garlic
1 tablespoon chili powder
½ teaspoon ground cumin
Sea salt and freshly ground black pepper, to taste
1 pound (454 g) top sirloin steak or flank steak, thinly sliced against the grain
1 red bell pepper, cored, seeded, and cut into ½-inch slices
1 green bell pepper, cored, seeded, and cut into ½-inch slices
1 large onion, sliced

1. In a small bowl or blender, combine the avocado oil, lime juice, garlic, chili powder, cumin, and salt and pepper to taste. 2. Place the sliced steak in a zip-top bag or shallow dish. Place the bell peppers and onion in a separate zip-top bag or dish. Pour half the marinade over the steak and the other half over the vegetables. Seal both bags and let the steak and vegetables marinate in the refrigerator for at least 1 hour or up to 4 hours. 3. Line the air fryer basket with an air fryer liner or aluminum foil. Remove the vegetables from their bag or dish and shake off any excess marinade. Set the air fryer to 400ºF (204ºC). Place the vegetables in the air fryer basket and cook for 13 minutes. 4. Remove the steak from its bag or dish and shake off any excess marinade. Place the steak on top of the vegetables in the air fryer, and cook for 7 to 10 minutes or until an instant-read thermometer reads 120ºF (49ºC) for medium-rare (or cook to your desired doneness). 5. Serve with desired fixings, such as keto tortillas, lettuce, sour cream, avocado slices, shredded Cheddar cheese, and cilantro.

Per Serving:
calories: 252 | fat: 18g | protein: 17g | carbs: 6g | fiber: 2g | sodium: 81mg

Broiled Dijon Burgers

Prep time: 25 minutes | Cook time: 10 minutes | Makes 6 burgers

1/4 cup fat-free egg product or 2 egg whites
2 tablespoons fat-free (skim) milk
2 teaspoons Dijon mustard or horseradish sauce
1/4 teaspoon salt
1/8 teaspoon pepper
1 cup soft bread crumbs (about 2 slices bread)
1 small onion, finely chopped (1/3 cup)
1 lb extra-lean (at least 90%) ground beef
6 whole-grain burger buns, split, toasted

1 Set oven control to broil. Spray broiler pan rack with cooking spray. 2 In medium bowl, mix egg product, milk, mustard, salt and pepper. Stir in bread crumbs and onion. Stir in beef. Shape mixture into 6 patties, each about 1/2 inch thick. Place patties on rack in broiler pan. 3 Broil with tops of patties about 5 inches from heat 6 minutes. Turn; broil until meat thermometer inserted in center of patties reads 160°F, 4 to 6 minutes longer. Serve patties in buns.

Per Serving:
calories: 250 | fat: 8g | protein: 22g | carbs: 23g | sugars: 5g | fiber: 3g | sodium: 450mg

Short Ribs with Chimichurri

Prep time: 30 minutes | Cook time: 13 minutes | Serves 4

1 pound (454 g) boneless short ribs
1½ teaspoons sea salt, divided
½ teaspoon freshly ground black pepper, divided
½ cup fresh parsley leaves
½ cup fresh cilantro leaves
1 teaspoon minced garlic

1 tablespoon freshly squeezed lemon juice
½ teaspoon ground cumin
¼ teaspoon red pepper flakes
2 tablespoons extra-virgin olive oil
Avocado oil spray

1. Pat the short ribs dry with paper towels. Sprinkle the ribs all over with 1 teaspoon salt and ¼ teaspoon black pepper. Let sit at room temperature for 45 minutes. 2. Meanwhile, place the parsley, cilantro, garlic, lemon juice, cumin, red pepper flakes, the remaining ½ teaspoon salt, and the remaining ¼ teaspoon black pepper in a blender or food processor. With the blender running, slowly drizzle in the olive oil. Blend for about 1 minute, until the mixture is smooth and well combined. 3. Set the air fryer to 400°F (204°C). Spray both sides of the ribs with oil. Place in the basket and air fry for 8 minutes. Flip and cook for another 5 minutes, until an instant-read thermometer reads 125°F (52°C) for medium-rare (or to your desired doneness). 4. Allow the meat to rest for 5 to 10 minutes, then slice. Serve warm with the chimichurri sauce.

Per Serving:
calories: 251 | fat: 17g | protein: 25g | carbs: 1g | fiber: 1g | sodium: 651mg

Red Wine Pot Roast with Winter Vegetables

Prep time: 10 minutes | Cook time: 1 hour 35 minutes | Serves 6

One 3-pound boneless beef chuck roast or bottom round roast (see Note)
2 teaspoons fine sea salt
1 teaspoon freshly ground black pepper
1 tablespoon cold-pressed avocado oil
4 large shallots, quartered
4 garlic cloves, minced

1 cup dry red wine
2 tablespoons Dijon mustard
2 teaspoons chopped fresh rosemary
1 pound parsnips or turnips, cut into ½-inch pieces
1 pound carrots, cut into ½-inch pieces
4 celery stalks, cut into ½-inch pieces

1. Put the beef onto a plate, pat it dry with paper towels, and then season all over with the salt and pepper. 2. Select the Sauté setting on the Instant Pot and heat the oil for 2 minutes. Using tongs, lower the roast into the pot and sear for about 4 minutes, until browned on the first side. Flip the roast and sear for about 4 minutes more, until browned on the second side. Return the roast to the plate. 3. Add the shallots to the pot and sauté for about 2 minutes, until they begin to soften. Add the garlic and sauté for about 1 minute more. Stir in the wine, mustard, and rosemary, using a wooden spoon to nudge any browned bits from the bottom of the pot. Return the roast to the pot, then spoon some of the cooking liquid over the top. 4. Secure the lid and set the Pressure Release to Sealing. Press the Cancel button to reset the cooking program, then select the Meat/Stew setting and set the cooking time for 1 hour 5 minutes at high pressure. (The pot will take about 5 minutes to come up to pressure before the

cooking program begins.) 5. When the cooking program ends, let the pressure release naturally for at least 15 minutes, then move the Pressure Release to Venting to release any remaining steam. Open the pot and, using tongs, carefully transfer the pot roast to a cutting board. Tent with aluminum foil to keep warm. 6. Add the parsnips, carrots, and celery to the pot. 7. Secure the lid and set the Pressure Release to Sealing. Press the Cancel button to reset the cooking program, then select the Pressure Cook or Manual setting and set the cooking time for 3 minutes at low pressure. (The pot will take about 10 minutes to come up to pressure before the cooking program begins.) 8. When the cooking program ends, perform a quick pressure release by moving the Pressure Release to Venting. Open the pot and, using a slotted spoon, transfer the vegetables to a serving dish. Wearing heat-resistant mitts, lift out the inner pot and pour the cooking liquid into a gravy boat or other serving vessel with a spout. (If you like, use a fat separator to remove the fat from the liquid before serving.) 9. If the roast was tied, snip the string and discard. Carve the roast against the grain into ½-inch-thick slices and arrange them on the dish with the vegetables. Pour some cooking liquid over the roast and serve, passing the remaining cooking liquid on the side.

Per Serving:
calorie: 448 | fat: 25g | protein: 26g | carbs: 26g | sugars: 7g | fiber: 6g | sodium: 945mg

Herb-Marinated Tenderloins

Prep time: 30 minutes | Cook time: 20 minutes | Serves 2

1 (8-ounce) beef tenderloin filet
6 fresh sage leaves
1 garlic clove, sliced into 6 pieces
4 fresh rosemary sprigs
Dash salt
Dash freshly ground black pepper

1 medium sweet potato
12 cherry tomatoes, chopped
1 tablespoon finely chopped fresh chives
2 teaspoons extra-virgin olive oil
4 cups baby spinach, divided

1. Cut 3 (2-inch-deep) slits in each side of the filet. Stuff 1 sage leave and 1 garlic slice into each slit. Wrap the rosemary sprigs around the filet. Season with salt and pepper. Refrigerate for 12 hours, or overnight, to allow the meat to absorb the seasoning flavors. 2. The next day, preheat the broiler to high. 3. Drain the steak. Place on an unheated rack in the broiler pan. Place the pan in the preheated oven. Broil the steak for 13 to 17 minutes for medium (160°F), 3 inches from the heat, turning once halfway through. Remove from the oven. Let the filet rest for 2 to 3 minutes before cutting in half. Tent with aluminum foil to keep warm. 4. While the filet cooks, poke the sweet potato all over with a fork. Microwave on high for about 6 minutes, or until soft. Thinly slice the cooked potato into rounds. Keep warm. 5. In a small bowl, mix together the tomatoes, chives, and olive oil. 6. Place 2 cups of spinach on each serving plate. Arrange half of the sweet potato slices in a half-moon shape on each plate. Spoon half of the tomatoes over the sweet potatoes. Place 1 filet half in the center of each plate. 7. Enjoy!

Per Serving:
calorie: 318 | fat: 13g | protein: 29g | carbs: 21g | sugars: 6g | fiber: 6g | sodium: 231mg

Bacon-Wrapped Vegetable Kebabs

Prep time: 10 minutes | Cook time: 10 to 12 minutes

| Serves 4

4 ounces (113 g) mushrooms, sliced	halved
1 small zucchini, sliced	Avocado oil spray
12 grape tomatoes	Sea salt and freshly ground black pepper, to taste
4 ounces (113 g) sliced bacon,	

1. Stack 3 mushroom slices, 1 zucchini slice, and 1 grape tomato. Wrap a bacon strip around the vegetables and thread them onto a skewer. Repeat with the remaining vegetables and bacon. Spray with oil and sprinkle with salt and pepper. 2. Set the air fryer to 400ºF (204ºC). Place the skewers in the air fryer basket in a single layer, working in batches if necessary, and air fry for 5 minutes. Flip the skewers and cook for 5 to 7 minutes more, until the bacon is crispy and the vegetables are tender. 3. Serve warm.

Per Serving:

calorie: 140 | fat: 11g | protein: 5g | carbs: 5g | sugars: 4g | fiber: 1g | sodium: 139mg

Garlic Balsamic London Broil

Prep time: 30 minutes | Cook time: 8 to 10 minutes |

Serves 8

2 pounds (907 g) London broil	2 tablespoons olive oil
3 large garlic cloves, minced	Sea salt and ground black pepper, to taste
3 tablespoons balsamic vinegar	
3 tablespoons whole-grain mustard	½ teaspoon dried hot red pepper flakes

1. Score both sides of the cleaned London broil. 2. Thoroughly combine the remaining ingredients; massage this mixture into the meat to coat it on all sides. Let it marinate for at least 3 hours. 3. Set the air fryer to 400ºF (204ºC); Then cook the London broil for 15 minutes. Flip it over and cook another 10 to 12 minutes. Bon appétit!

Per Serving:

calories: 240 | fat: 15g | protein: 23g | carbs: 2g | fiber: 0g | sodium: 141mg

Slow Cooker Chipotle Beef Stew

Prep time: 25 minutes | Cook time: 8 to 10 hours |

Serves 6

Stew	3 cloves garlic, chopped
1 package (12 oz) frozen whole kernel corn	2 cans (14.5 oz each) diced tomatoes, undrained
1 lb boneless beef top sirloin, trimmed of fat, cut into 1-inch cubes	1½ teaspoons ground cumin
	½ teaspoon salt
1 chipotle chile in adobo sauce (from 7-oz can), finely chopped	¼ teaspoon cracked black pepper
	Toppings
2 large onions, chopped (2 cups)	1 avocado, pitted, peeled cut into 12 wedges
2 poblano chiles, seeded, diced	12 baked tortilla chips, crushed

6 small cilantro sprigs, coarsely chopped	6 tablespoons reduced-fat sour cream

1 Spray 4- to 5-quart slow cooker with cooking spray. In small microwavable bowl, microwave corn uncovered on High 2 minutes or until thawed. In slow cooker, place corn and all remaining stew ingredients; mix well. Cover and cook on Low heat setting 8 to 10 hours (or High heat setting 4 to 5 hours). 2 Divide stew evenly among 6 bowls. To serve, top with avocado, tortilla chips, cilantro and sour cream.

Per Serving:

calories: 310 | fat: 10g | protein: 25g | carbs: 30g | sugars: 10g | fiber: 5g | sodium: 580mg

Kielbasa and Cabbage

Prep time: 10 minutes | Cook time: 20 to 25 minutes

| Serves 4

1 pound (454 g) smoked kielbasa sausage, sliced into ½-inch pieces	2 cloves garlic, chopped
	2 tablespoons olive oil
	½ teaspoon salt
1 head cabbage, very coarsely chopped	½ teaspoon freshly ground black pepper
½ yellow onion, chopped	¼ cup water

1. Preheat the air fryer to 400ºF (204ºC). 2. In a large bowl, combine the sausage, cabbage, onion, garlic, olive oil, salt, and black pepper. Toss until thoroughly combined. 3. Transfer the mixture to the basket of the air fryer and pour the water over the top. Pausing two or three times during the cooking time to shake the basket, air fry for 20 to 25 minutes, until the sausage is browned and the vegetables are tender.

Per Serving:

calories: 368 | fat: 28g | protein: 18g | carbs: 11g | net carbs: 6g | fiber: 5g

Lime-Parsley Lamb Cutlets

Prep time: 10 minutes | Cook time: 10 minutes | Serves 4

¼ cup extra-virgin olive oil	Pinch sea salt
¼ cup freshly squeezed lime juice	Pinch freshly ground black pepper
2 tablespoons lime zest	12 lamb cutlets (about 1½ pounds total)
2 tablespoons chopped fresh parsley	

1. In a medium bowl, whisk together the oil, lime juice, zest, parsley, salt, and pepper. 2. Transfer the marinade to a resealable plastic bag. 3. Add the cutlets to the bag and remove as much air as possible before sealing. 4. Marinate the lamb in the refrigerator for about 4 hours, turning the bag several times. 5. Preheat the oven to broil. 6. Remove the chops from the bag and arrange them on an aluminum foil–lined baking sheet. Discard the marinade. 7. Broil the chops for 4 minutes per side for medium doneness. 8. Let the chops rest for 5 minutes before serving.

Per Serving:

calorie: 333 | fat: 20g | protein: 36g | carbs: 20g | sugars: 0g | fiber: 0g | sodium: 182mg

BBQ Ribs and Broccoli Slaw

Prep time: 10 minutes | Cook time: 50 minutes | Serves 6

BBQ Ribs	1 pound broccoli florets (or
4 pounds baby back ribs	florets from 2 large crowns),
1 teaspoon fine sea salt	chopped
1 teaspoon freshly ground black	10 radishes, halved and thinly
pepper	sliced
Broccoli Slaw	1 red bell pepper, seeded and
½ cup plain 2 percent Greek	cut lengthwise into narrow
yogurt	strips
1 tablespoon olive oil	1 large apple (such as Fuji,
1 tablespoon fresh lemon juice	Jonagold, or Gala), thinly sliced
½ teaspoon fine sea salt	½ red onion, thinly sliced
¼ teaspoon freshly ground	¾ cup low-sugar or
black pepper	unsweetened barbecue sauce

1. To make the ribs: Pat the ribs dry with paper towels, then cut the racks into six sections (three to five ribs per section, depending on how big the racks are). Season the ribs all over with the salt and pepper. 2. Pour 1 cup water into the Instant Pot and place the wire metal steam rack into the pot. Place the ribs on top of the wire rack (it's fine to stack them up). 3. Secure the lid and set the Pressure Release to Sealing. Select the Pressure Cook or Manual setting and set the cooking time for 20 minutes at high pressure. (The pot will take about 15 minutes to come up to pressure before the cooking program begins.) 4. To make the broccoli slaw: While the ribs are cooking, in a small bowl, stir together the yogurt, oil, lemon juice, salt, and pepper, mixing well. In a large bowl, combine the broccoli, radishes, bell pepper, apple, and onion. Drizzle with the yogurt mixture and toss until evenly coated. 5. When the ribs have about 10 minutes left in their cooking time, preheat the oven to 400°F. Line a sheet pan with aluminum foil. 6. When the cooking program ends, perform a quick pressure release by moving the Pressure Release to Venting. Open the pot and, using tongs, transfer the ribs in a single layer to the prepared sheet pan. Brush the barbecue sauce onto both sides of the ribs, using 2 tablespoons of sauce per section of ribs. Bake, meaty-side up, for 15 to 20 minutes, until lightly browned. 7. Serve the ribs warm, with the slaw on the side.

Per Serving:

calories: 392 | fat: 15g | protein: 45g | carbs: 19g | sugars: 9g | fiber: 4g | sodium: 961mg

Teriyaki Rib-Eye Steaks

Prep time: 10 minutes | Cook time: 15 minutes | Serves 2

2 tablespoons water	¼ teaspoon garlic powder
1 tablespoon reduced-sodium	⅛ teaspoon ground
soy sauce	2 (6-ounce) lean beef rib-eye
1½ teaspoons Worcestershire	steaks
sauce	Extra-virgin olive oil cooking
1¼ teaspoons distilled white	spray
vinegar	2 cups sugar snap peas
1 teaspoon extra-virgin olive oil	1 cup sliced carrots
½ teaspoon granulated stevia	1 red bell pepper, sliced
½ teaspoon onion powder	

1. In a large bowl, whisk together the water, soy sauce,

Worcestershire sauce, white vinegar, olive oil, stevia, onion powder, garlic powder, and ginger. 2. With a fork, pierce the steaks several times. Add to the marinade. Let marinate in the refrigerator for at least 2 hours. 3. Spray a large skillet with cooking spray. Place it over medium heat. 4. Add the steaks. Cook for 7 minutes. Turn the steaks. Add the sugar snap peas, carrots, and bell pepper to the skillet. Cook for 7 minutes more, or until an instant-read thermometer inserted into the center of the steak reads 140°F. 5. Serve and savor!

Per Serving:

calorie: 630 | fat: 40g | protein: 40g | carbs: 29g | sugars: 12g | fiber: 9g | sodium: 271mg

Mustard Herb Pork Tenderloin

Prep time: 5 minutes | Cook time: 20 minutes | Serves 6

¼ cup mayonnaise	tenderloin
2 tablespoons Dijon mustard	½ teaspoon salt
½ teaspoon dried thyme	¼ teaspoon ground black
¼ teaspoon dried rosemary	pepper
1 (1-pound / 454-g) pork	

1. In a small bowl, mix mayonnaise, mustard, thyme, and rosemary. Brush tenderloin with mixture on all sides, then sprinkle with salt and pepper on all sides. 2. Place tenderloin into ungreased air fryer basket. Adjust the temperature to 400ºF (204ºC) and air fry for 20 minutes, turning tenderloin halfway through cooking. Tenderloin will be golden and have an internal temperature of at least 145ºF (63ºC) when done. Serve warm.

Per Serving:

calorie: 118 | fat: 5g | protein: 17g | carbs: 1g | sugars: 0g | fiber: 0g | sodium: 368mg

Pot Roast with Gravy and Vegetables

Prep time: 30 minutes | Cook time: 1 hour 15 minutes | Serves 6

1 tablespoon olive oil	or gravy browning seasoning
3–4 pound bottom round, rump,	sauce
or arm roast, trimmed of fat	1 garlic clove, minced
¼ teaspoon salt	2 medium onions, cut in wedges
2–3 teaspoons pepper	4 medium potatoes, cubed,
2 tablespoons flour	unpeeled
1 cup cold water	2 carrots, quartered
1 teaspoon Kitchen Bouquet,	1 green bell pepper, sliced

1. Press the Sauté button on the Instant Pot and pour the oil inside, letting it heat up. Sprinkle each side of the roast with salt and pepper, then brown it for 5 minutes on each side inside the pot. 2. Mix together the flour, water and Kitchen Bouquet and spread over roast. 3. Add garlic, onions, potatoes, carrots, and green pepper. 4. Secure the lid and make sure the vent is set to sealing. Press Manual and set the Instant Pot for 1 hour and 15 minutes. 5. When cook time is up, let the pressure release naturally.

Per Serving:

calories: 551 | fat: 30g | protein: 49g | carbs: 19g | sugars: 2g | fiber: 3g | sodium: 256mg

Couscous and Sweet Potatoes with Pork

Prep time: 20 minutes | Cook time: 10 minutes | Serves 5

1¼ cups uncooked couscous
1 lb pork tenderloin, thinly sliced
1 medium sweet potato, peeled, cut into julienne strips

1 cup chunky-style salsa
½ cup water
2 tablespoons honey
¼ cup chopped fresh cilantro

1 Cook couscous as directed on package. 2 While couscous is cooking, spray 12-inch skillet with cooking spray. Cook pork in skillet over medium heat 2 to 3 minutes, stirring occasionally, until brown. 3 Stir sweet potato, salsa, water and honey into pork. Heat to boiling; reduce heat to medium. Cover and cook 5 to 6 minutes, stirring occasionally, until potato is tender. Sprinkle with cilantro. Serve pork mixture over couscous.

Per Serving:
calorie: 320 | fat: 4g | protein: 23g | carbs: 48g | sugars: 11g | fiber: 3g | sodium: 420mg

Dry-Rubbed Sirloin

Prep time: 5 minutes | Cook time: 15 minutes | Serves 6

1⅛ pounds beef round sirloin tip
2 tablespoons Creole seasoning

1. Preheat the oven to 375°F. 2. Massage the beef all over with the Creole seasoning. 3. Put the beef in a Dutch oven, cover, and transfer to the oven. Cook for 15 minutes, or until the juices run clear when you pierce the beef. 4. Remove the beef from the oven, and let rest for 15 minutes. 5. Carve, and serve.

Per Serving:
calorie: 134 | fat: 4g | protein: 19g | carbs: 4g | sugars: 0g | fiber: 1g | sodium: 260mg

Garlic Beef Stroganoff

Prep time: 20 minutes | Cook time: 25 minutes | Serves 6

2 tablespoons canola oil
1½ pounds boneless round steak, cut into thin strips, trimmed of fat
2 teaspoons sodium-free beef bouillon powder
1 cup mushroom juice, with water added to make a full cup
2 (4½-ounce) jars sliced mushrooms, drained with juice

reserved
10¾-ounce can 98% fat-free, lower-sodium cream of mushroom soup
1 large onion, chopped
3 garlic cloves, minced
1 tablespoon Worcestershire sauce
6-ounces fat-free cream cheese, cubed and softened

1. Press the Sauté button and put the oil into the Instant Pot inner pot. 2. Once the oil is heated, sauté the beef until it is lightly browned, about 2 minutes on each side. Set the beef aside for a moment. Press Cancel and wipe out the Instant Pot with some paper towel. 3. Press Sauté again and dissolve the bouillon in the mushroom juice and water in inner pot of the Instant Pot. Once dissolved, press Cancel. 4. Add the mushrooms, soup, onion, garlic, and Worcestershire sauce and stir. Add the beef back to the pot. 5.

Secure the lid and make sure the vent is set to sealing. Press Manual and set for 15 minutes. 6. When cook time is up, let the pressure release naturally for 15 minutes, then perform a quick release. 7. Press Cancel and remove the lid. Press Sauté. Stir in cream cheese until smooth. 8. Serve over noodles.

Per Serving:
calories: 202 | fat: 8g | protein: 21g | carbs: 10g | sugars: 4g | fiber: 2g | sodium: 474mg

Marjoram-Pepper Steaks

Prep time: 5 minutes | Cook time: 8 minutes | Serves 2

1 tablespoon freshly ground black pepper
¼ teaspoon dried marjoram
2 (6-ounce, 1-inch-thick) beef tenderloins

1 tablespoon extra-virgin olive oil
¼ cup low-sodium beef broth
Fresh marjoram sprigs, for garnish

1. In a large bowl, mix together the pepper and marjoram. 2. Add the steaks. Coat both sides with the spice mixture. 3. In a skillet set over medium-high heat, heat the olive oil. 4. Add the steaks. Cook for 5 to 7 minutes, or until an instant-read thermometer inserted in the center registers 160°F (for medium). Remove from the skillet. Cover to keep warm. 5. Add the broth to the skillet. Increase the heat to high. Bring to a boil, scraping any browned bits from the bottom. Boil for about 1 minute, or until the liquid is reduced by half. 6. Spoon the broth sauce over the steaks. Garnish with marjoram sprigs and serve immediately.

Per Serving:
calorie: 339 | fat: 19g | protein: 38g | carbs: 2g | sugars: 0g | fiber: 1g | sodium: 209mg

Jalapeño Popper Pork Chops

Prep time: 15 minutes | Cook time: 6 to 8 minutes | Serves 4

1¾ pounds (794 g) bone-in, center-cut loin pork chops
Sea salt and freshly ground black pepper, to taste
6 ounces (170 g) cream cheese, at room temperature

4 ounces (113 g) sliced bacon, cooked and crumbled
4 ounces (113 g) Cheddar cheese, shredded
1 jalapeño, seeded and diced
1 teaspoon garlic powder

1. Cut a pocket into each pork chop, lengthwise along the side, making sure not to cut it all the way through. Season the outside of the chops with salt and pepper. 2. In a small bowl, combine the cream cheese, bacon, Cheddar cheese, jalapeño, and garlic powder. Divide this mixture among the pork chops, stuffing it into the pocket of each chop. 3. Set the air fryer to 400ºF (204ºC). Place the pork chops in the air fryer basket in a single layer, working in batches if necessary. Air fry for 3 minutes. Flip the chops and cook for 3 to 5 minutes more, until an instant-read thermometer reads 145ºF (63ºC). 4. Allow the chops to rest for 5 minutes, then serve warm.

Per Serving:
calorie: 469 | fat: 21g | protein: 60g | carbs: 5g | sugars: 3g | fiber: 0g | sodium: 576mg

Smoky Pork Tenderloin

Prep time: 5 minutes | Cook time: 19 to 22 minutes | Serves 6

1½ pounds (680 g) pork tenderloin
1 tablespoon avocado oil
1 teaspoon chili powder
1 teaspoon smoked paprika
1 teaspoon garlic powder
1 teaspoon sea salt
1 teaspoon freshly ground black pepper

1. Pierce the tenderloin all over with a fork and rub the oil all over the meat. 2. In a small dish, stir together the chili powder, smoked paprika, garlic powder, salt, and pepper. 3. Rub the spice mixture all over the tenderloin. 4. Set the air fryer to 400ºF (204ºC). Place the pork in the air fryer basket and air fry for 10 minutes. Flip the tenderloin and cook for 9 to 12 minutes more, until an instant-read thermometer reads at least 145ºF (63ºC). 5. Allow the tenderloin to rest for 5 minutes, then slice and serve.

Per Serving:
calories: 149 | fat: 5g | protein: 24g | carbs: 1g | fiber: 0g | sodium: 461mg

Apple Cinnamon Pork Chops

Prep time: 5 minutes | Cook time: 20 minutes | Serves 2

2 teaspoons extra-virgin olive oil
1 large apple, sliced
½ teaspoon organic cinnamon
⅛ teaspoon freshly grated nutmeg
Two 3-ounce lean boneless pork chops, trimmed of fat

1. In a medium nonstick skillet, heat the olive oil. Add the apple slices, and sauté until just tender. Sprinkle with cinnamon and nutmeg, remove from heat, and keep warm. 2. Place the pork chops in the skillet, and cook thoroughly; a meat thermometer inserted into the thickest part of the meat should reach 145 degrees. Remove the pork chops from the skillet, arrange on a serving platter, spoon the apple slices on top, and serve.

Per Serving:
calorie: 208 | fat: 8g | protein: 19g | carbs: 16g | sugars: 11g | fiber: 3g | sodium: 43mg

Zoodles Carbonara

Prep time: 10 minutes | Cook time: 25 minutes | Serves 4

6 slices bacon, cut into pieces
1 red onion, finely chopped
3 zucchini, cut into noodles
1 cup peas
½ teaspoon sea salt
3 garlic cloves, minced
3 large eggs, beaten
1 tablespoon heavy cream
Pinch red pepper flakes
½ cup grated Parmesan cheese (optional, for garnish)

1. In a large skillet over medium-high heat, cook the bacon until browned, about 5 minutes. With a slotted spoon, transfer the bacon to a plate. 2. Add the onion to the bacon fat in the pan and cook, stirring, until soft, 3 to 5 minutes. Add the zucchini, peas, and salt. Cook, stirring, until the zucchini softens, about 3 minutes. Add the garlic and cook, stirring constantly, for 5 minutes. 3. In a small bowl, whisk together the eggs, cream, and red pepper flakes. Add to the vegetables. 4. Remove the pan from the stove top and stir for 3 minutes, allowing the heat of the pan to cook the eggs without setting them. 5. Return the bacon to the pan and stir to mix. 6. Serve topped with Parmesan cheese, if desired.

Per Serving:
calorie: 294 | fat: 21g | protein: 14g | carbs: 14g | sugars: 7g | fiber: 4g | sodium: 544mg

Bavarian Beef

Prep time: 35 minutes | Cook time: 1 hour 15 minutes | Serves 8

1 tablespoon canola oil
3-pound boneless beef chuck roast, trimmed of fat
3 cups sliced carrots
3 cups sliced onions
2 large kosher dill pickles, chopped
1 cup sliced celery
½ cup dry red wine or beef
broth
⅓ cup German-style mustard
2 teaspoons coarsely ground black pepper
2 bay leaves
¼ teaspoon ground cloves
1 cup water
⅓ cup flour

1. Press Sauté on the Instant Pot and add in the oil. Brown roast on both sides for about 5 minutes. Press Cancel. 2. Add all of the remaining ingredients, except for the flour, to the Instant Pot. 3. Secure the lid and make sure the vent is set to sealing. Press Manual and set the time to 1 hour and 15 minutes. Let the pressure release naturally. 4. Remove meat and vegetables to large platter. Cover to keep warm. 5. Remove 1 cup of the liquid from the Instant Pot and mix with the flour. Press Sauté on the Instant Pot and add the flour/broth mixture back in, whisking. Cook until the broth is smooth and thickened. 6. Serve over noodles or spaetzle.

Per Serving:
calories: 251 | fat: 8g | protein: 26g | carbs: 17g | sugars: 7g | fiber: 4g | sodium: 525mg

Asian Steak Salad

Prep time: 20 minutes | Cook time: 5 minutes | Serves 6

1 lb cut-up lean beef for stir-fry
1 package (3 oz) Oriental-flavor ramen noodle soup mix
1/2 cup low-fat Asian marinade and dressing
1 bag (10 oz) romaine and leaf
lettuce mix
1 cup fresh snow pea pods
1/2 cup matchstick-cut carrots (from 10-oz bag)
1 can (11 oz) mandarin orange segments, drained

1 Spray 12-inch skillet with cooking spray; heat over medium-high heat. Place beef in skillet; sprinkle with 1 teaspoon seasoning mix from soup mix. (Discard remaining seasoning mix.) Cook beef 4 to 5 minutes, stirring occasionally, until brown. Stir in 1 tablespoon of the dressing. 2 Break block of noodles from soup mix into small pieces. Mix noodles, lettuce, pea pods, carrots, and orange segments in large bowl. Add remaining dressing; toss until well coated. Divide mixture among 6 serving plates. Top with beef.

Per Serving:
calories: 240 | fat: 7g | protein: 19g | carbs: 25g | sugars: 14g | fiber: 2g | sodium: 990mg

Beef Roast with Onions and Potatoes

Prep time: 30 minutes | Cook time: 9 to 10 hours | Serves 6

1 large sweet onion, cut in half, then cut into thin slices
1 boneless beef bottom round roast (3 lb), trimmed of excess fat
3 baking potatoes, cut into 1½- to 2-inch cubes
2 cloves garlic, finely chopped

1¾ cups beef-flavored broth
1 package (1 oz) onion soup mix (from 2-oz box)
¼ cup all-purpose flour

1. Spray 5- to 6-quart slow cooker with cooking spray. In slow cooker, place onion. If beef roast comes in netting or is tied, remove netting or strings. Place beef on onion. Place potatoes and garlic around beef. In small bowl, mix 1¼ cups of the broth and the dry soup mix; pour over beef. (Refrigerate remaining broth.) 2. Cover; cook on Low heat setting 9 to 10 hours. 3. Remove beef and vegetables from slow cooker; place on serving platter. Cover to keep warm. 4. In small bowl, mix remaining ½ cup broth and the flour; gradually stir into juices in slow cooker. Increase heat setting to High. Cover; cook about 15 minutes, stirring occasionally, until sauce has thickened. Serve sauce over beef and vegetables.

Per Serving:
calorie: 416 | fat: 9g | protein: 54g | carbs: 27g | sugars: 4g | fiber: 3g | sodium: 428mg

Bacon and Cheese Stuffed Pork Chops

Prep time: 10 minutes | Cook time: 12 minutes | Serves 4

½ ounce (14 g) plain pork rinds, finely crushed
½ cup shredded sharp Cheddar cheese
4 slices cooked sugar-free bacon, crumbled

4 (4-ounce / 113-g) boneless pork chops
½ teaspoon salt
¼ teaspoon ground black pepper

1. In a small bowl, mix pork rinds, Cheddar, and bacon. 2. Make a 3-inch slit in the side of each pork chop and stuff with ¼ pork rind mixture. Sprinkle each side of pork chops with salt and pepper. 3. Place pork chops into ungreased air fryer basket, stuffed side up. Adjust the temperature to 400°F (204°C) and air fry for 12 minutes. Pork chops will be browned and have an internal temperature of at least 145°F (63°C) when done. Serve warm.

Per Serving:
calorie: 366 | fat: 16g | protein: 51g | carbs: 0g | sugars: 0g | fiber: 0g | sodium: 531mg

Greek Stuffed Tenderloin

Prep time: 10 minutes | Cook time: 10 minutes | Serves 4

1½ pounds (680 g) venison or beef tenderloin, pounded to ¼ inch thick
3 teaspoons fine sea salt
1 teaspoon ground black pepper
2 ounces (57 g) creamy goat cheese
½ cup crumbled feta cheese (about 2 ounces / 57 g)
¼ cup finely chopped onions

2 cloves garlic, minced
For Garnish/Serving (Optional):
Prepared yellow mustard
Halved cherry tomatoes
Extra-virgin olive oil
Sprigs of fresh rosemary
Lavender flowers

1. Spray the air fryer basket with avocado oil. Preheat the air fryer to 400°F (204°C). 2. Season the tenderloin on all sides with the salt and pepper. 3. In a medium-sized mixing bowl, combine the goat cheese, feta, onions, and garlic. Place the mixture in the center of the tenderloin. Starting at the end closest to you, tightly roll the tenderloin like a jelly roll. Tie the rolled tenderloin tightly with kitchen twine. 4. Place the meat in the air fryer basket and air fry for 5 minutes. Flip the meat over and cook for another 5 minutes, or until the internal temperature reaches 135°F (57°C) for medium-rare. 5. To serve, smear a line of prepared yellow mustard on a platter, then place the meat next to it and add halved cherry tomatoes on the side, if desired. Drizzle with olive oil and garnish with rosemary sprigs and lavender flowers, if desired. 6. Best served fresh. Store leftovers in an airtight container in the fridge for 3 days. Reheat in a preheated 350°F (177°C) air fryer for 4 minutes, or until heated through.

Per Serving:
calories: 345 | fat: 17g | protein: 43g | carbs: 2g | fiber: 0g | sodium: 676mg

Chapter 7 Fish and Seafood

Cod with Mango Salsa

Prep time: 10 minutes | Cook time: 10 minutes | Serves 4

1 pound cod, cut into 4 fillets, pin bones removed
2 tablespoons extra-virgin olive oil
¾ teaspoon sea salt, divided
1 mango, pitted, peeled, and cut into cubes
¼ cup chopped cilantro
½ red onion, finely chopped
1 jalapeño, seeded and finely chopped
1 garlic clove, minced
Juice of 1 lime

1. Preheat the oven to 450°F. 2. In a medium bowl, whisk together the bread crumbs, salt, oregano, and cayenne until well combined. 3. Put the flour in a separate bowl. 4. In a small bowl, beat the eggs well. 5. Dip the scallops in the flour and pat off any excess. Dip them in the eggs, and then into the bread crumb mixture. Place on a rimmed baking sheet. 6. Bake until the breading is browned, 8 to 10 minutes. 7. Spoon the scallops into the lettuce leaves. Serve topped with the Remoulade.

Salmon en Papillote

Prep time: 15 minutes | Cook time: 15 minutes | Serves 2

For the roasted vegetables
½ pound fresh green beans, trimmed
½ onion, cut into ¼-inch-thick slices
1 tablespoon extra-virgin olive oil
1 teaspoon capers (optional)
For the salmon
2 teaspoons extra-virgin olive oil, divided
2 medium parsnips, cut into
¼-inch-thick rounds, divided
2 (4-ounce) salmon fillets
2 garlic cloves, thinly sliced, divided
1 lemon, divided (½ cut into slices, the other ½ cut into 2 wedges)
1 tablespoon chopped fresh thyme, divided
Kosher salt
Freshly ground black pepper

To make the roasted vegetables 1. Preheat the oven to 400°F. Line a baking sheet with parchment paper. 2. In a medium bowl, toss the green beans, onion, extra-virgin olive oil, and capers (if using) until well coated. 3. Spread the vegetables on half of the baking sheet and set aside until the salmon is ready to bake. To make the salmon 4. Cut two pieces of parchment paper, fold them in half, and cut each into a heart shape (about 10 to 12 inches in circumference). Lightly brush the parchment with ½ teaspoon of extra-virgin olive oil. 5. Open one of the hearts and place half the parsnips on the right half in the center, fanning them out. Place one piece of salmon on the fanned parsnips. Add half the garlic, half the lemon slices, half the thyme, ½ teaspoon of extra-virgin olive oil, and a pinch each of kosher salt and pepper. 6. Seal the packet by folding the left half of the heart over the right side. Fold along the edge of the heart and create a seal. Repeat with the other piece of parchment.

7. Place the packets on the empty side of the baking sheet and bake until the salmon is cooked through, 10 to 15 minutes. Allow the fish to rest a few minutes before serving with the roasted green beans and remaining lemon wedges. 8. Store any leftovers in an airtight container in the refrigerator for 1 to 2 days.

Per Serving:
calories: 389 | fat: 17g | protein: 28g | carbs: 35g | sugars: 11g | fiber: 10g | sodium: 261mg

Grilled Scallop Kabobs

Prep time: 15 minutes | Cook time: 20 minutes | Serves 6

15 ounces pineapple chunks, packed in their own juice, undrained
¼ cup dry white wine
¼ cup light soy sauce
2 tablespoons minced fresh parsley
4 garlic cloves, minced
⅛ teaspoon freshly ground black pepper
1 pound scallops
18 large cherry tomatoes
1 large green bell pepper, cut into 1-inch squares
18 medium mushroom caps

1. Drain the pineapple, reserving the juice. In a shallow baking dish, combine the pineapple juice, wine, soy sauce, parsley, garlic, and pepper. Mix well. 2. Add the pineapple, scallops, tomatoes, green pepper, and mushrooms to the marinade. Marinate 30 minutes at room temperature, stirring occasionally. 3. Alternate pineapple, scallops, and vegetables on metal or wooden skewers (remember to soak wooden skewers in water before using). 4. Grill the kabobs over medium-hot coals about 4–5 inches from the heat, turning frequently, for 5–7 minutes.

Per Serving:
calories: 132 | fat: 1g | protein: 13g | carbs: 18g | sugars: 10g | fiber: 3g | sodium: 587mg

Cajun Salmon

Prep time: 5 minutes | Cook time: 7 minutes | Serves 2

2 (4-ounce / 113-g) salmon fillets, skin removed
2 tablespoons unsalted butter, melted
⅛ teaspoon ground cayenne
pepper
½ teaspoon garlic powder
1 teaspoon paprika
¼ teaspoon ground black pepper

1. Brush each fillet with butter. 2. Combine remaining ingredients in a small bowl and then rub onto fish. Place fillets into the air fryer basket. 3. Adjust the temperature to 390ºF (199ºC) and air fry for 7 minutes. 4. When fully cooked, internal temperature will be 145ºF (63ºC). Serve immediately.

Per Serving:
calories: 213 | fat: 12g | protein: 24g | carbs: 1g | net carbs: 0g | fiber: 1g

Grilled Fish with Jicama Salsa

Prep time: 15 minutes | Cook time: 10 minutes | Serves 6

Jicama Salsa
2 cups chopped peeled jicama (3/4 lb)
1 medium cucumber, peeled, chopped (1 cup)
1 medium orange, peeled, chopped (3/4 cup)
1 tablespoon chopped fresh cilantro or parsley
1/2 teaspoon chili powder

1/4 teaspoon salt
1 tablespoon lime juice
Fish
1 1/2 lb swordfish, tuna or marlin steaks, 3/4 to 1 inch thick
2 tablespoons olive or canola oil
1 tablespoon lime juice
1/4 teaspoon salt
1/8 teaspoon crushed red pepper

1 In medium bowl, mix salsa ingredients. Cover and refrigerate at least 2 hours to blend flavors. 2 If fish steaks are large, cut into 6 serving pieces. Mix oil, lime juice, salt and red pepper in shallow glass or plastic dish or heavy-duty resealable food-storage plastic bag. Add fish; turn to coat with marinade. Cover dish or seal bag; refrigerate 30 minutes. 3 Heat charcoal or gas grill for direct heat. Remove fish from marinade; reserve marinade. Cover and grill fish 5 to 6 inches from medium heat about 10 minutes, brushing 2 or 3 times with marinade and turning once, until fish flakes easily with fork. Discard any remaining marinade. Serve fish with salsa.

Per Serving:

calories: 200 | fat: 10g | protein: 20g | carbs: 7g | sugars: 2g | fiber: 3g | sodium: 250mg

Seafood Stew

Prep time: 20 minutes | Cook time: 30 minutes | Serves 6

1 tablespoon extra-virgin olive oil
1 sweet onion, chopped
2 teaspoons minced garlic
3 celery stalks, chopped
2 carrots, peeled and chopped
1 (28-ounce) can sodium-free diced tomatoes, undrained
3 cups low-sodium chicken broth
1/2 cup clam juice
1/4 cup dry white wine
2 teaspoons chopped fresh basil

2 teaspoons chopped fresh oregano
2 (4-ounce) haddock fillets, cut into 1-inch chunks
1 pound mussels, scrubbed, debearded
8 ounces (16–20 count) shrimp, peeled, deveined, quartered
Sea salt
Freshly ground black pepper
2 tablespoons chopped fresh parsley

1. Place a large saucepan over medium-high heat and add the olive oil. 2. Sauté the onion and garlic until softened and translucent, about 3 minutes. 3. Stir in the celery and carrots and sauté for 4 minutes. 4. Stir in the tomatoes, chicken broth, clam juice, white wine, basil, and oregano. 5. Bring the sauce to a boil, then reduce the heat to low. Simmer for 15 minutes. 6. Add the fish and mussels, cover, and cook until the mussels open, about 5 minutes. 7. Discard any unopened mussels. Add the shrimp to the pan and cook until the shrimp are opaque, about 2 minutes. 8. Season with salt and pepper. Serve garnished with the chopped parsley.

Per Serving:

calories: 230 | fat: 6g | protein: 27g | carbs: 18g | sugars: 8g | fiber: 4g | sodium: 490mg

Cobia with Lemon-Caper Sauce

Prep time: 25 minutes | Cook time: 10 minutes | Serves 4

1/3 cup all-purpose flour
1/4 teaspoon salt
1/4 teaspoon pepper
1 1/4 lb cobia or sea bass fillets, cut into 4 pieces
2 tablespoons olive oil
1/3 cup dry white wine

1/2 cup reduced-sodium chicken broth
2 tablespoons lemon juice
1 tablespoon capers, rinsed, drained
1 tablespoon chopped fresh parsley

1 In shallow dish, stir flour, salt and pepper. Coat cobia pieces in flour mixture (reserve remaining flour mixture). In 12-inch nonstick skillet, heat oil over medium-high heat. Place coated cobia in oil. Cook 8 to 10 minutes, turning halfway through cooking, until fish flakes easily with fork; remove from heat. Lift fish from skillet to serving platter with slotted spatula (do not discard drippings); keep warm. 2 Heat skillet (with drippings) over medium heat. Stir in 1 tablespoon reserved flour mixture; cook and stir 30 seconds. Stir in wine; cook about 30 seconds or until thickened and slightly reduced. Stir in chicken broth and lemon juice; cook and stir 1 to 2 minutes until sauce is smooth and slightly thickened. Stir in capers. 3 Serve sauce over cobia; sprinkle with parsley.

Per Serving:

calories: 230 | fat: 9g | protein: 28g | carbs: 9g | sugars: 0g | fiber: 0g | sodium: 400mg

Citrus-Glazed Salmon

Prep time: 10 minutes | Cook time: 13 to 17 minutes | Serves 4

2 medium limes
1 small orange
1/3 cup agave syrup
1 teaspoon salt
1 teaspoon pepper
4 cloves garlic, finely chopped
1 1/4 lb salmon fillet, cut into 4 pieces

2 tablespoons sliced green onions
1 lime slice, cut into 4 wedges
1 orange slice, cut into 4 wedges
Hot cooked orzo pasta or rice, if desired

1 Heat oven to 400°F. Line 15x10x1-inch pan with cooking parchment paper or foil. In small bowl, grate lime peel from limes. Squeeze enough lime juice to equal 2 tablespoons; add to peel in bowl. Grate orange peel from oranges into bowl. Squeeze enough orange juice to equal 2 tablespoons; add to peel mixture. Stir in agave syrup, salt, pepper and garlic. In small cup, measure 1/4 cup citrus mixture for salmon (reserve remaining citrus mixture). 2 Place salmon fillets in pan, skin side down. Using 1/4 cup citrus mixture, brush tops and sides of salmon. Bake 13 to 17 minutes or until fish flakes easily with fork. Lift salmon pieces from skin with metal spatula onto serving plate. Sprinkle with green onions. Top each fish fillet with lime and orange wedges. Serve each fillet with 3 tablespoons reserved sauce and rice.

Per Serving:

calories: 320 | fat: 8g | protein: 31g | carbs: 30g | sugars: 23g | fiber: 3g | sodium: 680mg

Spicy Corn and Shrimp Salad in Avocado

Prep time: 10 minutes | Cook time: 0 minutes | Serves 2

¼ cup mayonnaise
1 teaspoon sriracha (or to taste)
½ teaspoon lemon zest
¼ teaspoon sea salt
4 ounces cooked baby shrimp

½ cup cooked and cooled corn kernels
½ red bell pepper, seeded and chopped
1 avocado, halved lengthwise

1. In a medium bowl, combine the mayonnaise, sriracha, lemon zest, and salt. 2. Add the shrimp, corn, and bell pepper. Mix to combine. 3. Spoon the mixture into the avocado halves.

Per Serving:

calories: 354 | fat: 25g | protein: 17g | carbs: 21g | sugars: 2g | fiber: 9g | sodium: 600mg

Lemon Pepper Salmon

Prep time: 5 minutes | Cook time: 20 minutes | Serves 4

Avocado oil cooking spray
20 Brussels sprouts, halved lengthwise
4 (4-ounce) skinless salmon fillets
½ teaspoon garlic powder

½ teaspoon freshly ground black pepper
¼ teaspoon salt
2 teaspoons freshly squeezed lemon juice

1. Heat a large skillet over medium-low heat. When hot, coat the cooking surface with cooking spray, and put the Brussels sprouts cut-side down in the skillet. Cover and cook for 5 minutes. 2. Meanwhile, season both sides of the salmon with the garlic powder, pepper, and salt. 3. Flip the Brussels sprouts, and move them to one side of the skillet. Add the salmon and cook, uncovered, for 4 to 6 minutes. 4. Check the Brussels sprouts. When they are tender, remove them from the skillet and set them aside. 5. Flip the salmon fillets. Cook for 4 to 6 more minutes, or until the salmon is opaque and flakes easily with a fork. Remove the salmon from the skillet, and let it rest for 5 minutes. 6. Divide the Brussels sprouts into four equal portions and add 1 salmon fillet to each portion. Sprinkle the lemon juice on top and serve.

Per Serving:

calories: 163 | fat: 7g | protein: 23g | carbs: 1g | sugars: 0g | fiber: 0g | sodium: 167mg

Tuna Steak

Prep time: 10 minutes | Cook time: 12 minutes | Serves 4

1 pound (454 g) tuna steaks, boneless and cubed
1 tablespoon mustard

1 tablespoon avocado oil
1 tablespoon apple cider vinegar

1. Mix avocado oil with mustard and apple cider vinegar. 2. Then brush tuna steaks with mustard mixture and put in the air fryer basket. 3. Cook the fish at 360ºF (182ºC) for 6 minutes per side.

Per Serving:

calories: 197 | fat: 9g | protein: 27g | carbs: 0g | fiber: 0g | sodium: 87mg

Blackened Salmon

Prep time: 10 minutes | Cook time: 8 minutes | Serves 2

10 ounces (283 g) salmon fillet
½ teaspoon ground coriander
1 teaspoon ground cumin

1 teaspoon dried basil
1 tablespoon avocado oil

1. In the shallow bowl, mix ground coriander, ground cumin, and dried basil. 2. Then coat the salmon fillet in the spices and sprinkle with avocado oil. 3. Put the fish in the air fryer basket and cook at 395ºF (202ºC) for 4 minutes per side.

Per Serving:

calories: 249 | fat: 13g | protein: 29g | carbs: 1g | fiber: 1g | sodium: 109mg

Scallops in Lemon-Butter Sauce

Prep time: 10 minutes | Cook time: 6 minutes | Serves 2

8 large dry sea scallops (about ¾ pound / 340 g)
Salt and freshly ground black pepper, to taste
2 tablespoons olive oil
2 tablespoons unsalted butter, melted

2 tablespoons chopped flat-leaf parsley
1 tablespoon fresh lemon juice
2 teaspoons capers, drained and chopped
1 teaspoon grated lemon zest
1 clove garlic, minced

1. Preheat the air fryer to 400ºF (204ºC). 2. Use a paper towel to pat the scallops dry. Sprinkle lightly with salt and pepper. Brush with the olive oil. Arrange the scallops in a single layer in the air fryer basket. Pausing halfway through the cooking time to turn the scallops, air fry for about 6 minutes until firm and opaque. 3. Meanwhile, in a small bowl, combine the oil, butter, parsley, lemon juice, capers, lemon zest, and garlic. Drizzle over the scallops just before serving.

Per Serving:

calories: 304 | fat: 22g | protein: 21g | carbs: 5g | net carbs: 4g | fiber: 1g

Air Fryer Fish Fry

Prep time: 5 minutes | Cook time: 15 minutes | Serves 4

2 cups low-fat buttermilk
½ teaspoon garlic powder
½ teaspoon onion powder
4 (4-ounce) flounder fillets

½ cup plain yellow cornmeal
½ cup chickpea flour
¼ teaspoon cayenne pepper
Freshly ground black pepper

1. In a large bowl, combine the buttermilk, garlic powder, and onion powder. 2. Add the flounder, turning until well coated, and set aside to marinate for 20 minutes. 3. In a shallow bowl, stir the cornmeal, chickpea flour, cayenne, and pepper together. 4. Dredge the fillets in the meal mixture, turning until well coated. Place in the basket of an air fryer. 5. Set the air fryer to 380°F, close, and cook for 12 minutes.

Per Serving:

calories: 266 | fat: 7g | protein: 27g | carbs: 24g | sugars: 8g | fiber: 2g | sodium: 569mg

Southern-Style Catfish

Prep time: 10 minutes | Cook time: 12 minutes | Serves 4

4 (7-ounce / 198-g) catfish fillets	almond flour
⅓ cup heavy whipping cream	2 teaspoons Old Bay seasoning
1 tablespoon lemon juice	½ teaspoon salt
1 cup blanched finely ground	¼ teaspoon ground black pepper

1. Place catfish fillets into a large bowl with cream and pour in lemon juice. Stir to coat. 2. In a separate large bowl, mix flour and Old Bay seasoning. 3. Remove each fillet and gently shake off excess cream. Sprinkle with salt and pepper. Press each fillet gently into flour mixture on both sides to coat. 4. Place fillets into ungreased air fryer basket. Adjust the temperature to 400°F (204°C) and air fry for 12 minutes, turning fillets halfway through cooking. Catfish will be golden brown and have an internal temperature of at least 145°F (63°C) when done. Serve warm.

Per Serving:

calories: 438 | fat: 28g | protein: 41g | carbs: 7g | fiber: 4g | sodium: 387mg

Quick Shrimp Skewers

Prep time: 10 minutes | Cook time: 5 minutes | Serves 5

4 pounds (1.8 kg) shrimp, peeled	1 tablespoon avocado oil
1 tablespoon dried rosemary	1 teaspoon apple cider vinegar

1. Mix the shrimps with dried rosemary, avocado oil, and apple cider vinegar. 2. Then sting the shrimps into skewers and put in the air fryer. 3. Cook the shrimps at 400°F (204°C) for 5 minutes.

Per Serving:

calories: 336 | fat: 5g | protein: 73g | carbs: 0g | fiber: 0g | sodium: 432mg

Stuffed Flounder Florentine

Prep time: 10 minutes | Cook time: 25 minutes | Serves 4

¼ cup pine nuts	pepper, to taste
2 tablespoons olive oil	2 tablespoons unsalted butter, divided
½ cup chopped tomatoes	
1 (6-ounce / 170-g) bag spinach, coarsely chopped	4 flounder fillets (about 1½ pounds / 680 g)
2 cloves garlic, chopped	Dash of paprika
Salt and freshly ground black	½ lemon, sliced into 4 wedges

1. Place the pine nuts in a baking dish that fits in your air fryer. Set the air fryer to 400°F (204°C) and air fry for 4 minutes until the nuts are lightly browned and fragrant. Remove the baking dish from the air fryer, tip the nuts onto a plate to cool, and continue preheating the air fryer. When the nuts are cool enough to handle, chop them into fine pieces. 2. In the baking dish, combine the oil, tomatoes, spinach, and garlic. Use tongs to toss until thoroughly combined. Air fry for 5 minutes until the tomatoes are softened and the spinach is wilted. 3. Transfer the vegetables to a bowl and stir in the toasted pine nuts. Season to taste with salt and freshly ground

black pepper. 4. Place 1 tablespoon of the butter in the bottom of the baking dish. Lower the heat on the air fryer to 350°F (177°C). 5. Place the flounder on a clean work surface. Sprinkle both sides with salt and black pepper. Divide the vegetable mixture among the flounder fillets and carefully roll up, securing with toothpicks. 6. Working in batches if necessary, arrange the fillets seam-side down in the baking dish along with 1 tablespoon of water. Top the fillets with remaining 1 tablespoon butter and sprinkle with a dash of paprika. 7.Cover loosely with foil and air fry for 10 to 15 minutes until the fish is opaque and flakes easily with a fork. Remove the toothpicks before serving with the lemon wedges.

Per Serving:

calories: 287 | fat: 21g | protein: 21g | carbs: 5g | sugars: 1g | fiber: 2g | sodium: 692mg

Poached Red Snapper

Prep time: 5 minutes | Cook time: 25 minutes | Serves 4

1 cup dry white wine	¼ teaspoon salt
1 medium lemon, sliced	1 cup water
6 parsley sprigs, plus additional for garnish	1 red snapper (about 1½–2 pounds), cleaned and scaled
5 peppercorns	with head and tail left on
5 scallions, sliced	1 lemon, sliced
2 bay leaves	

1. In a fish poacher or very large skillet, combine the wine, lemon slices, 6 parsley sprigs, peppercorns, scallions, bay leaves, salt, and water. Bring the mixture to a boil; add the snapper. 2. Cover the pan, lower the heat, and simmer the red snapper for 15–20 minutes until the fish flakes easily with a fork. 3. Carefully lift out the snapper, and transfer to a platter. Garnish with lemon slices and parsley.

Per Serving:

calories: 269 | fat: 3g | protein: 43g | carbs: 6g | sugars: 2g | fiber: 2g | sodium: 285mg

Catfish with Corn and Pepper Relish

Prep time: 10 minutes | Cook time: 10 minutes | Serves 4

3 tablespoons extra-virgin olive oil, divided	black beans, drained and rinsed
	1 cup frozen corn
4 (5-ounce) catfish fillets	1 medium red bell pepper, diced
¼ teaspoon salt	1 tablespoon apple cider vinegar
¼ teaspoon freshly ground black pepper	
1 (15-ounce) can low-sodium	3 tablespoons chopped scallions

1. Use 1½ tablespoons of oil to coat both sides of the catfish fillets, then season the fillets with the salt and pepper. 2. Heat a small saucepan over medium-high heat. Put the remaining 1½ tablespoons of oil, beans, corn, bell pepper, and vinegar in the pan and stir. Cover and cook for 5 minutes. 3. Place the catfish fillets on top of the relish mixture and cover. Cook for 5 to 7 minutes. 4. Serve each catfish fillet with one-quarter of the relish and top with the scallions.

Per Serving:

calories: 379 | fat: 15g | protein: 32g | carbs: 31g | sugars: 2g | fiber: 10g | sodium: 366mg

Salmon with Brussels Sprouts

Prep time: 5 minutes | Cook time: 20 minutes | Serves 4

2 tablespoons unsalted butter, divided
20 Brussels sprouts, halved lengthwise
4 (4-ounce) skinless salmon fillets
½ teaspoon salt
¼ teaspoon garlic powder

1. Heat a medium skillet over medium-low heat. When hot, melt 1 tablespoon of butter in the skillet, then add the Brussels sprouts cut-side down. Cook for 10 minutes. 2. Season both sides of the salmon fillets with the salt and garlic powder. 3. Heat another medium skillet over medium-low heat. When hot, melt the remaining 1 tablespoon of butter in the skillet, then add the salmon. Cover and cook for 6 to 8 minutes, or until the salmon is opaque and flakes easily with a fork. 4. Meanwhile, flip the Brussels sprouts and cover. Cook for 10 minutes or until tender. 5. Divide the Brussels sprouts into four equal portions and add 1 salmon fillet to each portion.

Per Serving:
calories: 236 | fat: 11g | protein: 27g | carbs: 9g | sugars: 2g | fiber: 4g | sodium: 400mg

Ahi Tuna Steaks

Prep time: 5 minutes | Cook time: 14 minutes | Serves 2

2 (6-ounce / 170-g) ahi tuna steaks
2 tablespoons olive oil
3 tablespoons everything bagel seasoning

1. Drizzle both sides of each steak with olive oil. Place seasoning on a medium plate and press each side of tuna steaks into seasoning to form a thick layer. 2. Place steaks into ungreased air fryer basket. Adjust the temperature to 400ºF (204ºC) and air fry for 14 minutes, turning steaks halfway through cooking. Steaks will be done when internal temperature is at least 145ºF (63ºC) for well-done. Serve warm.

Per Serving:
calories: 305 | fat: 14g | protein: 42g | carbs: 0g | fiber: 0g | sodium: 377mg

Baked Garlic Scampi

Prep time: 5 minutes | Cook time: 10 minutes | Serves 4

1 tablespoon extra-virgin olive oil
¼ teaspoon salt
7 garlic cloves, crushed
2 tablespoons chopped fresh
parsley, divided
1 pound large shrimp, shelled (with tails left on) and deveined
Juice and zest of 1 lemon
2 cups baby arugula

1. Preheat the oven to 350 degrees. Grease a 13-x-9-x-2-inch baking pan with the olive oil. Add the salt, garlic, and 1 tablespoon of the parsley in a medium bowl; mix well, and set aside. 2. Arrange the shrimp in a single layer in the baking pan, and bake for 3 minutes, uncovered. Turn the shrimp, and sprinkle with the lemon peel, lemon juice, and the remaining 1 tablespoon of parsley. Continue to bake 1–2 minutes more until the shrimp are bright pink and tender. 3. Remove the shrimp from the oven. Place the arugula on a serving platter, and top with the shrimp. Spoon the garlic mixture over the shrimp and arugula, and serve.

Per Serving:
calories: 140 | fat: 4g | protein: 23g | carbs: 3g | sugars: 1g | fiber: 0g | sodium: 285mg

Spicy Shrimp Fajitas

Prep time: 30 minutes | Cook time: 20 minutes | Makes 6 fajitas

Marinade
1 tablespoon lime juice
1 tablespoon olive or canola oil
¼ teaspoon salt
1 teaspoon chili powder
1 teaspoon ground cumin
2 cloves garlic, crushed
Pinch ground red pepper (cayenne)
Fajitas
2 lb uncooked deveined peeled
medium shrimp, thawed if frozen, tail shells removed
2 medium red bell peppers, cut into strips (2 cups)
1 medium red onion, sliced (2 cups)
Olive oil cooking spray
6 flour tortillas (8 inch)
¾ cup refrigerated guacamole (from 14-oz package)

1 Heat gas or charcoal grill. In 1-gallon resealable food-storage plastic bag, mix marinade ingredients. Add shrimp; seal bag and toss to coat. Set aside while grilling vegetables, turning bag once. 2 In medium bowl, place bell peppers and onion; spray with cooking spray. Place vegetables in grill basket (grill "wok"). Wrap tortillas in foil; set aside. 3 Place basket on grill rack over medium heat. Cover grill; cook 10 minutes, turning vegetables once. 4 Drain shrimp; discard marinade. Add shrimp to grill basket. Cover grill; cook 5 to 7 minutes longer, turning shrimp and vegetables once, until shrimp are pink. Place wrapped tortillas on grill. Cook 2 minutes, turning once, until warm. 5 On each tortilla, place shrimp, vegetables and guacamole; fold tortilla over filling.

Per Serving:
calories: 310 | fat: 10g | protein:27g | carbs: 29g | sugars: 4g | fiber: 2g | sodium: 770mg

Peppercorn-Crusted Baked Salmon

Prep time: 5 minutes | Cook time: 20 minutes | Serves 4

Nonstick cooking spray
½ teaspoon freshly ground black pepper
¼ teaspoon salt
Zest and juice of ½ lemon
¼ teaspoon dried thyme
1 pound salmon fillet

1. Preheat the oven to 425°F. Spray a baking sheet with nonstick cooking spray. 2. In a small bowl, combine the pepper, salt, lemon zest and juice, and thyme. Stir to combine. 3. Place the salmon on the prepared baking sheet, skin-side down. Spread the seasoning mixture evenly over the fillet. 4. Bake for 15 to 20 minutes, depending on the thickness of the fillet, until the flesh flakes easily.

Per Serving:
calories: 163 | fat: 7g | protein: 23g | carbs: 1g | sugars: 0g | fiber: 0g | sodium: 167mg

Baked Monkfish

Prep time: 20 minutes | Cook time: 12 minutes | Serves 2

2 teaspoons olive oil
1 cup celery, sliced
2 bell peppers, sliced
1 teaspoon dried thyme
½ teaspoon dried marjoram
½ teaspoon dried rosemary
2 monkfish fillets

1 tablespoon coconut aminos
2 tablespoons lime juice
Coarse salt and ground black pepper, to taste
1 teaspoon cayenne pepper
½ cup Kalamata olives, pitted and sliced

1. In a nonstick skillet, heat the olive oil for 1 minute. Once hot, sauté the celery and peppers until tender, about 4 minutes. Sprinkle with thyme, marjoram, and rosemary and set aside. 2. Toss the fish fillets with the coconut aminos, lime juice, salt, black pepper, and cayenne pepper. Place the fish fillets in the lightly greased air fryer basket and bake at 390ºF (199ºC) for 8 minutes. 3. Turn them over, add the olives, and cook an additional 4 minutes. Serve with the sautéed vegetables on the side. Bon appétit!

Per Serving:
calories: 263 | fat: 11g | protein: 27g | carbs: 13g | fiber: 5g | sodium: 332mg

Halibut Supreme

Prep time: 10 minutes | Cook time: 25 minutes | Serves 6

Nonstick cooking spray
1½ pound halibut steaks
1 cup sliced mushrooms
1 tablespoon extra-virgin olive oil
1 small onion, finely chopped
3 tablespoons white wine

¾ cup water
⅛ teaspoon freshly ground black pepper
¼ teaspoon salt
¼ cup toasted almond slivers
1 tablespoon chopped fresh parsley

1. Preheat the oven to 325 degrees. Coat a 13-x-9-x-2-inch baking dish with cooking spray, and place the halibut steaks in a baking dish. 2. Add the remaining ingredients except the almonds and parsley, and bake at 325 degrees, basting frequently, for 25 minutes until the fish flakes easily with a fork. 3. Remove from the oven, and top the halibut steaks with the toasted almond slivers. Garnish with parsley.

Per Serving:
calories: 267 | fat: 20g | protein: 18g | carbs: 3g | sugars: 1g | fiber: 1g | sodium: 190mg

Salmon Florentine

Prep time: 10 minutes | Cook time: 30 minutes | Serves 4

1 teaspoon extra-virgin olive oil
½ sweet onion, finely chopped
1 teaspoon minced garlic
3 cups baby spinach
1 cup kale, tough stems removed, torn into 3-inch

pieces
Sea salt
Freshly ground black pepper
4 (5-ounce) salmon fillets
Lemon wedges, for serving

1. Preheat the oven to 350°F. 2. Place a large skillet over medium-high heat and add the oil. 3. Sauté the onion and garlic until softened and translucent, about 3 minutes. 4. Add the spinach and kale and sauté until the greens wilt, about 5 minutes. 5. Remove the skillet from the heat and season the greens with salt and pepper. 6. Place the salmon fillets so they are nestled in the greens and partially covered by them. Bake the salmon until it is opaque, about 20 minutes. 7. Serve immediately with a squeeze of fresh lemon.

Per Serving:
calories: 211 | fat: 8g | protein: 30g | carbs: 5g | sugars: 2g | fiber: 1g | sodium: 129mg

Shrimp Étouffée

Prep time: 20 minutes | Cook time: 30 minutes | Serves 4 to 6

2 cups store-bought low-sodium vegetable broth, divided
¼ cup whole-wheat flour
1 small onion, finely chopped
2 celery stalks including leaves, finely chopped
1 medium green bell pepper, finely chopped

1 medium poblano pepper, finely chopped
3 garlic cloves, minced
1 tablespoon Creole seasoning
2 pounds medium shrimp, shelled and deveined
⅓ cup finely chopped chives, for garnish

1. In a Dutch oven, bring ½ cup of broth to a simmer over medium heat. 2. Stir in the flour and reduce the heat to low. Cook, stirring often, for 5 minutes, or until a thick paste is formed. 3. Add ½ cup of broth, the onion, celery, bell pepper, poblano pepper, and garlic and cook for 2 to 5 minutes, or until the vegetables have softened. 4. Slowly add the seasoning and remaining 1 cup of broth, ¼ cup at a time. 5. Add the shrimp and cook for about 5 minutes, or until just opaque. 6. Serve with the vegetable of your choice. Garnish with the chives.

Per Serving:
calories: 164 | fat: 1g | protein: 32g | carbs: 8g | sugars: 2g | fiber: 1g | sodium: 500mg

Herb-Crusted Halibut

Prep time: 10 minutes | Cook time: 20 minutes | Serves 4

4 (5-ounce) halibut fillets
Extra-virgin olive oil, for brushing
½ cup coarsely ground unsalted pistachios
1 tablespoon chopped fresh

parsley
1 teaspoon chopped fresh thyme
1 teaspoon chopped fresh basil
Pinch sea salt
Pinch freshly ground black pepper

1. Preheat the oven to 350°F. 2. Line a baking sheet with parchment paper. 3. Pat the halibut fillets dry with a paper towel and place them on the baking sheet. 4. Brush the halibut generously with olive oil. 5. In a small bowl, stir together the pistachios, parsley, thyme, basil, salt, and pepper. 6. Spoon the nut and herb mixture evenly on the fish, spreading it out so the tops of the fillets are covered. 7. Bake the halibut until it flakes when pressed with a fork, about 20 minutes. 8. Serve immediately.

Per Serving:
calories: 351 | fat: 27g | protein: 24g | carbs: 4g | sugars: 1g | fiber: 2g | sodium: 214mg

Salmon Fritters with Zucchini

Prep time: 15 minutes | Cook time: 12 minutes | Serves 4

2 tablespoons almond flour
1 zucchini, grated
1 egg, beaten
6 ounces (170 g) salmon fillet,
diced
1 teaspoon avocado oil
½ teaspoon ground black
pepper

1. Mix almond flour with zucchini, egg, salmon, and ground black pepper. 2. Then make the fritters from the salmon mixture. 3. Sprinkle the air fryer basket with avocado oil and put the fritters inside. 4. Cook the fritters at 375ºF (191ºC) for 6 minutes per side.

Per Serving:
calories: 102 | fat: 4g | protein: 11g | carbs: 4g | fiber: 1g | sodium: 52mg

Tuna Poke with Riced Broccoli

Prep time: 15 minutes | Cook time: 5 minutes | Serves 2

For the tuna poke
½ pound sushi-grade tuna (see tip), cut into ½-inch cubes
2 tablespoons soy sauce or tamari
1 tablespoon rice vinegar
1 teaspoon sesame oil
For the bowl
½ tablespoon extra-virgin olive oil
1 small head broccoli, grated
1 cup thawed (if frozen) edamame
1 medium carrot, julienned
1 cucumber, diced
2 scallions, both white and green parts, thinly sliced
Optional toppings
Avocado slices
Shaved radish
Toasted sesame seeds
Pickled ginger

To make the tuna poke 1. In a medium bowl, toss together the tuna, soy sauce, rice vinegar, and sesame oil. 2. Set aside. To make the bowl 3. Heat the oil in a large skillet over medium heat and sauté the broccoli until tender, 2 to 3 minutes. Remove the skillet from the heat and allow the broccoli to cool. 4. Assemble two bowls by placing riced broccoli as the base. Top each bowl with the tuna poke, edamame, carrot, and cucumber. Drizzle the remaining juices from the tuna marinade over the bowls and garnish with sliced scallions. 5. Store any leftovers in an airtight container in the refrigerator for up to 2 days.

Per Serving:
calories: 454 | fat: 18g | protein: 43g | carbs: 34g | sugars: 13g | fiber: 13g | sodium: 412mg

Grilled Rosemary Swordfish

Prep time: 5 minutes | Cook time: 15 minutes | Serves 4

2 scallions, thinly sliced
2 tablespoons extra-virgin olive oil
2 tablespoons white wine vinegar
1 teaspoon fresh rosemary, finely chopped
4 swordfish steaks (1 pound total)

1. In a small bowl, combine the scallions, olive oil, vinegar, and rosemary. Pour over the swordfish steaks. Let the steaks marinate for 30 minutes. 2. Remove the steaks from the marinade, and grill for 5–7 minutes per side, brushing with marinade. Transfer to a serving platter, and serve.

Per Serving:
calories: 225 | fat: 14g | protein: 22g | carbs: 0g | sugars: 0g | fiber: 0g | sodium: 92mg

Sesame-Crusted Halibut

Prep time: 5 minutes | Cook time: 15 minutes | Serves 2

1 tablespoon freshly squeezed lemon juice
1 tablespoon extra-virgin olive oil
1 garlic clove, minced
Freshly ground black pepper, to season
1 (8-ounce) halibut fillet, halved
2 tablespoons sesame seeds, toasted
1 teaspoon dried basil
1 teaspoon dried marjoram
½ cup minced chives
⅛ teaspoon salt
2 lemon wedges

1. Preheat the oven to 450°F. 2. Line a baking sheet with aluminum foil. 3. In a shallow glass dish, mix together the lemon juice, olive oil, and garlic. Season with pepper. 4. Add the halibut and turn to coat. Cover and refrigerate for 15 minutes. 5. In a small bowl, combine the sesame seeds, basil, marjoram, and chives. 6. Remove the fish from the refrigerator. Sprinkle with the salt. Coat evenly with the sesame seed mixture, covering the sides as well as the top. 7. Transfer the fish to the prepared baking sheet. Place the sheet in the preheated oven. Roast for 10 to 14 minutes, or until just cooked through. 8. Garnish each serving with 1 lemon wedge.

Per Serving:
calories: 331 | fat: 27g | protein: 18g | carbs: 3g | sugars: 0g | fiber: 2g | sodium: 251mg

Spicy Citrus Sole

Prep time: 10 minutes | Cook time: 10 minutes | Serves 4

1 teaspoon chili powder
1 teaspoon garlic powder
½ teaspoon lime zest
½ teaspoon lemon zest
¼ teaspoon freshly ground black pepper
¼ teaspoon smoked paprika
Pinch sea salt
4 (6-ounce) sole fillets, patted dry
1 tablespoon extra-virgin olive oil
2 teaspoons freshly squeezed lime juice

1. Preheat the oven to 450°F. 2. Line a baking sheet with aluminum foil and set it aside. 3. In a small bowl, stir together the chili powder, garlic powder, lime zest, lemon zest, pepper, paprika, and salt until well mixed. 4. Pat the fish fillets dry with paper towels, place them on the baking sheet, and rub them lightly all over with the spice mixture. 5. Drizzle the olive oil and lime juice on the top of the fish. 6. Bake until the fish flakes when pressed lightly with a fork, about 8 minutes. Serve immediately.

Per Serving:
calories: 155 | fat: 7g | protein: 21g | carbs: 1g | sugars: 0g | fiber: 1g | sodium: 524mg

Sole Piccata

Prep time: 10 minutes | Cook time: 20 minutes | Serves 4

1 teaspoon extra-virgin olive oil	2 tablespoons all-purpose flour
4 (5-ounce) sole fillets, patted dry	2 cups low-sodium chicken broth
3 tablespoons butter	Juice and zest of ½ lemon
2 teaspoons minced garlic	2 tablespoons capers

1. Place a large skillet over medium-high heat and add the olive oil. 2. Pat the sole fillets dry with paper towels then pan-sear them until the fish flakes easily when tested with a fork, about 4 minutes on each side. Transfer the fish to a plate and set it aside. 3. Return the skillet to the stove and add the butter. 4. Sauté the garlic until translucent, about 3 minutes. 5. Whisk in the flour to make a thick paste and cook, stirring constantly, until the mixture is golden brown, about 2 minutes. 6. Whisk in the chicken broth, lemon juice, and lemon zest. 7. Cook until the sauce has thickened, about 4 minutes. 8. Stir in the capers and serve the sauce over the fish.

Per Serving:

calories: 224 | fat: 13g | protein: 21g | carbs: 6g | sugars: 0g | fiber: 1g | sodium: 558mg

Tilapia with Pecans

Prep time: 20 minutes | Cook time: 16 minutes | Serves 5

2 tablespoons ground flaxseeds	2 tablespoons extra-virgin olive oil
1 teaspoon paprika	½ cup pecans, ground
Sea salt and white pepper, to taste	5 tilapia fillets, sliced into halves
1 teaspoon garlic paste	

1. Combine the ground flaxseeds, paprika, salt, white pepper, garlic paste, olive oil, and ground pecans in a Ziploc bag. Add the fish fillets and shake to coat well. 2. Spritz the air fryer basket with cooking spray. Cook in the preheated air fryer at 400°F (204°C) for 10 minutes; turn them over and cook for 6 minutes more. Work in batches. 3. Serve with lemon wedges, if desired. Enjoy!

Per Serving:

calories: 252 | fat: 17g | protein: 25g | carbs: 3g | fiber: 2g | sodium: 65mg

Ginger-Garlic Cod Cooked in Paper

Prep time: 10 minutes | Cook time: 15 minutes | Serves 4

1 chard bunch, stemmed, leaves and stems cut into thin strips	3 garlic cloves, minced
1 red bell pepper, seeded and cut into strips	2 tablespoons white wine vinegar
1 pound cod fillets cut into 4 pieces	2 tablespoons low-sodium tamari or gluten-free soy sauce
1 tablespoon grated fresh ginger	1 tablespoon honey

1. Preheat the oven to 425°F. 2. Cut four pieces of parchment paper, each about 16 inches wide. Lay the four pieces out on a large workspace. 3. On each piece of paper, arrange a small pile of chard leaves and stems, topped by several strips of bell pepper. Top with a piece of cod. 4. In a small bowl, mix the ginger, garlic, vinegar, tamari, and honey. Top each piece of fish with one-fourth of the mixture. 5. Fold the parchment paper over so the edges overlap. Fold the edges over several times to secure the fish in the packets. Carefully place the packets on a large baking sheet. 6. Bake for 12 minutes. Carefully open the packets, allowing steam to escape, and serve.

Per Serving:

calories: 118 | fat: 1g | protein: 19g | carbs: 9g | sugars: 6g | fiber: 1g | sodium: 715mg

Haddock with Creamy Cucumber Sauce

Prep time: 10 minutes | Cook time: 10 minutes | Serves 4

¼ cup 2 percent plain Greek yogurt	2 teaspoons chopped fresh mint
½ English cucumber, grated, liquid squeezed out	1 teaspoon honey
	Sea salt
½ scallion, white and green parts, finely chopped	4 (5-ounce) haddock fillets
	Freshly ground black pepper
	Nonstick cooking spray

1. In a small bowl, stir together the yogurt, cucumber, scallion, mint, honey, and a pinch of salt. Set it aside. 2. Pat the fish fillets dry with paper towels and season them lightly with salt and pepper. 3. Place a large skillet over medium-high heat and spray lightly with cooking spray. 4. Cook the haddock, turning once, until it is just cooked through, about 5 minutes per side. 5. Remove the fish from the heat and transfer to plates. 6. Serve topped with the cucumber sauce.

Per Serving:

calories: 123 | fat: 1g | protein: 24g | carbs: 3g | sugars: 3g | fiber: 0g | sodium: 310mg

Roasted Tilapia and Vegetables

Prep time: 15 minutes | Cook time: 20 minutes | Serves 4

1/2 lb fresh asparagus spears, trimmed, halved	wedges
	1 tablespoon olive oil
2 small zucchini, halved lengthwise, cut into 1/2-inch pieces	2 teaspoons Montreal steak seasoning
	4 tilapia fillets (about 11/2 lb)
1 red bell pepper, cut into 1/2-inch strips	2 teaspoons butter or margarine, melted
1 large onion, cut into 1/2-inch	1/2 teaspoon paprika

1 Heat oven to 450°F. In large bowl, toss asparagus, zucchini, bell pepper, onion and oil. Sprinkle with 1 teaspoon of the steak seasoning; toss to coat. Spread vegetables in ungreased 15x10x1-inch pan. Place on lower oven rack; roast 5 minutes. 2 Meanwhile, spray 13x9-inch (3-quart) glass baking dish with cooking spray. Pat tilapia fillets dry with paper towels. Brush with butter; sprinkle with remaining 1 teaspoon steak seasoning and the paprika. Place in baking dish. 3 Place baking dish on middle oven rack. Roast fish and vegetables 17 to 18 minutes longer or until fish flakes easily with fork and vegetables are tender.

Per Serving:

calories: 250 | fat: 8g | protein: 35g | carbs: 10g | sugars: 5g | fiber: 3g | sodium: 160mg

Salmon with Provolone Cheese

Prep time: 5 minutes | Cook time: 15 minutes | Serves 4

1 pound (454 g) salmon fillet, chopped

2 ounces (57 g) Provolone, grated

1 teaspoon avocado oil

¼ teaspoon ground paprika

1. Sprinkle the salmon fillets with avocado oil and put in the air fryer. 2. Then sprinkle the fish with ground paprika and top with Provolone cheese. 3. Cook the fish at 360°F (182°C) for 15 minutes.

Per Serving:

calories: 204 | fat: 10g | protein: 27g | carbs: 0g | fiber: 0g | sodium: 209mg

Chapter 8 Poultry

Chicken Enchilada Spaghetti Squash

Prep time: 5 minutes | Cook time: 40 minutes | Serves 4

1 (3-pound) spaghetti squash, halved lengthwise and seeded
1½ teaspoons ground cumin, divided
Avocado oil cooking spray
4 (4-ounce) boneless, skinless chicken breasts
1 large zucchini, diced
¾ cup canned red enchilada sauce
¾ cup shredded Cheddar or mozzarella cheese

1. Preheat the oven to 400ºF. 2. Season both halves of the squash with ½ teaspoon of cumin, and place them cut-side down on a baking sheet. Bake for 25 to 30 minutes. 3. Meanwhile, heat a large skillet over medium-low heat. When hot, spray the cooking surface with cooking spray and add the chicken breasts, zucchini, and 1 teaspoon of cumin. Cook the chicken for 4 to 5 minutes per side. Stir the zucchini when you flip the chicken. 4. Transfer the zucchini to a medium bowl and set aside. Remove the chicken from the skillet, and let it rest for 10 minutes or until it's cool enough to handle. Shred or dice the cooked chicken. 5. Place the chicken and zucchini in a large bowl, and add the enchilada sauce. 6. Remove the squash from the oven, flip it over, and comb through it with a fork to make thin strands. 7. Scoop the chicken mixture on top of the squash halves and top with the cheese. Return the squash to the oven and broil for 2 to 5 minutes, or until the cheese is bubbly.

Per Serving:
calorie: 391 | fat: 12g | protein: 35g | carbs: 40g | sugars: 3g | fiber: 7g | sodium: 368mg

Crispy Baked Drumsticks with Mustard Sauce

Prep time: 15 minutes | Cook time: 30 minutes | Serves 2

For the chicken
Extra-virgin olive oil cooking spray
⅓ cup almond meal
¼ teaspoon paprika
¼ teaspoon onion powder
¼ teaspoon salt
2 teaspoons extra-virgin olive oil
1 large egg
4 (4-ounce) skinless chicken drumsticks, trimmed
For the mustard sauce
2 tablespoons plain nonfat Greek yogurt
1 tablespoon Dijon mustard
¼ teaspoon liquid stevia
Freshly ground black pepper, to season

To make the chicken 1. Preheat the oven to 475ºF. 2. Coat a wire rack with cooking spray. Place the rack on a large rimmed baking sheet. 3. In a shallow dish, stir together the almond meal, paprika, onion powder, and salt. Drizzle with the olive oil. Mash together with a fork until the oil is thoroughly incorporated. 4. In another shallow dish, lightly beat the egg with a fork. 5. Working with 1 drumstick at a time, dip each into the egg, then press into the almond meal mixture, coating evenly on both sides. Place the chicken on the prepared rack. Repeat until all pieces are coated. 6. Place the sheet in the preheated oven. Bake for 25 to 30 minutes, or until golden and an instant-read thermometer inserted into the thickest part of a drumstick without touching the bone registers 165°F. To make the mustard sauce 1. In a small bowl, stir together the yogurt, mustard, and stevia. Season with pepper. 2. Serve the sauce with the drumsticks.

Per Serving:
calorie: 423 | fat: 22g | protein: 51g | carbs: 5g | sugars: 2g | fiber: 2g | sodium: 425mg

Chicken Salad Salad

Prep time: 15 minutes | Cook time: 0 minutes | Serves 4

2 cups shredded rotisserie chicken
1½ tablespoons plain low-fat Greek yogurt
⅛ teaspoon freshly ground black pepper
¼ cup halved purple seedless grapes
8 cups chopped romaine lettuce
1 medium tomato, sliced
1 avocado, sliced

1. In a large bowl, combine the chicken, yogurt, and pepper, and mix well. 2. Stir in the grapes. 3. Divide the lettuce into four portions. Spoon one-quarter of the chicken salad onto each portion and top with a couple slices of tomato and avocado.

Per Serving:
calorie: 305 | fat: 19g | protein: 24g | carbs: 11g | sugars: 4g | fiber: 6g | sodium: 79mg

Cilantro Lime Chicken Thighs

Prep time: 15 minutes | Cook time: 22 minutes | Serves 4

4 bone-in, skin-on chicken thighs
1 teaspoon baking powder
½ teaspoon garlic powder
2 teaspoons chili powder
1 teaspoon cumin
2 medium limes
¼ cup chopped fresh cilantro

1. Pat chicken thighs dry and sprinkle with baking powder. 2. In a small bowl, mix garlic powder, chili powder, and cumin and sprinkle evenly over thighs, gently rubbing on and under chicken skin. 3. Cut one lime in half and squeeze juice over thighs. Place chicken into the air fryer basket. 4. Adjust the temperature to 380ºF (193ºC) and roast for 22 minutes. 5. Cut other lime into four wedges for serving and garnish cooked chicken with wedges and cilantro.

Per Serving:
calories: 445 | fat: 32g | protein: 32g | carbs: 6g | fiber: 2g | sodium: 198mg

Buffalo Chicken Pizza

Prep time: 10 minutes | Cook time: 10 minutes |
Serves 6

1 ready-to-serve whole wheat pizza crust (10 oz)	sauce
1/4 cup fat-free ranch dressing	3/4 cup green and red bell pepper strips
1/4 cup finely chopped celery	3/4 cup shredded reduced-fat mozzarella cheese (3 oz)
1 cup cut-up cooked chicken breast	1 tablespoon crumbled blue cheese
3 tablespoons Buffalo wing	

1 Heat oven to 400°F. On large cookie sheet, place pizza crust. Spread ranch dressing over crust. Sprinkle with celery. 2 In small bowl, stir together chicken and wing sauce; arrange over crust. Top with bell pepper strips and cheeses. 3 Bake 10 minutes or until mozzarella cheese is melted and just beginning to brown. To serve, cut into wedges.

Per Serving:

calories: 230| fat: 6g | protein: 16g | carbs: 27g | sugars: 3g | fiber: 3g | sodium: 640mg

Pulled BBQ Chicken and Texas-Style Cabbage Slaw

Prep time: 5 minutes | Cook time: 20 minutes | Serves 6

Chicken	cut into narrow strips
1 cup water	2 carrots, julienned
1/4 teaspoon fine sea salt	1 large Fuji or Gala apple, julienned
3 garlic cloves, peeled	
2 bay leaves	1/2 cup chopped fresh cilantro
2 pounds boneless, skinless chicken thighs (see Note)	3 tablespoons fresh lime juice
	3 tablespoons extra-virgin olive oil
Cabbage Slaw	
1/2 head red or green cabbage, thinly sliced	1/2 teaspoon ground cumin
	1/4 teaspoon fine sea salt
1 red bell pepper, seeded and thinly sliced	3/4 cup low-sugar or unsweetened barbecue sauce
2 jalapeño chiles, seeded and	Cornbread, for serving

1. To make the chicken: Combine the water, salt, garlic, bay leaves, and chicken thighs in the Instant Pot, arranging the chicken in a single layer. 2. Secure the lid and set the Pressure Release to Sealing. Select the Poultry, Pressure Cook, or Manual setting and set the cooking time for 10 minutes at high pressure. (The pot will take about 10 minutes to come up to pressure before the cooking program begins.) 3. To make the slaw: While the chicken is cooking, in a large bowl, combine the cabbage, bell pepper, jalapeños, carrots, apple, cilantro, lime juice, oil, cumin, and salt and toss together until the vegetables and apples are evenly coated. 4. When the cooking program ends, perform a quick pressure release by moving the Pressure Release to Venting, or let the pressure release naturally. Open the pot and, using tongs, transfer the chicken to a cutting board. Using two forks, shred the chicken into bite-size pieces. Wearing heat-resistant mitts, lift out the inner pot and discard the cooking liquid. Return the inner pot to the housing. 5. Return the chicken to the pot and stir in the barbecue sauce. You can serve it right away or heat it for a minute or two on the Sauté setting, then return the pot to its Keep Warm setting until ready to serve. 6. Divide the chicken and slaw evenly among six plates. Serve with wedges of cornbread on the side.

Per Serving:

calories: 320 | fat: 14g | protein: 32g | carbs: 18g | sugars: 7g | fiber: 4g | sodium: 386mg

Tangy Barbecue Strawberry-Peach Chicken

Prep time: 20 minutes | Cook time: 40 minutes | Serves 4

For the barbecue sauce	1 teaspoon garlic powder
1 cup frozen peaches	1/2 teaspoon cayenne pepper
1 cup frozen strawberries	1/2 teaspoon onion powder
1/4 cup tomato purée	1/2 teaspoon freshly ground black pepper
1/2 cup white vinegar	
1 tablespoon yellow mustard	1 teaspoon celery seeds
1 teaspoon mustard seeds	For the chicken
1 teaspoon turmeric	4 boneless, skinless chicken thighs
1 teaspoon sweet paprika	

To make the barbecue sauce 1. In a stockpot, combine the peaches, strawberries, tomato purée, vinegar, mustard, mustard seeds, turmeric, paprika, garlic powder, cayenne, onion powder, black pepper, and celery seeds. Cook over low heat for 15 minutes, or until the flavors come together. 2. Remove the sauce from the heat, and let cool for 5 minutes. 3. Transfer the sauce to a blender, and purée until smooth. To make the chicken 1. Preheat the oven to 350°F. 2. Put the chicken in a medium bowl. Coat well with 1/2 cup of barbecue sauce. 3. Place the chicken on a rimmed baking sheet. 4. Place the baking sheet on the middle rack of the oven, and bake for about 20 minutes (depending on the thickness of thighs), or until the juices run clear. 5. Brush the chicken with additional sauce, return to the oven, and broil on high for 3 to 5 minutes, or until a light crust forms. 6. Serve.

Per Serving:

calorie: 389 | fat: 8g | protein: 63g | carbs: 13g | sugars: 7g | fiber: 3g | sodium: 175mg

Italian Chicken Thighs

Prep time: 5 minutes | Cook time: 20 minutes |
Serves 2

4 bone-in, skin-on chicken thighs	1 teaspoon dried basil
	1/2 teaspoon garlic powder
2 tablespoons unsalted butter, melted	1/4 teaspoon onion powder
	1/4 teaspoon dried oregano
1 teaspoon dried parsley	

1. Brush chicken thighs with butter and sprinkle remaining ingredients over thighs. Place thighs into the air fryer basket. 2. Adjust the temperature to 380ºF (193ºC) and roast for 20 minutes. 3. Halfway through the cooking time, flip the thighs. 4. When fully cooked, internal temperature will be at least 165ºF (74ºC) and skin will be crispy. Serve warm.

Per Serving:

calorie: 446 | fat: 34g | protein: 33g | carbs: 2g | sugars: 0g | fiber: 0g | sodium: 163mg

Turkey Divan Casserole

Prep time: 10 minutes | Cook time: 50 minutes | Serves 6

Nonstick cooking spray
3 teaspoons extra-virgin olive oil, divided
1 pound turkey cutlets
Pinch salt
¼ teaspoon freshly ground black pepper, divided
¼ cup chopped onion
2 garlic cloves, minced
2 tablespoons whole-wheat

flour
1 cup unsweetened plain almond milk
1 cup low-sodium chicken broth
½ cup shredded Swiss cheese, divided
½ teaspoon dried thyme
4 cups chopped broccoli
¼ cup coarsely ground almonds

1. Preheat the oven to 375°F. Spray a baking dish with nonstick cooking spray. 2. In a skillet, heat 1 teaspoon of oil over medium heat. Season the turkey with the salt and ⅛ teaspoon of pepper. Sauté the turkey cutlets for 5 to 7 minutes on each side until cooked through. Transfer to a cutting board, cool briefly, and cut into bite-size pieces. 3. In the same pan, heat the remaining 2 teaspoons of oil over medium-high heat. Sauté the onion for 3 minutes until it begins to soften. Add the garlic and continue cooking for another minute. 4. Stir in the flour and mix well. Whisk in the almond milk, broth, and remaining ⅛ teaspoon of pepper, and continue whisking until smooth. Add ¼ cup of cheese and the thyme, and continue stirring until the cheese is melted. 5. In the prepared baking dish, arrange the broccoli on the bottom. Cover with half the sauce. Place the turkey pieces on top of the broccoli, and cover with the remaining sauce. Sprinkle with the remaining ¼ cup of cheese and the ground almonds. 6. Bake for 35 minutes until the sauce is bubbly and the top is browned.

Per Serving:

calories: 207 | fat: 8g | protein: 25g | carbs: 9g | sugars: 2g | fiber: 3g | sodium: 128mg

Jerk Chicken Thighs

Prep time: 30 minutes | Cook time: 15 to 20 minutes | Serves 6

2 teaspoons ground coriander
1 teaspoon ground allspice
1 teaspoon cayenne pepper
1 teaspoon ground ginger
1 teaspoon salt
1 teaspoon dried thyme

½ teaspoon ground cinnamon
½ teaspoon ground nutmeg
2 pounds (907 g) boneless chicken thighs, skin on
2 tablespoons olive oil

1. In a small bowl, combine the coriander, allspice, cayenne, ginger, salt, thyme, cinnamon, and nutmeg. Stir until thoroughly combined. 2. Place the chicken in a baking dish and use paper towels to pat dry. Thoroughly coat both sides of the chicken with the spice mixture. Cover and refrigerate for at least 2 hours, preferably overnight. 3. Preheat the air fryer to 360ºF (182ºC). 4. Working in batches if necessary, arrange the chicken in a single layer in the air fryer basket and lightly coat with the olive oil. Pausing halfway through the cooking time to flip the chicken, air fry for 15 to 20 minutes, until a thermometer inserted into the thickest part registers 165ºF (74ºC).

Per Serving:

calories: 227 | fat: 11g | protein: 30g | carbs: 1g | fiber: 0g | sodium: 532mg

Coconut Lime Chicken

Prep time: 5 minutes | Cook time: 15 minutes | Serves 4

1 tablespoon coconut oil
4 (4-ounce) boneless, skinless chicken breasts
½ teaspoon salt
1 red bell pepper, cut into ¼-inch-thick slices
16 asparagus spears, bottom ends trimmed

1 cup unsweetened coconut milk
2 tablespoons freshly squeezed lime juice
½ teaspoon garlic powder
¼ teaspoon red pepper flakes
¼ cup chopped fresh cilantro

1. In a large skillet, heat the oil over medium-low heat. When hot, add the chicken. 2. Season the chicken with the salt. Cook for 5 minutes, then flip. 3. Push the chicken to the side of the skillet, and add the bell pepper and asparagus. Cook, covered, for 5 minutes. 4. Meanwhile, in a small bowl, whisk together the coconut milk, lime juice, garlic powder, and red pepper flakes. 5. Add the coconut milk mixture to the skillet, and boil over high heat for 2 to 3 minutes. 6. Top with the cilantro.

Per Serving:

calorie: 319 | fat: 21g | protein: 28g | carbs: 7g | sugars: 4g | fiber: 2g | sodium: 353mg

Asian Mushroom-Chicken Soup

Prep time: 30 minutes | Cook time: 15 minutes | Serves 6

1½ cups water
1 package (1 oz) dried portabella or shiitake mushrooms
1 tablespoon canola oil
¼ cup thinly sliced green onions (4 medium)
2 tablespoons gingerroot, peeled, minced
3 cloves garlic, minced
1 jalapeño chile, seeded, minced
1 cup fresh snow pea pods, sliced diagonally

3 cups reduced-sodium chicken broth
1 can (8 oz) sliced bamboo shoots, drained
2 tablespoons low-sodium soy sauce
½ teaspoon sriracha sauce
1 cup shredded cooked chicken breast
1 cup cooked brown rice
4 teaspoons lime juice
½ cup thinly sliced fresh basil leaves

1 In medium microwavable bowl, heat water uncovered on High 30 seconds or until hot. Add mushrooms; let stand 5 minutes or until tender. Drain mushrooms (reserve liquid). Slice any mushrooms that are large. Set aside. 2 In 4-quart saucepan, heat oil over medium heat. Add 2 tablespoons of the green onions, the gingerroot, garlic and chile to oil. Cook about 3 minutes, stirring occasionally, until vegetables are tender. Add snow pea pods; cook 2 minutes, stirring occasionally. Stir in mushrooms, reserved mushroom liquid and the remaining ingredients, except lime juice and basil. Heat to boiling; reduce heat. Cover and simmer 10 minutes or until hot. Stir in lime juice. 3 Divide soup evenly among 6 bowls. Top servings with basil and remaining green onions.

Per Serving:

calories: 150 | fat: 4g | protein: 11g | carbs: 16g | sugars: 3g | fiber: 3g | sodium: 490mg

Chicken Paprika

Prep time: 5 minutes | Cook time: 35 minutes | Serves 8

1 tablespoon extra-virgin olive oil	teaspoon salt
1 large onion, minced	⅛ teaspoon freshly ground black pepper
1 medium red bell pepper, julienned	Four 8-ounce boneless, skinless chicken breasts, halved
1 cup sliced fresh mushrooms	8 ounces plain low-fat Greek yogurt
1–2 teaspoons smoked paprika	
2 tablespoons lemon juice	

1. Heat the oil in a large skillet over medium heat. Add the onion, red pepper, and mushrooms, and sauté until tender, about 3–4 minutes. 2. Add 1 cup of water, the paprika, lemon juice, salt, and pepper, blending well. Bring the mixture to a boil over high heat, and reduce the heat to medium. Add the chicken; cover, and let simmer for 25–30 minutes or until the chicken is no longer pink. 3. Reduce the heat to low, quickly stir in the Greek yogurt, mixing well, and continue to cook for 1–2 minutes. Do not boil. Serve hot.

Per Serving:
calorie: 184 | fat: 5g | protein: 29g | carbs: 4g | sugars: 3g | fiber: 1g | sodium: 209mg

Taco Stuffed Sweet Potatoes

Prep time: 5 minutes | Cook time: 15 minutes | Serves 4

4 medium sweet potatoes	2 teaspoons ground cumin
2 tablespoons extra-virgin olive oil	1 teaspoon chili powder
1 pound 93% lean ground turkey	½ teaspoon salt
	½ teaspoon freshly ground black pepper

1. Pierce the potatoes with a fork, and microwave them on the potato setting, or for 10 minutes on high power. 2. Meanwhile, heat a medium skillet over medium heat. When hot, put the oil, turkey, cumin, chili powder, salt, and pepper into the skillet, stirring and breaking apart the meat, as needed. 3. Remove the potatoes from the microwave and halve them lengthwise. Depress the centers with a spoon, and fill each half with an equal amount of cooked turkey.

Per Serving:
calorie: 348 | fat: 17g | protein: 24g | carbs: 27g | sugars: 6g | fiber: 4g | sodium: 462mg

Turkey and Quinoa Caprese Casserole

Prep time: 10 minutes | Cook time: 35 minutes | Serves 8

⅔ cup quinoa	4 cups spinach leaves, finely sliced
1⅓ cups water	3 garlic cloves, minced
Nonstick cooking spray	¼ cup sliced fresh basil
2 teaspoons extra-virgin olive oil	¼ cup chicken or vegetable broth
1 pound lean ground turkey	2 large ripe tomatoes, sliced
¼ cup chopped red onion	4 ounces mozzarella cheese, thinly sliced
½ teaspoon salt	
1 (15-ounce can) fire-roasted tomatoes, drained	

1. In a small pot, combine the quinoa and water. Bring to a boil, reduce the heat, cover, and simmer for 10 minutes. Turn off the heat, and let the quinoa sit for 5 minutes to absorb any remaining water. 2. Preheat the oven to 400°F. Spray a baking dish with nonstick cooking spray. 3. In a large skillet, heat the oil over medium heat. Add the turkey, onion, and salt. Cook until the turkey is cooked through and crumbled. 4. Add the tomatoes, spinach, garlic, and basil. Stir in the broth and cooked quinoa. Transfer the mixture to the prepared baking dish. Arrange the tomato and cheese slices on top. 5. Bake for 15 minutes until the cheese is melted and the tomatoes are softened. Serve.

Per Serving:
calories: 218 | fat: 9g | protein: 18g | carbs: 17g | sugars: 3g | fiber: 3g | sodium: 340mg

Slow-Roasted Turkey Breast in Beer-Mustard Sauce

Prep time: 5 minutes | Cook time: 2 hour 30 minutes | Serves 10

5-pound, bone-in turkey breast, skin removed	tomato paste
1 tablespoon prepared mustard	½ cup spicy no-added-salt tomato juice (or spice up mild juice with several drops of hot pepper sauce)
½ cup light beer	
¼ cup red wine vinegar	
¾ cup ketchup	¼ teaspoon freshly ground black pepper
1 tablespoon no-added-salt	

1. Preheat the oven to 350 degrees. 2. Spread the turkey breast with mustard. 3. In a small bowl, combine the beer, vinegar, ketchup, tomato paste, and tomato juice. Pour the mixture over the turkey, and then sprinkle with pepper. 4. Roast, covered, for 1½ hours at 350 degrees. Remove the cover, and roast an additional 1 hour, basting occasionally. Transfer to a serving platter, and serve.

Per Serving:
calorie: 280 | fat: 4g | protein: 52g | carbs: 6g | sugars: 4g | fiber: 0g | sodium: 450mg

Greek Chicken

Prep time: 25 minutes | Cook time: 20 minutes | Serves 6

4 potatoes, unpeeled, quartered	3 teaspoons dried oregano
2 pounds chicken pieces, trimmed of skin and fat	¾ teaspoons salt
2 large onions, quartered	½ teaspoons pepper
1 whole bulb garlic, cloves minced	1 tablespoon olive oil
	1 cup water

1. Place potatoes, chicken, onions, and garlic into the inner pot of the Instant Pot, then sprinkle with seasonings. Top with oil and water. 2. Secure the lid and make sure vent is set to sealing. Cook on Manual mode for 20 minutes. 3. When cook time is over, let the pressure release naturally for 5 minutes, then release the rest manually.

Per Serving:
calorie: 278 | fat: 6g | protein: 27g | carbs: 29g | sugars: 9g | fiber: 4g | sodium: 358mg

Turkey Bolognese with Chickpea Pasta

Prep time: 5 minutes | Cook time: 25 minutes | Serves 4

1 onion, coarsely chopped	½ cup milk
1 large carrot, coarsely chopped	¾ cup red or white wine
2 celery stalks, coarsely chopped	1 (28-ounce) can diced tomatoes
1 tablespoon extra-virgin olive oil	10 ounces cooked chickpea pasta
1 pound ground turkey	

1. Place the onion, carrots, and celery in a food processor and pulse until finely chopped. 2. Heat the extra-virgin olive oil in a Dutch oven or medium skillet over medium-high heat. Sauté the chopped vegetables for 3 to 5 minutes, or until softened. Add the ground turkey, breaking the poultry into smaller pieces, and cook for 5 minutes. 3. Add the milk and wine and cook until the liquid is nearly evaporated (turn up the heat to high to quicken the process). 4. Add the tomatoes and bring the sauce to a simmer. Reduce the heat to low and simmer for 10 to 15 minutes. 5. Meanwhile, cook the pasta according to the package instructions and set aside. 6. Serve the sauce with the cooked chickpea pasta. 7. Store any leftovers in an airtight container in the refrigerator for 3 to 4 days.

Per Serving:
calorie: 419 | fat: 15g | protein: 31g | carbs: 34g | sugars: 8g | fiber: 11g | sodium: 150mg

Roast Chicken with Pine Nuts and Fennel

Prep time: 20 minutes | Cook time: 30 minutes | Serves 2

For the herb paste	2 teaspoons extra-virgin olive oil
2 tablespoons fresh rosemary leaves	For the vegetables
1 tablespoon freshly grated lemon zest	1 large fennel bulb, cored and chopped (about 3 cups)
2 garlic cloves, quartered	1 cup sliced fresh mushrooms
½ teaspoon freshly ground black pepper	½ cup sliced carrots
¼ teaspoon salt	¼ cup chopped sweet onion
1 teaspoon extra-virgin olive oil	2 teaspoons extra-virgin olive oil
For the chicken	2 tablespoons pine nuts
4 (6-ounce) skinless chicken drumsticks	2 teaspoons white wine vinegar

To make the vegetables 1. Preheat the oven to 450°F. 2. In a 9-by-13-inch baking dish, toss together the fennel, mushrooms, carrots, onion, and olive oil. Place the dish in the preheated oven. Bake for 10 minutes. 3. Stir in the pine nuts. 4. Top with the browned drumsticks. Return the dish to the oven. Bake for 15 to 20 minutes more, or until the fennel is golden and an instant-read thermometer inserted into the thickest part of a drumstick without touching the bone registers 165°F. 5. Remove the chicken from the pan. 6. Stir the white wine vinegar into the pan. Toss the vegetables to coat, scraping up any browned bits. 7. Serve the chicken with the vegetables and enjoy!

Per Serving:
calorie: 316 | fat: 15g | protein: 35g | carbs: 10g | sugars: 4g | fiber: 3g | sodium: 384mg

Grain-Free Parmesan Chicken

Prep time: 5 minutes | Cook time: 20 minutes | Serves 4

1½ cups (144 g) almond flour	[13-mm]-thick) boneless, skinless chicken breasts
½ cup (50 g) grated Parmesan cheese	½ cup (120 ml) no-added-sugar marinara sauce
1 tbsp (3 g) Italian seasoning	½ cup (56 g) shredded mozzarella cheese
1 tsp garlic powder	2 tbsp (8 g) minced fresh herbs of choice (optional)
½ tsp black pepper	
2 large eggs	
4 (6-oz [170-g], ½-inch	

1. Preheat the oven to 375°F (191°C). Line a large, rimmed baking sheet with parchment paper. 2. In a shallow dish, mix together the almond flour, Parmesan cheese, Italian seasoning, garlic powder, and black pepper. In another shallow dish, whisk the eggs. Dip a chicken breast into the egg wash, then gently shake off any extra egg. Dip the chicken breast into the almond flour mixture, coating it well. Place the chicken breast on the prepared baking sheet. Repeat this process with the remaining chicken breasts. 3. Bake the chicken for 15 to 20 minutes, or until the meat is no longer pink in the center. 4. Remove the chicken from the oven and flip each breast. Top each breast with 2 tablespoons (30 ml) of marinara sauce and 2 tablespoons (14 g) of mozzarella cheese. 5. Increase the oven temperature to broil and place the chicken back in the oven. Broil it until the cheese is melted and just starting to brown. Carefully remove the chicken from the oven, top it with the herbs (if using), and let it rest for about 10 minutes before serving.

Per Serving:
calorie: 572 | fat: 32g | protein: 60g | carbs: 13g | sugars: 4g | fiber:5g | sodium: 560mg

Wine-Poached Chicken with Herbs and Vegetables

Prep time: 5 minutes | Cook time: 1 hour | Serves 8

4 quarts low-sodium chicken broth	dry
2 cups dry white wine	½ pound carrots, peeled and julienned
4 large bay leaves	½ pound turnips, peeled and julienned
4 sprigs fresh thyme	½ pound parsnips, peeled and julienned
¼ teaspoon freshly ground black pepper	4 small leeks, washed and trimmed
4-pound chicken, giblets removed, washed and patted	

1. In a large stockpot, combine the broth, wine, bay leaves, thyme, dash salt (optional), and pepper. Let simmer over medium heat while you prepare the chicken. 2. Stuff the cavity with ⅓ each of the carrots, turnips, and parsnips; then truss. Add the stuffed chicken to the stockpot, and poach, covered, over low heat for 30 minutes. 3. Add the remaining vegetables with the leeks, and continue to simmer for 25–30 minutes, or until juices run clear when the chicken is pierced with a fork. 4. Remove the chicken and vegetables to a serving platter. Carve the chicken, remove the skin, and surround the sliced meat with poached vegetables to serve.

Per Serving:
calorie: 476 | fat: 13g | protein: 57g | carbs: 24g | sugars: 6g | fiber: 4g | sodium: 387mg

Shredded Buffalo Chicken

Prep time: 10 minutes | Cook time: 20 minutes | Serves 8

2 tablespoons avocado oil
½ cup finely chopped onion
1 celery stalk, finely chopped
1 large carrot, chopped
⅓ cup mild hot sauce (such as Frank's RedHot)

½ tablespoon apple cider vinegar
¼ teaspoon garlic powder
2 bone-in, skin-on chicken breasts (about 2 pounds)

1. Set the electric pressure cooker to the Sauté setting. When the pot is hot, pour in the avocado oil. 2. Sauté the onion, celery, and carrot for 3 to 5 minutes or until the onion begins to soften. Hit Cancel. 3. Stir in the hot sauce, vinegar, and garlic powder. Place the chicken breasts in the sauce, meat-side down. 4. Close and lock the lid of the pressure cooker. Set the valve to sealing. 5. Cook on high pressure for 20 minutes. 6. When cooking is complete, hit Cancel and quick release the pressure. Once the pin drops, unlock and remove the lid. 7. Using tongs, transfer the chicken breasts to a cutting board. When the chicken is cool enough to handle, remove the skin, shred the chicken and return it to the pot. Let the chicken soak in the sauce for at least 5 minutes. 8. Serve immediately.

Per Serving:

calorie: 235 | fat: 14g | protein: 24g | carbs: 2g | sugars: 1g | fiber: 1g | sodium: 142mg

Kung Pao Chicken and Zucchini Noodles

Prep time: 15 minutes | Cook time: 15 minutes | Serves 2

For the noodles
2 medium zucchini, ends trimmed
For the sauce
1½ tablespoons low-sodium soy sauce
1 tablespoon balsamic vinegar
1 teaspoon hoisin sauce
2½ tablespoons water
1½ teaspoons red chili paste
2 teaspoons granulated stevia
2 teaspoons cornstarch
For the chicken
6 ounces boneless skinless chicken breast, cut into ½-inch pieces
Salt, to season

Freshly ground black pepper, to season
1 teaspoon extra-virgin olive oil
1 teaspoon sesame oil
2 garlic cloves, minced
1 tablespoon chopped fresh ginger
½ red bell pepper, cut into ½-inch pieces
½ (8-ounce) can water chestnuts, drained and sliced
1 celery stalk, cut into ¾-inch dice
2 tablespoons crushed dry-roasted peanuts, divided
2 tablespoons scallions, divided

To make the noodles With a spiralizer or julienne peeler, cut the zucchini lengthwise into spaghetti-like strips. Set aside. To make the sauce In a small bowl, whisk together the soy sauce, balsamic vinegar, hoisin sauce, water, red chili paste, stevia, and cornstarch. Set aside. To make the chicken 1. Season the chicken with salt and pepper. 2. In a large, deep nonstick pan or wok set over medium-high heat, heat the olive oil. 3. Add the chicken. Cook for 4 to 5 minutes, stirring, or until browned and cooked through. Transfer the chicken to a plate. Set aside. 4. Return the pan to the stove. Reduce the heat to medium. 5. Add the sesame oil, garlic, and ginger. Cook for about 30 seconds, or until fragrant. 6. Add the red bell pepper, water chestnuts, and celery. 7. Stir in the sauce. Bring

to a boil. Reduce the heat to low. Simmer for 1 to 2 minutes, until thick and bubbling. 8. Stir in the zucchini noodles. Cook for about 2 minutes, tossing, until just tender and mixed with the sauce. 9. Add the chicken and any accumulated juices. Stir to combine. Cook for about 2 minutes, or until heated through. 10. Divide the mixture between 2 bowls. Top each serving with 1 tablespoon of peanuts and 1 tablespoon of scallions. Enjoy!

Per Serving:

calorie: 322 | fat: 13g | protein: 29g | carbs: 28g | sugars: 12g | fiber: 8g | sodium: 553mg

One-Pot Roast Chicken Dinner

Prep time: 10 minutes | Cook time: 40 minutes | Serves 6

½ head cabbage, cut into 2-inch chunks
1 sweet onion, peeled and cut into eighths
1 sweet potato, peeled and cut into 1-inch chunks
4 garlic cloves, peeled and lightly crushed

2 tablespoons extra-virgin olive oil, divided
2 teaspoons minced fresh thyme
Sea salt
Freshly ground black pepper
2½ pounds bone-in chicken thighs and drumsticks

1. Preheat the oven to 450°F. 2. Lightly grease a large roasting pan and arrange the cabbage, onion, sweet potato, and garlic in the bottom. Drizzle with 1 tablespoon of oil, sprinkle with the thyme, and season the vegetables lightly with salt and pepper. 3. Season the chicken with salt and pepper. 4. Place a large skillet over medium-high heat and brown the chicken on both sides in the remaining 1 tablespoon of oil, about 10 minutes in total. 5. Place the browned chicken on top of the vegetables in the roasting pan. Roast until the chicken is cooked through, about 30 minutes.

Per Serving:

calorie: 328 | fat: 13g | protein: 38g | carbs: 14g | sugars: 6g | fiber: 3g | sodium: 217mg

Lemon Chicken

Prep time: 5 minutes | Cook time: 20 to 25 minutes | Serves 4

8 bone-in chicken thighs, skin on
1 tablespoon olive oil
1½ teaspoons lemon-pepper seasoning

½ teaspoon paprika
½ teaspoon garlic powder
¼ teaspoon freshly ground black pepper
Juice of ½ lemon

1. Preheat the air fryer to 360°F (182°C). 2. Place the chicken in a large bowl and drizzle with the olive oil. Top with the lemon-pepper seasoning, paprika, garlic powder, and freshly ground black pepper. Toss until thoroughly coated. 3. Working in batches if necessary, arrange the chicken in a single layer in the basket of the air fryer. Pausing halfway through the cooking time to turn the chicken, air fry for 20 to 25 minutes, until a thermometer inserted into the thickest piece registers 165°F (74°C). 4. Transfer the chicken to a serving platter and squeeze the lemon juice over the top.

Per Serving:

calories: 399 | fat: 19g | protein: 56g | carbs: 1g | fiber: 0g | sodium: 367mg

Thanksgiving Turkey Breast

Prep time: 5 minutes | Cook time: 30 minutes | Serves 4

1½ teaspoons fine sea salt	1 teaspoon chopped fresh thyme
1 teaspoon ground black pepper	leaves
1 teaspoon chopped fresh	1 (2-pound / 907-g) turkey
rosemary leaves	breast
1 teaspoon chopped fresh sage	3 tablespoons ghee or unsalted
1 teaspoon chopped fresh	butter, melted
tarragon	3 tablespoons Dijon mustard

1. Spray the air fryer with avocado oil. Preheat the air fryer to 390°F (199°C). 2. In a small bowl, stir together the salt, pepper, and herbs until well combined. Season the turkey breast generously on all sides with the seasoning. 3. In another small bowl, stir together the ghee and Dijon. Brush the ghee mixture on all sides of the turkey breast. 4. Place the turkey breast in the air fryer basket and air fry for 30 minutes, or until the internal temperature reaches 165°F (74°C). Transfer the breast to a cutting board and allow it to rest for 10 minutes before cutting it into ½-inch-thick slices. 5. Store leftovers in an airtight container in the refrigerator for up to 4 days or in the freezer for up to a month. Reheat in a preheated 350°F (177°C) air fryer for 4 minutes, or until warmed through.

Per Serving:

calorie: 418 | fat: 22g | protein: 51g | carbs: 1g | sugars: 0g | fiber: 1g | sodium: 603mg

Ground Turkey Tetrazzini

Prep time: 5 minutes | Cook time: 20 minutes |

Serves 6

1 tablespoon extra-virgin olive	wheat elbow pasta
oil	2 cups low-sodium chicken
2 garlic cloves, minced	broth
1 yellow onion, diced	1½ cups frozen green peas,
8 ounces cremini or button	thawed
mushrooms, sliced	3 cups baby spinach
½ teaspoon fine sea salt	Three ¾-ounce wedges
¼ teaspoon freshly ground	Laughing Cow creamy light
black pepper	Swiss cheese, or 2 tablespoons
1 pound 93 percent lean ground	Neufchâtel cheese, at room
turkey	temperature
1 teaspoon poultry seasoning	⅓ cup grated Parmesan cheese
6 ounces whole-grain extra-	1 tablespoon chopped fresh flat-
broad egg-white pasta (such	leaf parsley
as No Yolks brand) or whole-	

1. Select the Sauté setting on the Instant Pot and heat the oil and garlic for 2 minutes, until the garlic is bubbling but not browned. Add the onion, mushrooms, salt, and pepper and sauté for about 5 minutes, until the mushrooms have wilted and begun to give up their liquid. Add the turkey and poultry seasoning and sauté, using a wooden spoon or spatula to break up the meat as it cooks, for about 4 minutes more, until cooked through and no streaks of pink remain. 2. Stir in the pasta. Pour in the broth and use the spoon or spatula to nudge the pasta into the liquid as much as possible. It's fine if some pieces are not completely submerged. 3. Secure the lid and set the Pressure Release to Sealing. Press the Cancel button to reset the cooking program, then select the Pressure Cook or Manual

setting and set the cooking time for 5 minutes at high pressure. (The pot will take about 5 minutes to come up to pressure before the cooking program begins.) 4. When the cooking program ends, let the pressure release naturally for 5 minutes, then move the Pressure Release to Venting to release any remaining steam. Open the pot and stir in the peas, spinach, Laughing Cow cheese, and Parmesan. Let stand for 2 minutes, then stir the mixture once more. 5. Ladle into bowls or onto plates and sprinkle with the parsley. Serve right away.

Per Serving:

calories: 321 | fat: 11g | protein: 26g | carbs: 35g | sugars: 4g | fiber: 5g | sodium: 488mg

Chicken Nuggets

Prep time: 10 minutes | Cook time: 15 minutes | Serves 4

1 pound (454 g) ground chicken	1 large egg, whisked
thighs	½ teaspoon salt
½ cup shredded Mozzarella	¼ teaspoon dried oregano
cheese	¼ teaspoon garlic powder

1. In a large bowl, combine all ingredients. Form mixture into twenty nugget shapes, about 2 tablespoons each. 2. Place nuggets into ungreased air fryer basket, working in batches if needed. Adjust the temperature to 375°F (191°C) and air fry for 15 minutes, turning nuggets halfway through cooking. Let cool 5 minutes before serving.

Per Serving:

calories: 195 | fat: 8g | protein: 28g | carbs: 1g | fiber: 0g | sodium: 419mg

Easy Chicken Cacciatore

Prep time: 5 minutes | Cook time: 20 minutes |

Serves 2

Extra-virgin olive oil cooking	chicken breasts, cubed
spray	1 cup sliced cremini mushrooms
1 garlic clove, chopped	½ cup chopped tomatoes, with
½ cup chopped red onion	juice
¾ cup chopped green bell	1 cup green beans
pepper	1 teaspoon dried oregano
2 (6-ounce) boneless skinless	1 teaspoon dried rosemary

1. Coat a skillet with cooking spray. Place it over medium heat. 2. Add the garlic. Sauté for about 1 minute, or until browned. 3. Add the red onion, green bell pepper, and chicken. Cook for about 6 minutes, or until the chicken is slightly browned, tossing to cook all sides. 4. Stir in the mushrooms, tomatoes, green beans, oregano, and rosemary. Reduce the heat to medium-low. Simmer for 8 to 10 minutes, stirring constantly. 5. Remove from the heat and serve hot. 6. Enjoy!

Per Serving:

calorie: 265 | fat: 5g | protein: 42g | carbs: 13g | sugars: 6g | fiber: 4g | sodium: 91mg

Teriyaki Turkey Meatballs

Prep time: 20 minutes | Cook time: 20 minutes | Serves 6

1 pound lean ground turkey
¼ cup finely chopped scallions, both white and green parts
1 egg
2 garlic cloves, minced
1 teaspoon grated fresh ginger
2 tablespoons reduced-sodium tamari or gluten-free soy sauce
1 tablespoon honey
2 teaspoons mirin
1 teaspoon toasted sesame oil

1. Preheat the oven to 400°F. Line a baking sheet with parchment paper. 2. In a large mixing bowl, combine the turkey, scallions, egg, garlic, ginger, tamari, honey, mirin, and sesame oil. Mix well. 3. Using your hands, form the meat mixture into balls about the size of a tablespoon. Arrange on the prepared baking sheet. 4. Bake for 10 minutes, flip with a spatula, and continue baking for an additional 10 minutes until the meatballs are cooked through.

Per Serving:
calories: 153 | fat: 8g | protein: 16g | carbs: 5g | sugars: 4g | fiber: 0g | sodium: 270mg

Chicken Provençal

Prep time: 5 minutes | Cook time: 25 minutes | Serves 4

2 tablespoons extra-virgin olive oil
Two 8-ounce boneless, skinless chicken breasts, halved
1 medium garlic clove, minced
¼ cup minced onion
¼ cup minced green bell pepper
½ cup dry white wine
1 cup canned diced tomatoes
¼ cup pitted Kalamata olives
¼ cup finely chopped fresh basil
⅛ teaspoon freshly ground black pepper

1. Heat the oil in a skillet over medium heat. Add the chicken, and brown about 3–5 minutes. 2. Add the remaining ingredients, and cook uncovered over medium heat for 20 minutes or until the chicken is no longer pink. Transfer to a serving platter and season with additional pepper to taste, if desired, before serving.

Per Serving:
calorie: 245 | fat: 11g | protein: 26g | carbs: 5g | sugars: 2g | fiber: 2g | sodium: 121mg

Pizza in a Pot

Prep time: 25 minutes | Cook time: 15 minutes | Serves 8

1 pound bulk lean sweet Italian turkey sausage, browned and drained
28-ounce can crushed tomatoes
15½-ounce can chili beans
2¼-ounce can sliced black olives, drained
1 medium onion, chopped
1 small green bell pepper, chopped
2 garlic cloves, minced
¼ cup grated Parmesan cheese
1 tablespoon quick-cooking tapioca
1 tablespoon dried basil
1 bay leaf

1. Set the Instant Pot to Sauté, then add the turkey sausage. Sauté until browned. 2. Add the remaining ingredients into the Instant Pot and stir. 3. Secure the lid and make sure the vent is set to sealing. Cook on Manual for 15 minutes. 4. When cook time is up, let the pressure release naturally for 5 minutes then perform a quick release. Discard bay leaf.

Per Serving:
calorie: 251 | fat: 10g | protein: 18g | carbs: 23g | sugars: 8g | fiber: 3g | sodium: 936mg

Mild Chicken Curry with Coconut Milk

Prep time: 10 minutes | Cook time: 14 minutes | Serves 4 to 6

1 large onion, diced
6 cloves garlic, crushed
¼ cup coconut oil
½ teaspoon black pepper
½ teaspoon turmeric
½ teaspoon paprika
¼ teaspoon cinnamon
¼ teaspoon cloves
¼ teaspoon cumin
¼ teaspoon ginger
½ teaspoon salt
1 tablespoon curry powder (more if you like more flavor)
½ teaspoon chili powder
24-ounce can of low-sodium diced or crushed tomatoes
13½-ounce can of light coconut milk (I prefer a brand that has no unwanted ingredients, like guar gum or sugar)
4 pounds boneless skinless chicken breasts, cut into chunks

1. Sauté onion and garlic in the coconut oil, either with Sauté setting in the inner pot of the Instant Pot or on stove top, then add to pot. 2. Combine spices in a small bowl, then add to the inner pot. 3. Add tomatoes and coconut milk and stir. 4. Add chicken, and stir to coat the pieces with the sauce. 5. Secure the lid and make sure vent is at sealing. Set to Manual mode (or Pressure Cook on newer models) for 14 minutes. 6. Let pressure release naturally (if you're crunched for time, you can do a quick release). 7. Serve with your favorite sides, and enjoy!

Per Serving:
calorie: 535 | fat: 21g | protein: 71g | carbs: 10g | sugars: 5g | fiber: 2g | sodium: 315mg

Greek Chicken Stir-Fry

Prep time: 15 minutes | Cook time: 15 minutes | Serves 2

1 (6-ounce / 170-g) chicken breast, cut into 1-inch cubes
½ medium zucchini, chopped
½ medium red bell pepper, seeded and chopped
¼ medium red onion, peeled
and sliced
1 tablespoon coconut oil
1 teaspoon dried oregano
½ teaspoon garlic powder
¼ teaspoon dried thyme

1. Place all ingredients into a large mixing bowl and toss until the coconut oil coats the meat and vegetables. Pour the contents of the bowl into the air fryer basket. 2. Adjust the temperature to 375°F (191°C) and air fry for 15 minutes. 3. Shake the basket halfway through the cooking time to redistribute the food. Serve immediately.

Per Serving:
calories: 183 | fat: 9g | protein: 20g | carbs: 4g | fiber: 1g | sodium: 44mg

Chicken Satay Stir-Fry

Prep time: 10 minutes | Cook time: 15 minutes | Serves 4

3 tablespoons extra-virgin olive oil
1 pound chicken breasts or thighs, cut into ¾-inch pieces
½ teaspoon sea salt
2 cups broccoli florets
1 red bell pepper, seeded and

chopped
6 scallions, green and white parts, sliced on the bias (cut diagonally into thin slices)
1 head cauliflower, riced
Peanut Sauce

1. In a large skillet over medium-high heat, heat the olive oil until it shimmers. 2. Season the chicken with the salt. Add the chicken to the oil and cook, stirring occasionally, until opaque, about 5 minutes. Remove the chicken from the oil with a slotted spoon and set it aside on a plate. Return the pan to the heat. 3. Add the broccoli, bell pepper, and scallions. Cook, stirring, until the vegetables are crisp-tender, 3 to 5 minutes. Add the cauliflower and cook for 3 minutes more. 4. Return the chicken to the skillet. Stir in the Peanut Sauce. Bring to a simmer and reduce heat to medium-low. Simmer to heat through, about 2 minutes more.

Per Serving:
calorie: 283 | fat: 15g | protein: 26g | carbs: 11g | sugars: 4g | fiber: 4g | sodium: 453mg

Chicken with Spiced Sesame Sauce

Prep time: 20 minutes | Cook time: 8 minutes | Serves 5

2 tablespoons tahini (sesame sauce)
¼ cup water
1 tablespoon low-sodium soy sauce
¼ cup chopped onion

1 teaspoon red wine vinegar
2 teaspoons minced garlic
1 teaspoon shredded ginger root (Microplane works best)
2 pounds chicken breast, chopped into 8 portions

1. Place first seven ingredients in bottom of the inner pot of the Instant Pot. 2. Add coarsely chopped chicken on top. 3. Secure the lid and make sure vent is at sealing. Set for 8 minutes using Manual setting. When cook time is up, let the pressure release naturally for 10 minutes, then perform a quick release. 4. Remove ingredients and shred chicken with fork. Combine with other ingredients in pot for a tasty sandwich filling or sauce.

Per Serving:
calorie: 215 | fat: 7g | protein: 35g | carbs: 2g | sugars: 0g | fiber: 0g | sodium: 178mg

Baked Turkey Spaghetti

Prep time: 5 minutes | Cook time: 20 minutes | Serves 4

1 (10-ounce) package zucchini noodles
2 tablespoons extra-virgin olive oil, divided
1 pound 93% lean ground turkey

½ teaspoon dried oregano
2 cups low-sodium spaghetti sauce
½ cup shredded sharp Cheddar cheese

1. Pat zucchini noodles dry between two paper towels. 2. In an oven-safe medium skillet, heat 1 tablespoon of olive oil over medium heat. When hot, add the zucchini noodles. Cook for 3 minutes, stirring halfway through. 3. Add the remaining 1 tablespoon of oil, ground turkey, and oregano. Cook for 7 to 10 minutes, stirring and breaking apart, as needed. 4. Add the spaghetti sauce to the skillet and stir. 5. If your broiler is in the top of your oven, place the oven rack in the center position. Set the broiler on high. 6. Top the mixture with the cheese, and broil for 5 minutes or until the cheese is bubbly.

Per Serving:
calorie: 365 | fat: 23g | protein: 27g | carbs: 13g | sugars: 9g | fiber: 3g | sodium: 214mg

Chicken in Wine

Prep time: 10 minutes | Cook time: 12 minutes | Serves 6

2 pounds chicken breasts, trimmed of skin and fat
10¾-ounce can 98% fat-free, reduced-sodium cream of mushroom soup

10¾-ounce can French onion soup
1 cup dry white wine or chicken broth

1. Place the chicken into the Instant Pot. 2. Combine soups and wine. Pour over chicken. 3. Secure the lid and make sure vent is set to sealing. Cook on Manual mode for 12 minutes. 4. When cook time is up, let the pressure release naturally for 5 minutes and then release the rest manually.

Per Serving:
calories: 225 | fat: 5g | protein: 35g | carbs: 7g | sugars: 3g | fiber: 1g | sodium: 645mg

Peanut Chicken Satay

Prep time: 20 minutes | Cook time: 10 minutes | Serves 8

FOR THE PEANUT SAUCE
1 cup natural peanut butter
2 tablespoons low-sodium tamari or gluten-free soy sauce
1 teaspoon red chili paste
1 tablespoon honey
Juice of 2 limes
½ cup hot water
FOR THE CHICKEN
2 pounds boneless, skinless chicken thighs, trimmed of fat

and cut into 1-inch pieces
½ cup plain nonfat Greek yogurt
2 garlic cloves, minced
1 teaspoon minced fresh ginger
½ onion, coarsely chopped
1½ teaspoons ground coriander
2 teaspoons ground cumin
½ teaspoon salt
1 teaspoon extra-virgin olive oil
Lettuce leaves, for serving

TO MAKE THE PEANUT SAUCE In a medium mixing bowl, combine the peanut butter, tamari, chili paste, honey, lime juice, and hot water. Mix until smooth. Set aside. TO MAKE THE CHICKEN 1. In a large mixing bowl, combine the chicken, yogurt, garlic, ginger, onion, coriander, cumin, and salt, and mix well. 2. Cover and marinate in the refrigerator for at least 2 hours. 3. Thread the chicken pieces onto bamboo skewers. 4. In a grill pan or large skillet, heat the oil. Cook the skewers for 3 to 5 minutes on each side until the pieces are cooked through. 5. Remove the chicken from the skewers and place a few pieces on each lettuce leaf. Drizzle with the peanut sauce and serve.

Per Serving:
calories: 386| fat: 26g | protein: 16g | carbs: 14g | sugars: 6g | fiber: 2g | sodium: 442mg

Prep time: 30 minutes | Cook time: 18 minutes | Serves 6 to 8

1–2 heads savoy cabbage
1 pound ground turkey
1 egg
1 cup reduced-fat shredded cheddar cheese
2 tablespoons evaporated skim milk
¼ cup reduced-fat shredded Parmesan cheese
¼ cup reduced-fat shredded mozzarella cheese
¼ cup finely diced onion

¼ cup finely diced bell pepper
¼ cup finely diced mushrooms
1 teaspoon salt
½ teaspoon black pepper
1 teaspoon garlic powder
6 basil leaves, fresh and cut chiffonade
1 tablespoon fresh parsley, chopped
1 quart of your favorite pasta sauce

1. Remove the core from the cabbages. 2. Boil pot of water and place 1 head at a time into the water for approximately 10 minutes. 3. Allow cabbage to cool slightly. Once cooled, remove the leaves carefully and set aside. You'll need about 15 or 16. 4. Mix together the meat and all remaining ingredients except the pasta sauce. 5. One leaf at a time, put a heaping tablespoon of meat mixture in the center. 6. Tuck the sides in and then roll tightly. 7. Add ½ cup sauce to the bottom of the inner pot of the Instant Pot. 8. Place the rolls, fold-side down, into the pot and layer them, putting a touch of sauce between each layer and finally on top. (You may want to cook the rolls in two batches.) 9. Lock lid and make sure vent is at sealing. Set timer on 18 minutes on Manual at high pressure, then manually release the pressure when cook time is over.

Per Serving:

calories: 199| fat: 8g | protein: 2mg | carbs: 14g | sugars: 7g | fiber: 3g | sodium: 678mg

Chapter 9 Salads

Couscous Salad

Prep time: 10 minutes | Cook time: 6 minutes | Serves ½ cup

1 cup whole-wheat couscous
2 cups boiling water
¼ cup finely chopped red or yellow bell pepper
¼ cup chopped carrots
¼ cup finely chopped celery
2 tablespoons minced Italian parsley
1 tablespoon extra-virgin olive

oil
4 tablespoons rice vinegar
2 garlic cloves, minced
3 tablespoons finely minced scallions
¼ cup slivered almonds
¼ teaspoon freshly ground black pepper

1. Place dry couscous in a heat-proof bowl. Pour boiling water over it, and let sit for 5–10 minutes until all the water is absorbed. 2. In a large bowl, combine the couscous, bell pepper, carrots, celery, and parsley together. 3. In a blender or food processor, combine the olive oil, vinegar, garlic, and scallions, and process for 1 minute. Pour over the couscous and vegetables, toss well, garnish with almonds, and season with the pepper. Serve.

Per Serving:
calorie: 373 | fat: 15g | protein: 12g | carbs: 51g | sugars: 3g | fiber: 10g | sodium: 34mg

Greek Rice Salad

Prep time: 10 minutes | Cook time: 0 minutes | Serves 4

3 tablespoons fresh lemon juice
1½ tablespoons coconut nectar or pure maple syrup
1 tablespoon red wine vinegar
1 teaspoon sea salt
1 teaspoon Dijon mustard
¼ teaspoon allspice
½–1 teaspoon grated fresh garlic
Freshly ground black pepper to taste (optional)
4 cups cooked brown rice

1 cup chopped cucumber (seeds removed, if you prefer)
1 cup sliced grape or cherry tomatoes or chopped tomatoes (can substitute chopped red pepper)
½ cup sliced kalamata olives
½ tablespoon chopped fresh oregano
2 tablespoons chopped fresh dill

1. In a large bowl, whisk together the lemon juice, nectar or syrup, vinegar, salt, mustard, allspice, garlic, and pepper (if using). Add the rice, cucumber, tomatoes, olives, oregano, and dill, and stir to combine. Taste, and add extra salt or lemon juice, if desired. Serve as a side or as a hearty lunch over greens.

Per Serving:
calorie: 306 | fat: 4g | protein: 6g | carbs: 62g | sugars: 7g | fiber: 5g | sodium: 751mg

Curried Chicken Salad

Prep time: 15 minutes | Cook time: 40 minutes | Serves 2

4 ounces chicken breast, rinsed and drained
1 small apple, peeled, cored, and finely chopped
2 tablespoons slivered almonds
1 tablespoon dried cranberries
2 tablespoons chia seeds
¼ cup plain nonfat Greek

yogurt
1 tablespoon curry powder
1½ teaspoons Dijon mustard
⅛ teaspoon salt
¼ teaspoon freshly ground black pepper
4 cups chopped romaine lettuce, divided

1. Preheat the oven to 400°F. 2. To a small baking dish, add the chicken. Place the dish in the preheated oven. Bake for 30 to 40 minutes, or until the chicken is completely opaque and registers 165°F on an instant-read thermometer. Remove from the oven. Chop into cubes. Set aside. 3. In a medium bowl, mix together the chicken, apple, almonds, cranberries, and chia seeds. 4. Add the yogurt, curry powder, mustard, salt, and pepper. Toss to coat. 5. On 2 plates, arrange 2 cups of lettuce on each. 6. Top each with one-half of the curried chicken salad. 7. Serve immediately.

Per Serving:
calorie: 240 | fat: 9g | protein: 19g | carbs: 25g | sugars: 14g | fiber: 8g | sodium: 258mg

Salmon and Baby Greens with Edamame

Prep time: 15 minutes | Cook time: 10 minutes | Serves 2

3 teaspoons extra-virgin olive oil, divided
4 cups mixed baby greens, divided
¼ cup edamame
1 teaspoon balsamic vinegar

¼ teaspoon salt
1 (6-ounce) salmon fillet
Extra-virgin olive oil cooking spray
2 tablespoons chopped fresh dill

1. In a large skillet set over medium heat, heat 1½ teaspoons of olive oil. 2. Add 2 cups of baby greens. Cook for 1 minute. Transfer to a medium salad bowl. Repeat with the remaining 1½ teaspoons of olive oil and 2 cups of baby greens. 3. Add the edamame, balsamic vinegar, and salt to the greens. Toss to combine. 4. Place an oven rack about 8 inches from the broiler. 5. Preheat the broiler to high. 6. To a small ovenproof dish, add the salmon. Coat the salmon with cooking spray. 7. Put the dish under the preheated broiler. Broil for 8 to 10 minutes, depending on its thickness, or until the fish is just cooked. 8. Cut the fish in half. Place it on top of the greens. 9. Top with the fresh dill. 10. Serve immediately.

Per Serving:
calorie: 225 | fat: 12g | protein: 22g | carbs: 9g | sugars: 2g | fiber: 4g | sodium: 389mg

Herbed Tomato Salad

Prep time: 7 minutes | Cook time: 0 minutes | Serves 2 to 4

1 pint cherry tomatoes, halved
1 bunch fresh parsley, leaves only (stems discarded)
1 cup cilantro, leaves only (stems discarded)
¼ cup fresh dill

1 teaspoon sumac (optional)
2 tablespoons extra-virgin olive oil
Kosher salt
Freshly ground black pepper

1. In a medium bowl, carefully toss together the tomatoes, parsley, cilantro, dill, sumac (if using), extra-virgin olive oil, and salt and pepper to taste. 2. Store any leftovers in an airtight container in the refrigerator for up to 3 days, but the salad is best consumed on the day it is dressed.

Per Serving:
calorie: 113 | fat: 10g | protein: 2g | carbs: 7g | sugars: 3g | fiber: 3g | sodium: 30mg

Carrot and Cashew Chicken Salad

Prep time: 20 minutes | Cook time: 25 minutes | Serves 2

Extra-virgin olive oil cooking spray
1 cup carrots rounds
1 red bell pepper, thinly sliced
1½ teaspoons granulated stevia
1 tablespoon extra-virgin olive oil, divided
¼ teaspoon salt, divided
⅜ teaspoon freshly ground black pepper, divided

1 (6-ounce) boneless skinless chicken breast, thinly sliced across the grain
2 tablespoons chopped scallions
1 tablespoon apple cider vinegar
1 cup sugar snap peas
4 cups baby spinach
4 tablespoons chopped cashews, divided

1. Preheat the oven to 425°F. 2. Coat an 8-by-8-inch baking pan and a rimmed baking sheet with cooking spray. 3. In the prepared baking pan, add the carrots and red bell pepper. Sprinkle with the stevia, 1 teaspoon of olive oil, ⅛ teaspoon of salt, and ⅛ teaspoon of pepper. Toss to coat. 4. Place the pan in the preheated oven. Roast for about 25 minutes, stirring several times, or until tender. 5. About 5 minutes before the vegetables are done, place the sliced chicken in a medium bowl and drizzle with 1 teaspoon of olive oil. Sprinkle with the scallions. Season with the remaining ⅛ teaspoon of salt and ⅛ teaspoon of pepper. Toss to mix. Arrange in a single layer on the prepared baking sheet. 6. Place the sheet in the preheated oven. Roast for 5 to 7 minutes, turning once, or until cooked through. 7. Remove the pan with the vegetables and the baking sheet from the oven. Cool for about 3 minutes. 8. In a large salad bowl, mix together the apple cider vinegar, the remaining 1 teaspoon of olive oil, the sugar snap peas, and remaining ⅛ teaspoon of pepper. Let stand 5 minutes to blend the flavors. 9. To finish, add the spinach to the bowl with the dressing and peas. Toss to mix well. 10. Evenly divide between 2 serving plates. Top each with half of the roasted carrots, half of the roasted red bell peppers, and half of the cooked chicken. 11. Sprinkle each with about 2 tablespoons of cashews. Serve warm.

Per Serving:
calorie: 335 | fat: 17g | protein: 26g | carbs: 21g | sugars: 8g | fiber: 6g | sodium: 422mg

Chinese Chicken Salad

Prep time: 10 minutes | Cook time: 0 minutes | Serves 4

2 cups cooked chicken, diced
1 cup finely chopped celery
1 cup shredded carrots
¼ cup crushed unsweetened pineapple, drained
2 tablespoons finely diced pimiento

Two 8-ounce cans water chestnuts, drained and chopped
2 scallions, chopped
⅓ cup low-fat mayonnaise
1 tablespoon light soy sauce
1 teaspoon lemon juice
8 large tomatoes, hollowed

1. In a large bowl, combine the chicken, celery, carrots, pineapple, pimiento, water chestnuts, and scallions. 2. In a separate bowl, combine the mayonnaise, soy sauce, and lemon juice. Mix well. Add the dressing to the salad, and toss. Cover, and chill in the refrigerator for 2–3 hours. 3. For each serving, place a small scoop of chicken salad into a hollowed-out tomato.

Per Serving:
calorie: 365 | fat: 16g | protein: 27g | carbs: 32g | sugars: 17g | fiber: 9g | sodium: 476mg

Kidney Bean Salad

Prep time: 10 minutes | Cook time: 0 minutes | Serves 4

3 cups diced cucumber
1 (15-ounce) can low-sodium dark red kidney beans, drained and rinsed
2 avocados, diced
1½ cups diced tomatoes

1 cup cooked corn
¾ cup sliced red onion
1 tablespoon extra-virgin olive oil
1 tablespoon apple cider vinegar

1. In a large bowl, combine the cucumber, kidney beans, avocados, tomatoes, corn, onion, olive oil, and vinegar.

Per Serving:
calorie: 394 | fat: 20g | protein: 13g | carbs: 47g | sugars: 10g | fiber: 16g | sodium: 261mg

Ham and Egg Calico Salad

Prep time: 15 minutes | Cook time: 0 minutes | Serves 4

2 tablespoons pickle relish
2 tablespoons apple cider vinegar
1 (15-ounce) can sweet peas, drained
1 (15-ounce) can cut green beans, drained
1 (8-ounce) can water chestnuts, drained and chopped

1 (15-ounce) can light red kidney beans, rinsed and drained
½ cup diced onion
2 cups diced ham
4 hardboiled eggs, halved lengthwise
¼ teaspoon freshly ground black pepper

1. In a large bowl, stir together the pickle relish and vinegar. 2. Add the peas, green beans, water chestnuts, kidney beans, onion, and ham and stir together until everything is coated. 3. Portion into 4 bowls and top each with 2 egg halves. 4. Add a pinch of pepper to each serving.

Per Serving:
calorie: 373 | fat: 10g | protein: 32g | carbs: 41g | sugars: 10g | fiber: 14g | sodium: 557mg

Mediterranean Chicken Salad

Prep time: 5 minutes | Cook time: 0 minutes | Serves 3

8 ounces boneless, skinless, cooked chicken breast
2 tablespoons extra-virgin olive oil
2 tablespoons balsamic vinegar
¼ teaspoon dried basil
2 small garlic cloves, minced
¼ teaspoon freshly ground

black pepper
1 cup cooked green beans, cut into 2-inch pieces
1 cup cooked artichokes
¼ cup pine nuts, toasted
¼ cup sliced black olives
3 cherry tomatoes, halved
Tomato wedges (optional)

1. Cut the cooked chicken into bite-sized chunks, and set aside. 2. In a medium bowl, whisk together the oil, vinegar, basil, garlic, and pepper. Add the chicken, and toss with the dressing. 3. Add the green beans, artichokes, pine nuts, olives, and cherry tomatoes; toss well. Chill in the refrigerator for several hours. Garnish the salad with tomato wedges, and serve.

Per Serving:

calorie: 307 | fat: 19g | protein: 21g | carbs: 14g | sugars: 4g | fiber: 7g | sodium: 73mg

First-of-the-Season Tomato, Peach, and Strawberry Salad

Prep time: 15 minutes | Cook time: 0 minutes | Serves 6

6 cups mixed spring greens
4 large ripe plum tomatoes, thinly sliced
4 large ripe peaches, pitted and thinly sliced
12 ripe strawberries, thinly sliced

½ Vidalia onion, thinly sliced
2 tablespoons white balsamic vinegar
2 tablespoons extra-virgin olive oil
Freshly ground black pepper

1. Put the greens in a large salad bowl, and layer the tomatoes, peaches, strawberries, and onion on top. 2. Dress with the vinegar and oil, toss together, and season with pepper.

Per Serving:

calorie: 122 | fat: 5g | protein: 3g | carbs: 19g | sugars: 14g | fiber: 4g | sodium: 20mg

Italian Bean Salad

Prep time: 15 minutes | Cook time: 0 minutes | Serves 4

2 tablespoons lemon juice
1 tablespoon red wine vinegar
1 tablespoon pure maple syrup
1½ teaspoons Dijon mustard
Rounded ¼ teaspoon sea salt
½ teaspoon dried oregano
¼ teaspoon garlic powder
Freshly ground black pepper to taste (optional)
1 can (15 ounces) chickpeas, rinsed
1 can (15 ounces) white beans, rinsed

1 cup chopped red, yellow, or orange bell pepper
½ cup chopped fresh tomatoes
1–1½ cups quartered or roughly chopped artichoke hearts (frozen or canned, not marinated in oil)
¼ cup chopped or sliced dry-pack sun-dried tomatoes
¼ cup sliced green portion of green onion or chives
⅓ cup sliced kalamata olives
¼ cup chopped fresh basil

leaves
3 tablespoons raisins or ¼ cup

sliced grapes (optional)

1. In a large bowl, combine the lemon juice, vinegar, syrup, mustard, salt, oregano, garlic powder, and black pepper (if using). Whisk to thoroughly combine. Add the chickpeas, beans, bell pepper, fresh tomatoes, artichoke hearts, sun-dried tomatoes, green onion or chives, olives, basil, and raisins or grapes (if using). Mix well to fully coat with the dressing. Taste, and season with extra salt and black pepper, if desired. Serve, or refrigerate for up to 4 days.

Per Serving:

calorie: 275 | fat: 4g | protein: 15g | carbs: 49g | sugars: 10g | fiber: 15g | sodium: 801mg

Moroccan Carrot Salad

Prep time: 15 minutes | Cook time: 0 minutes | Serves 5

Dressing
¼ cup orange juice
2 tablespoons olive oil
1 teaspoon orange peel
1 teaspoon ground cumin
1 teaspoon paprika
¼ teaspoon salt
⅛ to ¼ teaspoon ground red pepper (cayenne)
⅛ teaspoon ground cinnamon
Salad
1 bag (10 oz) julienne

(matchstick-cut) carrots (5 cups)
1 can (15 oz) chickpeas (garbanzo beans), drained, rinsed
¼ cup golden raisins
3 tablespoons salted roasted whole almonds, coarsely chopped
¼ cup coarsely chopped fresh cilantro or parsley

1 In small bowl, combine all dressing ingredients with whisk until blended; set aside. 2 In large bowl, combine carrots, chickpeas and raisins; toss to combine. Add dressing; mix thoroughly. Cover and refrigerate at least 2 hours or overnight, stirring occasionally. Just before serving, sprinkle with almonds and cilantro.

Per Serving:

calorie: 310 | fat: 11g | protein: 10g | carbs: 44g | sugars: 12g | fiber: 10g | sodium: 230mg

Mandarin Orange Chicken Salad

Prep time: 10 minutes | Cook time: 0 minutes | Serves 4

1 (8-ounce) container plain Greek yogurt
½ teaspoon ground ginger
1½ cups cooked cubed chicken
1 (8-ounce) package frozen peas in the pod, thawed
1 (8-ounce) can water chestnuts,

drained and chopped
1 (11-ounce) can mandarin orange segments, drained
½ cup unsalted peanuts
1 (10-ounce) bag chopped romaine lettuce, divided

1. In a large bowl, mix the Greek yogurt with the ground ginger. Add the chicken and mix to coat. 2. Add the pea pods, water chestnuts, mandarin oranges, and peanuts. Stir all the ingredients together until well mixed. 3. Divide ¼ of the bag of romaine into 4 bowls and top with the chicken salad.

Per Serving:

calorie: 338 | fat: 18g | protein: 28g | carbs: 19g | sugars: 10g | fiber: 5g | sodium: 85mg

Warm Barley and Squash Salad with Balsamic Vinaigrette

Prep time: 20 minutes | Cook time: 40 minutes | Serves 8

1 small butternut squash
3 teaspoons plus 2 tablespoons extra-virgin olive oil, divided
2 cups broccoli florets
1 cup pearl barley
1 cup toasted chopped walnuts
2 cups baby kale

½ red onion, sliced
2 tablespoons balsamic vinegar
2 garlic cloves, minced
½ teaspoon salt
¼ teaspoon freshly ground black pepper

1. Preheat the oven to 400°F. Line a baking sheet with parchment paper. 2. Peel and seed the squash, and cut it into dice. In a large bowl, toss the squash with 2 teaspoons of olive oil. Transfer to the prepared baking sheet and roast for 20 minutes. 3. While the squash is roasting, toss the broccoli in the same bowl with 1 teaspoon of olive oil. After 20 minutes, flip the squash and push it to one side of the baking sheet. Add the broccoli to the other side and continue to roast for 20 more minutes until tender. 4. While the veggies are roasting, in a medium pot, cover the barley with several inches of water. Bring to a boil, then reduce the heat, cover, and simmer for 30 minutes until tender. Drain and rinse. 5. Transfer the barley to a large bowl, and toss with the cooked squash and broccoli, walnuts, kale, and onion. 6. In a small bowl, mix the remaining 2 tablespoons of olive oil, balsamic vinegar, garlic, salt, and pepper. Toss the salad with the dressing and serve.

Per Serving:

calories: 274 | fat: 15g | protein: 6g | carbs: 32g | sugars: 3g | fiber: 7g | sodium: 144mg

Roasted Carrot and Quinoa with Goat Cheese

Prep time: 10 minutes | Cook time: 20 minutes | Serves 4

4 large carrots, cut into ⅛-inch-thick rounds
4 tablespoons oil (olive, safflower, or grapeseed), divided
2 teaspoons paprika
1 teaspoon turmeric

2 teaspoons ground cumin
2 cups water
1 cup quinoa, rinsed
½ cup shelled pistachios, toasted
4 ounces goat cheese
12 ounces salad greens

1. Preheat the oven to 400°F. Line a baking sheet with parchment paper. 2. In a large bowl, toss together the carrots, 2 tablespoons of oil, the paprika, turmeric, and cumin until the carrots are well coated. Spread them evenly on the prepared baking sheet and roast until tender, 15 to 17 minutes. 3. In a medium saucepan, combine the water and quinoa over high heat. Bring to a boil, reduce the heat to low and simmer until tender, about 15 minutes. 4. Transfer the roasted carrots to a large bowl and add the cooked quinoa, remaining 2 tablespoons of oil, the pistachios, and goat cheese and toss to combine. 5. Evenly divide the greens among four plates and top with the carrot mixture. Serve. 6. Store any leftovers in an airtight container in the refrigerator for up to 2 days.

Per Serving:

calorie: 544 | fat: 33g | protein: 21g | carbs: 43g | sugars: 6g | fiber: 9g | sodium: 202mg

Salmon Niçoise Salad

Prep time: 10 minutes | Cook time: 30 minutes | Serves 1

salad
4 oz (113 g) fresh salmon fillets
Cooking oil spray, as needed
1 tsp olive oil
Sea salt, as needed
Black pepper, as needed
2 cups (60 g) arugula
⅛ cup (17 g) assorted olives
½ cup (60 g) coarsely chopped cucumber
1 large hard-boiled egg
½ cup (65 g) quartered baby

potatoes
2 tsp (2 g) dried rosemary
2½ oz (71 g) fresh green beans
dressing
1 tbsp (15 g) tahini
½ tbsp (8 g) Dijon mustard
1 tbsp (15 ml) fresh lemon juice
3 tbsp (45 ml) water
½ tsp dried dill
Sea salt, as needed
Black pepper, as needed

1. Preheat the oven to 400°F (204°C). Line a large baking sheet with parchment paper. 2. Bring a large pot of water to a boil over high heat. 3. To make the salad, heat a medium skillet over medium-high heat. Spray the salmon with the cooking oil spray and drizzle the oil on top. Place it in the skillet and cook for 2 to 3 minutes on each side (depending how thick the fillet is), until the outside is an opaque pink color and just barely starts to brown. Season the salmon with the salt and black pepper. 4. On a serving plate, arrange a bed of arugula. On the arugula, arrange the olives, cucumber, egg, and salmon. Set the plate aside. 5. Place the potatoes in a medium bowl. Add the rosemary and toss to coat the potatoes. Transfer them to the prepared baking sheet and bake them for 20 to 25 minutes, or until the potatoes are brown and crispy on the outside. 6. While the potatoes are roasting, prepare a large bowl of ice water. Add the green beans to the boiling water and cook them for 2 minutes. Quickly transfer the green beans to the bowl of ice water. Once they have cooled, add the green beans to the salad. 7. To make the dressing, mix together the tahini, mustard, lemon juice, water, dill, sea salt, and black pepper in a medium jar. 8. Add the potatoes to the salad, toss the salad with the dressing, and serve.

Per Serving:

calorie: 471 | fat: 23g | protein: 37g | carbs: 31g | sugars: 6g | fiber: 7g | sodium: 555mg

Winter Chicken and Citrus Salad

Prep time: 10 minutes | Cook time: 0 minutes | Serves 4

4 cups baby spinach
2 tablespoons extra-virgin olive oil
1 tablespoon freshly squeezed lemon juice
⅛ teaspoon salt

Freshly ground black pepper
2 cups chopped cooked chicken
2 mandarin oranges, peeled and sectioned
½ peeled grapefruit, sectioned
¼ cup sliced almonds

1. In a large mixing bowl, toss the spinach with the olive oil, lemon juice, salt, and pepper. 2. Add the chicken, oranges, grapefruit, and almonds to the bowl. Toss gently. 3. Arrange on 4 plates and serve.

Per Serving:

calories: 249 | fat: 12g | protein: 24g | carbs: 11g | sugars: 7g | fiber: 3g | sodium: 135mg

Warm Sweet Potato and Black Bean Salad

Prep time: 5 minutes | Cook time: 35 minutes | Serves 2

Extra-virgin olive oil cooking spray
1 large sweet potato, peeled and cubed
1 tablespoon extra-virgin olive oil
1 tablespoon balsamic vinegar
1 teaspoon dried rosemary

¼ teaspoon garlic powder
⅛ teaspoon salt
⅛ teaspoon freshly ground black pepper
1 cup canned black beans, drained and rinsed
2 tablespoons chopped chives

1. Preheat the oven to 450°F. 2. In a small baking dish coated with cooking spray, place the sweet potato cubes. Put the dish in the preheated oven. Bake for 20 to 35 minutes, uncovered, or until tender. 3. In a medium serving bowl, whisk together the olive oil, balsamic vinegar, rosemary, garlic powder, salt, and pepper. 4. Add the black beans and cooked sweet potato to the oil and herb mixture. Toss to coat. 5. Sprinkle with the chives. 6. Serve immediately and enjoy!

Per Serving:

calorie: 235 | fat: 7g | protein: 8g | carbs: 35g | sugars: 4g | fiber: 10g | sodium: 359mg

Strawberry-Blueberry-Orange Salad

Prep time: 15 minutes | Cook time: 0 minutes | Serves 8

1/4 cup fat-free or reduced-fat mayonnaise
3 tablespoons sugar
1 tablespoon white vinegar
2 teaspoons poppy seed

2 cups fresh strawberry halves
2 cups fresh blueberries
1 orange, peeled, chopped
Sliced almonds, if desired

1 In small bowl, mix mayonnaise, sugar, vinegar and poppy seed with whisk until well blended. 2 In medium bowl, mix strawberries, blueberries and orange. Just before serving, pour dressing over fruit; toss. Sprinkle with almonds.

Per Serving:

calorie: 70 | fat: 1g | protein: 0g | carbs: 16g | sugars: 12g | fiber: 2g | sodium: 60mg

Mediterranean Vegetable Salad

Prep time: 10 minutes | Cook time: 0 minutes | Serves 6

1/3 cup tarragon vinegar or white wine vinegar
2 tablespoons canola or soybean oil
2 tablespoons chopped fresh or 2 teaspoons dried oregano leaves
1/2 teaspoon sugar
1/2 teaspoon salt
1/2 teaspoon ground mustard
1/2 teaspoon pepper

2 cloves garlic, finely chopped
3 large tomatoes, sliced
2 large yellow bell peppers, sliced into thin rings
6 oz fresh spinach leaves (from 10-oz bag), stems removed (about 1 cup)
1/2 cup crumbled feta cheese (2 oz)
Kalamata olives, if desired

1 In small bowl, mix vinegar, oil, oregano, sugar, salt, mustard,

pepper and garlic. In glass or plastic container, place tomatoes and bell peppers. Pour vinegar mixture over vegetables. Cover and refrigerate at least 1 hour to blend flavors. 2 Line serving platter with spinach. Drain vegetables; place on spinach. Sprinkle with cheese; garnish with olives.

Per Serving:

calorie: 110 | fat: 8g | protein: 3g | carbs: 8g | sugars: 6g | fiber: 1g | sodium: 340mg

Wild Rice Salad

Prep time: 5 minutes | Cook time: 45 minutes | Serves 6

1 cup raw wild rice (rinsed)
4 cups cold water
1 cup mandarin oranges, packed in their own juice (drain and reserve 2 tablespoons of liquid)
½ cup chopped celery

¼ cup minced red bell pepper
1 shallot, minced
1 teaspoon minced thyme
2 tablespoons raspberry vinegar
1 tablespoon extra-virgin olive oil

1. Place the rinsed, raw rice and the water in a saucepan. Bring to a boil, lower the heat, cover the pan, and cook for 45–50 minutes until the rice has absorbed the water. Set the rice aside to cool. 2. In a large bowl, combine the mandarin oranges, celery, red pepper, and shallot. 3. In a small bowl, combine the reserved juice, thyme, vinegar, and oil. 4. Add the rice to the mandarin oranges and vegetables. Pour the dressing over the salad, toss, and serve.

Per Serving:

calorie: 134 | fat: 3g | protein: 4g | carbs: 24g | sugars: 4g | fiber: 3g | sodium: 12mg

Broccoli "Tabouli"

Prep time: 15 minutes | Cook time: 0 minutes | Serves 2

1 broccoli head, trimmed into florets (about 2 cups)
1 large jicama, peeled
1 cup chickpeas, drained and rinsed
2 plum tomatoes, diced
1 medium cucumber, peeled, seeded, and diced
½ cup chopped fresh parsley
½ cup chopped fresh mint

¼ cup chopped red onion
¼ cup freshly squeezed lemon juice
2 tablespoons sunflower seeds
1 tablespoon extra-virgin olive oil
Salt, to season
Freshly ground black pepper, to season
4 cups baby spinach, divided

1. With a grater or food processor, grate the broccoli into grain-size pieces until it resembles rice. 2. Repeat with the jicama. You should have about 1 cup. 3. To a large bowl, add the grated broccoli, grated jicama, chickpeas, tomatoes, cucumber, parsley, mint, red onion, lemon juice, sunflower seeds, and olive oil. Toss until well mixed. Season with salt and pepper. 4. Arrange 2 cups of spinach on each of 2 plates. 5. Top each with half of the tabouli mixture. 6. Serve immediately.

Per Serving:

calorie: 265 | fat: 8g | protein: 9g | carbs: 44g | sugars: 10g | fiber: 21g | sodium: 138mg

Rainbow Quinoa Salad

Prep time: 10 minutes | Cook time: 0 minutes | Serves 3

Dressing
3½ tablespoons orange juice
1 tablespoon apple cider vinegar
1 tablespoon pure maple syrup
1½ teaspoons yellow mustard
Couple pinches of cloves
Rounded ½ teaspoon sea salt
Freshly ground black pepper to taste
Salad
2 cups cooked quinoa, cooled

½ cup corn kernels
½ cup diced apple tossed in ½ teaspoon lemon juice
¼ cup diced red pepper
¼ cup sliced green onions or chives
1 can (15 ounces) black beans, rinsed and drained
Sea salt to taste
Freshly ground black pepper to taste

1. To make the dressing: In a large bowl, whisk together the orange juice, vinegar, syrup, mustard, cloves, salt, and pepper. 2. To make the salad: Add the quinoa, corn, apple, red pepper, green onion or chives, and black beans, and stir to combine well. Season with the salt and black pepper to taste. Serve, or store in an airtight container in the fridge.

Per Serving:
calorie: 355 | fat: 4g | protein: 15g | carbs: 68g | sugars: 12g | fiber: 15g | sodium: 955mg

Young Kale and Cabbage Salad with Toasted Peanuts

Prep time: 15 minutes | Cook time: 0 minutes | Serves 6

2 bunches baby kale, thinly sliced
½ head green savoy cabbage, cored and thinly sliced
¼ cup apple cider vinegar
Juice of 1 lemon

1 teaspoon ground cumin
¼ teaspoon smoked paprika
1 medium red bell pepper, thinly sliced
1 cup toasted peanuts
1 garlic clove, thinly sliced

1. In a large salad bowl, toss the kale and cabbage together. 2. In a small bowl, to make the dressing, whisk the vinegar, lemon juice, cumin, and paprika together. 3. Pour the dressing over the greens, and gently massage with your hands. 4. Add the pepper, peanuts, and garlic, and toss to combine.

Per Serving:
calorie: 177 | fat: 12g | protein: 8g | carbs: 13g | sugars: 5g | fiber: 5g | sodium: 31mg

Thai Broccoli Slaw

Prep time: 20 minutes | Cook time: 0 minutes | Serves 8

Dressing
2 tablespoons reduced-fat creamy peanut butter
1 tablespoon grated gingerroot
1 tablespoon rice vinegar
1 tablespoon orange marmalade
1½ teaspoons reduced-sodium soy sauce

1/4 to 1/2 teaspoon chili garlic sauce
Slaw
3 cups broccoli slaw mix (from 10-oz bag)
1/2 cup bite-size thin strips red bell pepper
1/2 cup julienne (matchstick-cut) carrots
1/2 cup shredded red cabbage

2 tablespoons chopped fresh cilantro

1 In small bowl, combine all dressing ingredients. Beat with whisk, until blended. 2 In large bowl, toss all slaw ingredients. Pour dressing over slaw mixture; toss until coated. Cover and refrigerate at least 1 hour to blend flavors but no longer than 6 hours, tossing occasionally to blend dressing from bottom of bowl back into slaw mixture.

Per Serving:
calorie: 50 | fat: 1.5g | protein: 2g | carbs: 7g | sugars: 3g | fiber: 1g | sodium: 75mg

Italian Potato Salad

Prep time: 10 minutes | Cook time: 25 minutes | Serves 8

12 new red potatoes, 3–4 ounces each, washed and skins left on
3 celery stalks, chopped
1 red bell pepper, minced
¼ cup chopped scallions
2 tablespoons olive oil
1 tablespoon balsamic vinegar

½ tablespoon red vinegar
1 teaspoon chopped fresh parsley
⅛ teaspoon freshly ground black pepper

1. Boil the potatoes for 20 minutes in a large pot of boiling water. Drain, and let cool for 30 minutes. 2. Cut the potatoes into large chunks, and toss the potatoes with the celery, bell pepper, and scallions. 3. In a medium bowl, combine the olive oil, balsamic vinegar, red vinegar, parsley, and pepper; pour the dressing over the potato salad. Serve at room temperature.

Per Serving:
calorie: 128 | fat: 4g | protein: 3g | carbs: 22g | sugars: 3g | fiber: 3g | sodium: 30mg

Pomegranate "Tabbouleh" with Cauliflower

Prep time: 20 minutes | Cook time: 5 minutes | Serves 4 to 6

⅓ cup extra-virgin olive oil, divided
4 cups grated cauliflower (about 1 medium head)
Juice of 1 lemon
¼ red onion, minced
4 large tomatoes, diced

3 large bunches flat-leaf parsley, chopped
1 large bunch mint, chopped
½ cup pomegranate arils
Kosher salt
Freshly ground black pepper

1. In a large skillet, heat 2 tablespoons of extra-virgin olive oil. When it's hot, add the cauliflower and sauté for 3 to 5 minutes or until it starts to crisp. Remove the skillet from the heat and allow the cauliflower to cool while you prep the remaining ingredients. 2. In a large bowl, combine the remaining extra-virgin olive oil with the lemon juice and red onion. Mix well, then mix in the tomatoes, parsley, mint, and pomegranate arils. 3. After the cauliflower cools, 5 to 7 minutes, add it to the bowl with the other ingredients. Season with salt and pepper to taste and serve. 4. Store any leftovers in an airtight container in the refrigerator for 3 to 5 days.

Per Serving:
calorie: 205 | fat: 15g | protein: 4g | carbs: 17g | sugars: 9g | fiber: 5g | sodium: 50mg

Tu-No Salad

Prep time: 10 minutes | Cook time: 0 minutes | Serves 2

1 can (15 ounces) chickpeas, rinsed and drained
1 tablespoon tahini
2 tablespoons water
1 tablespoon red wine vinegar (can substitute apple cider vinegar)
1 tablespoon chickpea miso (or other mild-flavored miso)
1 teaspoon vegan

Worcestershire sauce (optional)
½ teaspoon Dijon mustard
½ teaspoon coconut nectar
2 tablespoons minced celery
2 tablespoons minced cucumber
2 tablespoons minced apple
⅛ teaspoon sea salt
Freshly ground black pepper to taste

1. In a small food processor, pulse the chickpeas until fairly crumbly but not finely ground. (Alternatively, you can mash by hand.) In a large bowl, combine the chickpeas, tahini, water, vinegar, miso, Worcestershire sauce, mustard, nectar, celery, cucumber, apple, and salt. Mix together well. Season with additional salt and pepper to taste, and serve!

Per Serving:
calorie: 264 | fat: 8g | protein: 12g | carbs: 37g | sugars: 8g | fiber: 10g | sodium: 800mg

Fiery Black Bean Salad

Prep time: 10 minutes | Cook time: 0 minutes | Serves 8

3 cups cooked black beans
2 tomatoes, chopped
2 red bell peppers, finely chopped
1 cup yellow corn
3 garlic cloves, minced
1 jalapeño pepper, minced

¼ cup fresh lime juice
2 tablespoons red wine vinegar
1 tablespoon cumin
1 tablespoon extra-virgin olive oil
2 tablespoons freshly chopped cilantro (optional)

1. Combine all ingredients in a bowl, and chill in the refrigerator for several hours to blend the flavors. Serve.

Per Serving:
calorie: 138 | fat: 3g | protein: 7g | carbs: 23g | sugars: 3g | fiber: 7g | sodium: 8mg

Savory Skillet Corn Bread

Prep time: 15 minutes | Cook time: 20 minutes | Serves 8

Nonstick cooking spray
1 cup whole-wheat all-purpose flour
1 cup yellow cornmeal
1¾ teaspoons baking powder
¾ teaspoon baking soda
½ teaspoon salt

1 large zucchini, grated
1 cup reduced-fat Cheddar cheese, grated
¼ bunch chives, finely chopped
1 cup buttermilk
2 large eggs
3 tablespoons canola oil

1. Preheat the oven to 420°F. Lightly spray a cast iron skillet with cooking spray. 2. In a medium bowl, whisk the flour, cornmeal, baking powder, baking soda, and salt together. 3. In a large bowl, gently whisk the zucchini, cheese, chives, buttermilk, eggs, and oil together. 4. Add the dry ingredients to the wet ingredients, and stir

until just combined, taking care not to overmix, and pour into the prepared skillet. 5. Transfer the skillet to the oven, and bake for 20 minutes, or until a knife inserted into the center comes out clean. Remove from the oven, and let sit for 10 minutes before serving.

Per Serving:
calorie: 239 | fat: 8g | protein: 10g | carbs: 31g | sugars: 3g | fiber: 2g | sodium: 470mg

Mozzarella-Tomato Salad

Prep time: 15 minutes | Cook time: 0 minutes | Serves 2

Fresh mozzarella cheese (2 ounces), cut into ¾-inch cubes
½ cup cherry tomatoes, halved
½ cup cannellini beans, drained and rinsed
½ cup artichoke hearts, drained
¼ cup jarred roasted red peppers
¼ cup chopped scallions

1 tablespoon minced fresh basil
1 tablespoon extra-virgin olive oil
2 teaspoons balsamic vinegar
⅛ teaspoon salt
4 cups baby spinach, divided

1. In a small bowl, stir together the mozzarella cheese, tomatoes, beans, artichoke hearts, red peppers, and scallions. 2. In another small bowl, whisk the basil, olive oil, balsamic vinegar, and salt until combined. 3. Drizzle the dressing over the cheese and vegetables. Toss to coat. Chill for 15 minutes. 4. Using 2 plates, arrange 2 cups of spinach on each. Top with half of the cheese and vegetable mixture. 5. Serve immediately.

Per Serving:
calorie: 199 | fat: 8g | protein: 9g | carbs: 26g | sugars: 6g | fiber: 10g | sodium: 387mg

Zucchini, Carrot, and Fennel Salad

Prep time: 10 minutes | Cook time: 8 minutes | Serves ½ cup

2 medium carrots, peeled and julienned
1 medium zucchini, julienned
½ medium fennel bulb, core removed and julienned
1 tablespoon fresh orange juice
2 tablespoons Dijon mustard
3 tablespoons extra-virgin olive oil
1 teaspoon white wine vinegar

½ teaspoon dried thyme
1 tablespoon finely minced parsley
 teaspoon salt
¼ teaspoon freshly ground black pepper
¼ cup chopped walnuts
1 medium head romaine lettuce, washed and leaves separated

1. Place the carrots, zucchini, and fennel in a medium bowl; set aside. 2. In a medium bowl, combine the orange juice, mustard, olive oil, vinegar, thyme, parsley, salt, and pepper; mix well. 3. Pour the dressing over the vegetables and toss. Add the walnuts, and mix again. Refrigerate until ready to serve. 4. To serve, line a bowl or plates with lettuce leaves, and spoon ½ cup of salad on top.

Per Serving:
calorie: 201 | fat: 16g | protein: 5g | carbs: 14g | sugars: 6g | fiber: 6g | sodium: 285mg

Shaved Brussels Sprouts and Kale with Poppy Seed Dressing

Prep time: 20 minutes | Cook time: 0 minutes |

Serves 4 to 6

1 pound Brussels sprouts, shaved	4 ounces shredded Romano cheese
1 bunch kale, thinly shredded	Poppy seed dressing
4 scallions, both white and green parts, thinly sliced	Kosher salt
	Freshly ground black pepper

1. In a large bowl, toss together the Brussels sprouts, kale, scallions, and Romano cheese. Add the dressing to the greens and toss to combine. Season with salt and pepper to taste.

Per Serving:

calorie: 139 | fat: 7g | protein: 11g | carbs: 11g | sugars: 3g | fiber: 4g | sodium: 357mg

Rotisserie Chicken and Avocado Salad

Prep time: 15 minutes | Cook time: 0 minutes | Serves 4

½ cup plain Greek yogurt	1 cup shredded rotisserie chicken meat
1 tablespoon freshly squeezed lime juice	½ medium red onion, chopped
4 teaspoons chopped fresh cilantro	1 large tomato, diced
2 ripe avocados, peeled, pitted, and cubed	4 cups mixed leafy greens, divided

1. In a large bowl, stir together the Greek yogurt, lime juice, and cilantro to make a dressing. 2. Add the avocado, chicken, onion, and tomato and mix gently into the dressing. 3. Divide 1 cup of the greens into 4 bowls and top with the chicken salad.

Per Serving:

calorie: 269 | fat: 18g | protein: 14g | carbs: 16g | sugars: 5g | fiber: 9g | sodium: 93mg

Romaine Lettuce Salad with Cranberry, Feta, and Beans

Prep time: 10 minutes | Cook time: 0 minutes | Serves 2

1 cup chopped fresh green beans	½ cup cranberries, fresh or frozen
6 cups washed and chopped romaine lettuce	¼ cup crumbled fat-free feta cheese
1 cup sliced radishes	1 tablespoon extra-virgin olive oil
2 scallions, sliced	Salt, to season
¼ cup chopped fresh oregano	Freshly ground black pepper, to season
1 cup canned kidney beans, drained and rinsed	

1. In a microwave-safe dish, add the green beans and a small amount of water. Microwave on high for about 2 minutes, or until tender. 2. In a large bowl, toss together the romaine lettuce, radishes, scallions, and oregano. 3. Add the green beans, kidney beans, cranberries, feta cheese, and olive oil. Season with salt and

pepper. Toss to coat. 4. Evenly divide between 2 plates and enjoy immediately.

Per Serving:

calorie: 271 | fat: 9g | protein: 16g | carbs: 36g | sugars: 10g | fiber: 13g | sodium: 573mg

Haricot Verts, Walnut, and Feta Salad

Prep time: 10 minutes | Cook time: 15 minutes |

Serves 12

½ cup walnuts, toasted	⅓ cup crumbled fat-free feta cheese
1½ pounds fresh haricot verts, trimmed and halved	¼ cup extra-virgin olive oil
½ cup cooked green lentils	¼ cup white wine vinegar
1 medium red onion, sliced into rings	¼ cup chopped fresh mint leaves
½ cup peeled, seeded, and diced cucumber	1 garlic clove, minced

1. Place the walnuts in a small baking dish in a 350-degree oven for 5–10 minutes until lightly browned. Remove from the oven, and set aside. 2. Steam the haricot verts about 4–5 minutes, or until desired degree of crispness. 3. In a salad bowl, combine the haricot verts with the walnuts, lentils, red onion rings, cucumber, and feta cheese. 4. Combine all the dressing ingredients together, and toss with the vegetables. Chill in the refrigerator for 2–3 hours before serving.

Per Serving:

calorie: 119 | fat: 7g | protein: 5g | carbs: 11g | sugars: 3g | fiber: 4g | sodium: 61mg

Pasta Salad–Stuffed Tomatoes

Prep time: 10 minutes | Cook time: 0 minutes |

Serves 4

1 cup uncooked whole-wheat fusilli	parsley
2 small carrots, sliced	¼ cup calorie-free, fat-free Italian salad dressing
2 scallions, chopped	2 tablespoons low-fat mayonnaise
¼ cup chopped pimiento	¼ teaspoon dried marjoram
1 cup cooked kidney beans	¼ teaspoon freshly ground black pepper
½ cup sliced celery	
¼ cup cooked peas	4 medium tomatoes
2 tablespoons chopped fresh	

1. Cook the fusilli in boiling water until cooked, about 7–8 minutes; drain. 2. In a large bowl, combine the macaroni with the remaining salad ingredients (except the tomatoes), and toss well. Cover, and chill in the refrigerator 1 hour or more. 3. With the stem end down, cut each tomato into 6 wedges, cutting to, but not through, the base of the tomato. Spread the wedges slightly apart, and spoon the pasta mixture into the tomatoes. Chill until ready to serve.

Per Serving:

calorie: 214 | fat: 3g | protein: 10g | carbs: 40g | sugars: 6g | fiber: 8g | sodium: 164mg

Blueberry and Chicken Salad on a Bed of Greens

Prep time: 10 minutes | Cook time: 0 minutes | Serves 4

2 cups chopped cooked chicken
1 cup fresh blueberries
¼ cup finely chopped almonds
1 celery stalk, finely chopped
¼ cup finely chopped red onion
1 tablespoon chopped fresh basil

1 tablespoon chopped fresh cilantro
½ cup plain, nonfat Greek yogurt or vegan mayonnaise
¼ teaspoon salt
¼ teaspoon freshly ground black pepper
8 cups salad greens (baby spinach, spicy greens, romaine)

1. In a large mixing bowl, combine the chicken, blueberries, almonds, celery, onion, basil, and cilantro. Toss gently to mix. 2. In a small bowl, combine the yogurt, salt, and pepper. Add to the chicken salad and stir to combine. 3. Arrange 2 cups of salad greens on each of 4 plates and divide the chicken salad among the plates to serve.

Per Serving:

calories: 207 | fat: 6g | protein: 28g | carbs: 11g | sugars: 6g | fiber: 3g | sodium: 235mg

BLT Potato Salad

Prep time: 20 minutes | Cook time: 10 to 15 minutes | Serves 6

4 small new red potatoes (about 12 oz), cut into 1/2-inch cubes
1/4 cup reduced-fat mayonnaise or salad dressing
1 teaspoon Dijon mustard
2 teaspoons chopped fresh or 1/2 teaspoon dried dill weed
1/4 teaspoon salt

1/8 teaspoon pepper
1/2 cup grape tomatoes or halved cherry tomatoes
11/2 cups bite-size pieces romaine lettuce
2 slices turkey bacon, cooked, crumbled

1 In 2-quart saucepan, place potatoes. Add enough water to cover. Heat to boiling; reduce heat to low. Cover; cook 10 to 15 minutes or until potatoes are tender. Drain; cool about 10 minutes. 2 Meanwhile, in medium bowl, mix mayonnaise, mustard, dill weed, salt and pepper. Stir in potatoes, tomatoes and lettuce until coated. Sprinkle with bacon.

Per Serving:

calorie: 100 | fat: 5g | protein: 3g | carbs: 12g | sugars: 2g | fiber: 1g | sodium: 300mg

Chapter 10 Snacks and Appetizers

Southern Boiled Peanuts

Prep time: 5 minutes | Cook time: 1 hour 20 minutes | Makes 8 cups

1 pound raw jumbo peanuts in the shell

3 tablespoons fine sea salt

1. Remove the inner pot from the Instant Pot and add the peanuts to it. Cover the peanuts with water and use your hands to agitate them, loosening any dirt. Drain the peanuts in a colander, rinse out the pot, and return the peanuts to it. Return the inner pot to the Instant Pot housing. 2. Add the salt and 9 cups water to the pot and stir to dissolve the salt. Select a salad plate just small enough to fit inside the pot and set it on top of the peanuts to weight them down, submerging them all in the water. 3. Secure the lid and set the Pressure Release to Sealing. Select the Steam setting and set the cooking time for 1 hour at low pressure. (The pot will take about 20 minutes to come up to pressure before the cooking program begins.) 4. When the cooking program ends, let the pressure release naturally (this will take about 1 hour). Open the pot and, wearing heat-resistant mitts, remove the inner pot from the housing. Let the peanuts cool to room temperature in the brine (this will take about 1½ hours). 5. Serve at room temperature or chilled. Transfer the peanuts with their brine to an airtight container and refrigerate for up to 1 week.

Per Serving:

calories: 306 | fat: 17g | protein: 26g | carbs: 12g | sugars: 2g | fiber: 4g | sodium: 303mg

Garlic Kale Chips

Prep time: 5 minutes | Cook time: 15 minutes | Serves 1

1 (8-ounce) bunch kale, trimmed and cut into 2-inch pieces
1 tablespoon extra-virgin olive oil

½ teaspoon sea salt
¼ teaspoon garlic powder
Pinch cayenne (optional, to taste)

1. Preheat the oven to 350°F. Line two baking sheets with parchment paper. 2. Wash the kale and pat it completely dry. 3. In a large bowl, toss the kale with the olive oil, sea salt, garlic powder, and cayenne, if using. 4. Spread the kale in a single layer on the prepared baking sheets. 5. Bake until crisp, 12 to 15 minutes, rotating the sheets once.

Per Serving:

calorie: 78 | fat: 5g | protein: 3g | carbs: 7g | sugars: 2g | fiber: 3g | sodium: 416mg

Sweet Potato Oven Fries with Spicy Sour Cream

Prep time: 10 minutes | Cook time: 35 minutes | Serves 4

1 teaspoon salt-free southwest chipotle seasoning
2 large dark-orange sweet potatoes (1 lb), peeled, cut into 1/2-inch-thick slices

Olive oil cooking spray
1/2 cup reduced-fat sour cream
1 tablespoon sriracha sauce
1 tablespoon chopped fresh cilantro

1 Heat oven to 425°F. Spray large cookie sheet with cooking spray. Place 3/4 teaspoon of the seasoning in 1-gallon resealable food-storage plastic bag; add potatoes. Seal bag; shake until potatoes are evenly coated. Place potatoes in single layer on cookie sheet; spray lightly with cooking spray. Bake 20 minutes or until bottoms are golden brown. Turn potatoes; bake 10 to 15 minutes longer or until tender and bottoms are golden brown. 2 Meanwhile, in small bowl, stir sour cream, sriracha sauce, cilantro and remaining 1/4 teaspoon seasoning; refrigerate until ready to serve. 3 Serve fries warm with spicy sour cream.

Per Serving:

calories: 120 | fat: 4g | protein: 2g | carbs: 20g | sugars: 7g | fiber: 3g | sodium: 140mg

Caramelized Onion–Shrimp Spread

Prep time: 30 minutes | Cook time: 20 minutes | Serves 18

1 tablespoon butter (do not use margarine)
1/2 medium onion, thinly sliced (about 1/2 cup)
1 clove garlic, finely chopped
1/4 cup apple jelly
1 container (8 oz) reduced-fat

cream cheese, softened
1 bag (4 oz) frozen cooked salad shrimp, thawed, well drained (about 1 cup)
1 teaspoon chopped fresh chives
36 whole-grain crackers

1 In 1-quart saucepan, melt butter over medium-low heat. Add onion; cook 15 minutes, stirring frequently. Add garlic; cook 1 minute, stirring occasionally, until onion and garlic are tender and browned. Stir in apple jelly. Cook, stirring constantly, until melted. Remove from heat. Let stand 5 minutes to cool. 2 Meanwhile, in small bowl, stir together cream cheese and shrimp. On 8-inch plate, spread shrimp mixture into a 5-inch round. 3 Spoon onion mixture over shrimp mixture. Sprinkle with chives. Serve with crackers.

Per Serving:

calories: 90| fat: 4g | protein: 3g | carbs: 10g | sugars: 3g | fiber: 1g | sodium: 140mg

Hummus

Prep time: 5 minutes | Cook time: 5 minutes | Serves 12

One 15-ounce can chickpeas, drained (reserve a little liquid)
3 cloves garlic
Juice of 1 lemon

Juice of 1 lime
1 teaspoon extra-virgin olive oil
1 teaspoon ground cumin

1. In a blender or food processor, combine all the ingredients until smooth, adding chickpea liquid or water if necessary to blend, and create a creamy texture. Refrigerate until ready to serve. Serve with crunchy vegetables, crackers, or pita bread.

Per Serving:
calorie: 56 | fat: 1g | protein: 3g | carbs: 9g | sugars: 2g | fiber: 2g | sodium: 76mg

Crab-Filled Mushrooms

Prep time: 5 minutes | Cook time: 25 minutes | Serves 10

20 large fresh mushroom caps
6 ounces canned crabmeat, rinsed, drained, and flaked
½ cup crushed whole-wheat crackers
2 tablespoons chopped fresh parsley
2 tablespoons finely chopped

green onion
⅛ teaspoon freshly ground black pepper
¼ cup chopped pimiento
3 tablespoons extra-virgin olive oil
10 tablespoons wheat germ

1. Preheat the oven to 350 degrees. Clean the mushrooms by dusting off any dirt on the cap with a mushroom brush or paper towel; remove the stems. 2. In a small mixing bowl, combine the crabmeat, crackers, parsley, onion, and pepper. 3. Place the mushroom caps in a 13-x-9-x-2-inch baking dish, crown side down. Stuff some of the crabmeat filling into each cap. Place a little pimiento on top of the filling. 4. Drizzle the olive oil over the caps and sprinkle each cap with ½ tablespoon wheat germ. Bake for 15–17 minutes. Transfer to a serving platter, and serve hot.

Per Serving:
calorie: 113 | fat: 6g | protein: 7g | carbs: 9g | sugars: 1g | fiber: 2g | sodium: 77mg

Cinnamon Toasted Pumpkin Seeds

Prep time: 5 minutes | Cook time: 45 minutes | Serves 4

1 cup pumpkin seeds
2 tablespoons canola oil
1 teaspoon cinnamon

2 (1-gram) packets stevia
¼ teaspoon sea salt

1. Preheat the oven to 300°F. 2. In a bowl, toss the pumpkin seeds with the oil, cinnamon, stevia, and salt. 3. Spread the seeds in a single layer on a rimmed baking sheet. Bake until browned and fragrant, stirring once or twice, about 45 minutes.

Per Serving:
calorie: 233 | fat: 21g | protein: 9g | carbs: 5g | sugars: 0g | fiber: 2g | sodium: 151mg

Vegetable Kabobs with Mustard Dip

Prep time: 35 minutes | Cook time: 10 minutes | Serves 9

Dip
⅔ cup plain fat-free yogurt
⅓ cup fat-free sour cream
1 tablespoon finely chopped fresh parsley
1 teaspoon onion powder
1 teaspoon garlic salt
1 tablespoon Dijon mustard
Kabobs

1 medium bell pepper, cut into 6 strips, then cut into thirds
1 medium zucchini, cut diagonally into ½-inch slices
1 package (8 oz) fresh whole mushrooms
9 large cherry tomatoes
2 tablespoons olive or vegetable oil

1 In small bowl, mix dip ingredients. Cover; refrigerate at least 1 hour. 2 Heat gas or charcoal grill. On 5 (12-inch) metal skewers, thread vegetables so that one kind of vegetable is on the same skewer (use 2 skewers for mushrooms); leave space between each piece. Brush vegetables with oil. 3 Place skewers of bell pepper and zucchini on grill over medium heat. Cover grill; cook 2 minutes. Add skewers of mushrooms and tomatoes. Cover grill; cook 4 to 5 minutes, carefully turning every 2 minutes, until vegetables are tender. Transfer vegetables from skewers to serving plate. Serve with dip.

Per Serving:
calories: 60 | fat: 3.5g | protein: 2g | carbs: 6g | sugars: 3g | fiber: 1g | sodium: 180mg

Creamy Cheese Dip

Prep time: 5 minutes | Cook time: 5 minutes | Serves 40

1 cup plain fat-free yogurt, strained overnight in cheesecloth over a bowl set in

the refrigerator
1 cup fat-free ricotta cheese
1 cup low-fat cottage cheese

1. Combine all the ingredients in a food processor; process until smooth. Place in a covered container, and refrigerate until ready to use (this cream cheese can be refrigerated for up to 1 week).

Per Serving:
calorie: 21 | fat: 1g | protein: 2g | carbs: 1g | sugars: 1g | fiber: 0g | sodium: 81mg

No-Added-Sugar Berries and Cream Yogurt Bowl

Prep time: 5 minutes | Cook time: 0 minutes | Serves 1

1 cup (200 g) plain nonfat Greek yogurt
1 tbsp (15 g) almond butter

½ cup (50 g) frozen mixed berries, thawed
Zest of ½ medium lemon

1. In a small bowl, combine the yogurt, almond butter, berries, and lemon zest.

Per Serving:
calorie: 270 | fat: 10g | protein: 27g | carbs: 21g | sugars: 15g | fiber: 3g | sodium: 89mg

Candied Pecans

Prep time: 5 minutes | Cook time: 20 minutes | Serves 10

4 cups raw pecans
1½ teaspoons liquid stevia
½ cup plus 1 tablespoon water, divided
1 teaspoon vanilla extract
1 teaspoon cinnamon
¼ teaspoon nutmeg
⅛ teaspoon ground ginger
⅛ teaspoon sea salt

1. Place the raw pecans, liquid stevia, 1 tablespoon water, vanilla, cinnamon, nutmeg, ground ginger, and sea salt into the inner pot of the Instant Pot. 2. Press the Sauté button on the Instant Pot and sauté the pecans and other ingredients until the pecans are soft. 3. Pour in the ½ cup water and secure the lid to the locked position. Set the vent to sealing. 4. Press Manual and set the Instant Pot for 15 minutes. 5. Preheat the oven to 350°F. 6. When cooking time is up, turn off the Instant Pot, then do a quick release. 7. Spread the pecans onto a greased, lined baking sheet. 8. Bake the pecans for 5 minutes or less in the oven, checking on them frequently so they do not burn.

Per Serving:

calories: 275 | fat: 28g | protein: 4g | carbs: 6g | sugars: 2g | fiber: 4g | sodium: 20mg

Green Goddess White Bean Dip

Prep time: 1 minutes | Cook time: 45 minutes |

Makes 3 cups

1 cup dried navy, great Northern, or cannellini beans
4 cups water
2 teaspoons fine sea salt
3 tablespoons fresh lemon juice
¼ cup extra-virgin olive oil,
plus 1 tablespoon
¼ cup firmly packed fresh flat-leaf parsley leaves
1 bunch chives, chopped
Leaves from 2 tarragon sprigs
Freshly ground black pepper

1. Combine the beans, water, and 1 teaspoon of the salt in the Instant Pot and stir to dissolve the salt. 2. Secure the lid and set the Pressure Release to Sealing. Select the Bean/Chili, Pressure Cook, or Manual setting and set the cooking time for 30 minutes at high pressure if using navy or Great Northern beans or 40 minutes at high pressure if using cannellini beans. (The pot will take about 15 minutes to come up to pressure before the cooking program begins.) 3. When the cooking program ends, let the pressure release naturally for 15 minutes, then move the Pressure Release to Venting to release any remaining steam. Open the pot and scoop out and reserve ½ cup of the cooking liquid. Wearing heat-resistant mitts, lift out the inner pot and drain the beans in a colander. 4. In a food processor or blender, combine the beans, ½ cup cooking liquid, lemon juice, ¼ cup olive oil, ½ teaspoon parsley, chives, tarragon, remaining 1 teaspoon salt, and ½ teaspoon pepper. Process or blend on medium speed, stopping to scrape down the sides of the container as needed, for about 1 minute, until the mixture is smooth. 5. Transfer the dip to a serving bowl. Drizzle with the remaining 1 tablespoon olive oil and sprinkle with a few grinds of pepper. The dip will keep in an airtight container in the refrigerator for up to 1 week. Serve at room temperature or chilled.

Per Serving:

calorie: 70 | fat: 5g | protein: 3g | carbs: 8g | sugars: 1g | fiber: 4g | sodium: 782mg

Chilled Shrimp

Prep time: 5 minutes | Cook time: 5 minutes | Serves 20

5 pounds jumbo shrimp, unshelled
¼ cup plus 2 tablespoons extra-virgin olive oil, divided
4 medium lemons, thinly sliced
3 tablespoons minced garlic
3 medium red onions, thinly sliced
½ cup minced parsley
Parsley sprigs (for garnish)

1. Preheat the oven to 400 degrees. Peel, and devein shrimp, leaving the tails intact. 2. Arrange the shrimp on a baking sheet and brush with 2 tablespoons of the olive oil. Bake the shrimp for 3 minutes or until they turn bright pink. 3. Place the lemon slices in a large bowl. Add the remaining ¼ cup of olive oil, garlic, onions, and minced parsley. Add the shrimp and toss vigorously to coat. Cover, and let marinate, refrigerated, for 6–8 hours. 4. Just before serving, arrange the shrimp on a serving platter. Garnish with parsley sprigs and some of the red onions and lemons from the bowl.

Per Serving:

calorie: 127 | fat: 3g | protein: 23g | carbs: 2g | sugars: 0g | fiber: 0g | sodium: 136mg

Fresh Dill Dip

Prep time: 5 minutes | Cook time: 5 minutes | Serves 6

1 cup plain fat-free yogurt
¼ teaspoon salt
¼ teaspoon freshly ground black pepper
¼ cup minced parsley
2 tablespoons finely chopped
fresh chives
1 tablespoon finely chopped fresh dill
1 tablespoon apple cider vinegar

1. In a small bowl, combine all the ingredients. Chill for 2–4 hours. Serve with fresh cut vegetables.

Per Serving:

calorie: 20 | fat: 0g | protein: 2g | carbs: 3g | sugars: 2g | fiber: 0g | sodium: 120mg

No-Bake Coconut and Cashew Energy Bars

Prep time: 5 minutes | Cook time: 0 minutes | Makes

12 energy bars

1 cup (110 g) raw cashews
1 cup (80 g) unsweetened shredded coconut
½ cup (120 g) unsweetened nut butter of choice
2 tbsp (30 ml) pure maple syrup

1. Line an 8 x 8–inch (20 x 20–cm) baking pan with parchment paper. 2. In a large food processor, combine the cashews and coconut. Pulse them for 15 to 20 seconds to form a powder. 3. Add the nut butter and maple syrup and process until a doughy paste is formed, scraping down the sides if needed. 4. Spread the dough into the prepared baking pan. Cover the dough with another sheet of parchment paper and press it flat. 5. Freeze the dough for 1 hour. Cut the dough into bars.

Per Serving:

calorie: 169 | fat: 14g | protein: 4g | carbs: 10g | sugars: 3g | fiber: 2g | sodium: 6mg

Cucumber Pâté

Prep time: 10 minutes | Cook time: 20 minutes | Serves 12

1 large cucumber, peeled, seeded, and quartered
1 small green bell pepper, seeded and quartered
3 stalks celery, quartered
1 medium onion, quartered
1 cup low-fat cottage cheese
½ cup plain nonfat Greek yogurt
1 package unflavored gelatin
¼ cup boiling water
¼ cup cold water

1. Spray a 5-cup mold or a 1½-quart mixing bowl with nonstick cooking spray. 2. In a food processor, coarsely chop the cucumber, green pepper, celery, and onion. Remove the vegetables from the food processor and set aside. 3. In a food processor, combine the cottage cheese and yogurt, and blend until smooth. 4. In a medium bowl, dissolve the gelatin in the boiling water; slowly stir in the cold water. Add the chopped vegetables and cottage cheese mixture, and mix thoroughly. 5. Pour the mixture into the prepared mold and refrigerate overnight or until firm. To serve, carefully invert the mold onto a serving plate, and remove the mold. Surround the pâté with assorted crackers, and serve.

Per Serving:

calorie: 57 | fat: 2g | protein: 6g | carbs: 3g | sugars: 2g | fiber: 1g | sodium: 107mg

Vietnamese Meatball Lollipops with Dipping Sauce

Prep time: 30 minutes | Cook time: 20 minutes | Serves 12

Meatballs
1 1/4 lb lean (at least 90%) ground turkey
1/4 cup chopped water chestnuts (from 8-oz can), drained
1/4 cup chopped fresh cilantro
1 tablespoon cornstarch
2 tablespoons fish sauce
1/2 teaspoon pepper
3 cloves garlic, finely chopped
Dipping Sauce
1/4 cup water
1/4 cup reduced-sodium soy sauce
2 tablespoons packed brown sugar
2 tablespoons chopped fresh chives or green onions
2 tablespoons lime juice
2 cloves garlic, finely chopped
1/2 teaspoon crushed red pepper
About 24 (6-inch) bamboo skewers

1 Heat oven to 400°F. Line cookie sheet with foil; spray with cooking spray (or use nonstick foil). 2 In large bowl, combine all meatball ingredients until well mixed. Shape into 1 1/4-inch meatballs. On cookie sheet, place meatballs 1 inch apart. Bake 20 minutes, turning halfway through baking, until thermometer inserted in center of meatballs reads at least 165°F. 3 Meanwhile, in 1-quart saucepan, heat all dipping sauce ingredients over low heat until sugar is dissolved; set aside. 4 Insert bamboo skewers into cooked meatballs; place on serving plate. Serve with warm dipping sauce.

Per Serving:

calorie: 80 | fat: 2g | protein: 10g | carbs: 5g | sugars: 3g | fiber: 0g | sodium: 440mg

Blackberry Baked Brie

Prep time: 5 minutes | Cook time: 15 minutes | Serves 5

8-ounce round Brie
1 cup water
¼ cup sugar-free blackberry
preserves
2 teaspoons chopped fresh mint

1. Slice a grid pattern into the top of the rind of the Brie with a knife. 2. In a 7-inch round baking dish, place the Brie, then cover the baking dish securely with foil. 3. Insert the trivet into the inner pot of the Instant Pot; pour in the water. 4. Make a foil sling and arrange it on top of the trivet. Place the baking dish on top of the trivet and foil sling. 5. Secure the lid to the locked position and turn the vent to sealing. 6. Press Manual and set the Instant Pot for 15 minutes on high pressure. 7. When cooking time is up, turn off the Instant Pot and do a quick release of the pressure. 8. When the valve has dropped, remove the lid, then remove the baking dish. 9. Remove the top rind of the Brie and top with the preserves. Sprinkle with the fresh mint.

Per Serving:

calorie: 133 | fat: 10g | protein: 8g | carbs: 4g | sugars: 0g | fiber: 0g | sodium: 238mg

Lemon Cream Fruit Dip

Prep time: 5 minutes | Cook time: 0 minutes | Serves 4

1 cup (200 g) plain nonfat Greek yogurt
¼ cup (28 g) coconut flour
1 tbsp (15 ml) pure maple syrup
½ tsp pure vanilla extract
½ tsp pure almond extract
Zest of 1 medium lemon
Juice of ½ medium lemon

1. In a medium bowl, whisk together the yogurt, coconut flour, maple syrup, vanilla, almond extract, lemon zest, and lemon juice. Serve the dip with fruit or crackers.

Per Serving:

calorie: 80 | fat: 1g | protein: 7g | carbs: 10g | sugars: 6g | fiber: 3g | sodium: 37mg

Ginger and Mint Dip with Fruit

Prep time: 20 minutes | Cook time: 0 minutes | Serves 6

Dip
1 1/4 cups plain fat-free yogurt
1/4 cup packed brown sugar
2 teaspoons chopped fresh mint leaves
2 teaspoons grated gingerroot
1/2 teaspoon grated lemon peel
Fruit Skewers
12 bamboo skewers (6 inch)
1 cup fresh raspberries
2 cups melon cubes (cantaloupe and/or honeydew)

1 In small bowl, mix dip ingredients with whisk until smooth. Cover; refrigerate at least 15 minutes to blend flavors. 2 On each skewer, alternately thread 3 raspberries and 2 melon cubes. Serve with dip.

Per Serving:

calories: 100 | fat: 0g | protein: 3g | carbs: 20g | sugars: 17g | fiber: 2g | sodium: 50mg

Blood Sugar–Friendly Nutty Trail Mix

Prep time: 5 minutes | Cook time: 0 minutes | Serves 4

¼ cup (31 g) raw shelled pistachios
¼ cup (30 g) raw pecans
¼ cup (43 g) raw almonds

¼ cup (38 g) raisins
¼ cup (45 g) dairy-free dark chocolate chips

1. In a medium bowl, combine the pistachios, pecans, almonds, raisins, and chocolate chips. 2. Divide the trail mix into four portions.

Per Serving:
calorie: 234 | fat: 17g | protein: 5g | carbs: 21g | sugars: 15g | fiber: 4g | sodium: 6mg

Baked Scallops

Prep time: 5 minutes | Cook time: 10 minutes | Serves 4

12 ounces fresh bay or dry sea scallops
1½ teaspoons salt-free pickling spices
½ cup cider vinegar
¼ cup water
1 tablespoon finely chopped

onion
1 red bell pepper, cut into thin strips
1 head butter lettuce, rinsed and dried
⅓ cup sesame seeds, toasted

1. Preheat the oven to 350 degrees. Wash the scallops in cool water, and cut any scallops that are too big in half. 2. Spread the scallops out in a large baking dish (be careful not to overlap them). In a small bowl, combine the spices, cider vinegar, water, onion, and pepper; pour the mixture over the scallops. Season with salt, if desired. 3. Cover the baking dish and bake for 7 minutes. Remove from the oven, and allow the scallops to chill in the refrigerator (leave them in the cooking liquid/vegetable mixture). 4. Just before serving, place the lettuce leaves on individual plates or a platter, and place the scallops and vegetables over the top. Sprinkle with sesame seeds before serving.

Per Serving:
calorie: 159 | fat: 8g | protein: 14g | carbs: 7g | sugars: 2g | fiber: 3g | sodium: 344mg

Ground Turkey Lettuce Cups

Prep time: 5 minutes | Cook time: 30 minutes | Serves 8

3 tablespoons water
2 tablespoons soy sauce, tamari, or coconut aminos
3 tablespoons fresh lime juice
2 teaspoons Sriracha, plus more for serving
2 tablespoons cold-pressed avocado oil
2 teaspoons toasted sesame oil
4 garlic cloves, minced
1-inch piece fresh ginger, peeled and minced
2 carrots, diced

2 celery stalks, diced
1 yellow onion, diced
2 pounds 93 percent lean ground turkey
½ teaspoon fine sea salt
Two 8-ounce cans sliced water chestnuts, drained and chopped
1 tablespoon cornstarch
2 hearts romaine lettuce or 2 heads butter lettuce, leaves separated
½ cup roasted cashews (whole or halves and pieces), chopped

1 cup loosely packed fresh   cilantro leaves

1. In a small bowl, combine the water, soy sauce, 2 tablespoons of the lime juice, and the Sriracha and mix well. Set aside. 2. Select the Sauté setting on the Instant Pot and heat the avocado oil, sesame oil, garlic, and ginger for 2 minutes, until the garlic is bubbling but not browned. Add the carrots, celery, and onion and sauté for about 3 minutes, until the onion begins to soften. 3. Add the turkey and salt and sauté, using a wooden spoon or spatula to break up the meat as it cooks, for about 5 minutes, until cooked through and no streaks of pink remain. Add the water chestnuts and soy sauce mixture and stir to combine, working quickly so not too much steam escapes. 4. Secure the lid and set the Pressure Release to Sealing. Press the Cancel button to reset the cooking program, then select the Pressure Cook or Manual setting and set the cooking time for 5 minutes at high pressure. (The pot will take about 10 minutes to come up to pressure before the cooking program begins.) 5. When the cooking program ends, perform a quick pressure release by moving the Pressure Release to Venting, or let the pressure release naturally. Open the pot. 6. In a small bowl, stir together the remaining 1 tablespoon lime juice and the cornstarch, add the mixture to the pot, and stir to combine. Press the Cancel button to reset the cooking program, then select the Sauté setting. Let the mixture come to a boil and thicken, stirring often, for about 2 minutes, then press the Cancel button to turn off the pot. 7. Spoon the turkey mixture onto the lettuce leaves and sprinkle the cashews and cilantro on top. Serve right away, with additional Sriracha at the table.

Per Serving:
calories: 127 | fat: 7g | protein: 6g | carbs: 10g | sugars: 2g | fiber: 3g | sodium: 392mg

Creamy Apple-Cinnamon Quesadilla

Prep time: 15 minutes | Cook time: 10 minutes | Serves 4

1 tablespoon granulated sugar
½ teaspoon ground cinnamon
¼ cup reduced-fat cream cheese (from 8-oz container)
1 tablespoon packed brown

sugar
2 whole wheat tortillas (8 inch)
½ small apple, cut into ¼-inch slices (½ cup)
Cooking spray

1 In small bowl, mix granulated sugar and ¼ teaspoon of the cinnamon; set aside. In another small bowl, mix cream cheese, brown sugar and remaining ¼ teaspoon cinnamon with spoon. 2 Spread cream cheese mixture over tortillas. Place apple slices on cream cheese mixture on 1 tortilla. Top with remaining tortilla, cheese side down. Spray both sides of quesadilla with cooking spray; sprinkle with cinnamon-sugar mixture. 3 Heat 10-inch nonstick skillet over medium heat. Add quesadilla; cook 2 to 3 minutes or until bottom is brown and crisp. Turn quesadilla; cook 2 to 3 minutes longer or until bottom is brown and crisp. 4 Transfer quesadilla from skillet to cutting board; let stand 2 to 3 minutes. Cut into 8 wedges to serve.

Per Serving:
calories: 110 | fat: 3g | protein: 3g | carbs: 19g | sugars: 9g | fiber: 2g | sodium: 170mg

Cucumber Roll-Ups

Prep time: 5 minutes | Cook time: 0 minutes | Serves 2 to 4

2 (6-inch) gluten-free wraps
2 tablespoons cream cheese
1 medium cucumber, cut into

long strips
2 tablespoons fresh mint

1. Place the wraps on your work surface and spread them evenly with the cream cheese. Top with the cucumber and mint. 2. Roll the wraps up from one side to the other, kind of like a burrito. Slice into 1-inch bites or keep whole. 3. Serve. 4. Store any leftovers in an airtight container in the refrigerator for 1 to 2 days.

Per Serving:
calorie: 70 | fat: 1g | protein: 4g | carbs: 12g | sugars: 3g | fiber: 2g | sodium: 183mg

Monterey Jack Cheese Quiche Squares

Prep time: 10 minutes | Cook time: 15 minutes | Serves 12

4 egg whites
1 cup plus 2 tablespoons low-fat cottage cheese
¼ cup plus 2 tablespoons flour
¾ teaspoon baking powder
1 cup shredded reduced-fat Monterey Jack cheese

½ cup diced green chilies
1 red bell pepper, diced
1 cup lentils, cooked
1 tablespoon extra-virgin olive oil
Parsley sprigs

1. Preheat the oven to 350 degrees. 2. In a medium bowl, beat the egg whites and cottage cheese for 2 minutes, until smooth. 3. Add the flour and baking powder, and beat until smooth. Stir in the cheese, green chilies, red pepper, and lentils. 4. Coat a 9-inch-square pan with the olive oil, and pour in the egg mixture. Bake for 30–35 minutes, until firm. 5. Remove the quiche from the oven, and allow to cool for 10 minutes (it will be easier to cut). Cut into 12 squares and transfer to a platter, garnish with parsley sprigs, and serve.

Per Serving:
calorie: 104 | fat: 6g | protein: 8g | carbs: 4g | sugars: 0g | fiber: 0g | sodium: 215mg

Creamy Spinach Dip

Prep time: 13 minutes | Cook time: 5 minutes | Serves 11

8 ounces low-fat cream cheese
1 cup low-fat sour cream
½ cup finely chopped onion
½ cup no-sodium vegetable broth
5 cloves garlic, minced
½ teaspoon salt

¼ teaspoon black pepper
10 ounces frozen spinach
12 ounces reduced-fat shredded Monterey Jack cheese
12 ounces reduced-fat shredded Parmesan cheese

1. Add cream cheese, sour cream, onion, vegetable broth, garlic, salt, pepper, and spinach to the inner pot of the Instant Pot. 2. Secure lid, make sure vent is set to sealing, and set to the Bean/Chili setting on high pressure for 5 minutes. 3. When done, do a manual release. 4. Add the cheeses and mix well until creamy and well combined.

Per Serving:
calorie: 274 | fat: 18g | protein: 19g | carbs: 10g | sugars: 3g | fiber: 1g | sodium: 948mg

Chicken Kabobs

Prep time: 5 minutes | Cook time: 20 minutes | Serves 6

1 pound boneless, skinless chicken breast
3 tablespoons light soy sauce
One 1-inch cube of fresh ginger root, finely chopped
3 tablespoons extra-virgin olive

oil
3 tablespoons dry vermouth
1 large clove garlic, finely chopped
12 watercress sprigs
2 large lemons, cut into wedges

1. Cut the chicken into 1-inch cubes and place in a shallow bowl. 2. In a small bowl, combine the soy sauce, ginger root, oil, vermouth, and garlic and pour over the chicken. Cover the chicken, and let marinate for at least 1 hour (or overnight). 3. Thread the chicken onto 12 metal or wooden skewers (remember to soak wooden skewers in water before using). Grill or broil 6 inches from the heat source for 8 minutes, turning frequently. 4. Arrange the skewers on a platter and garnish with the watercress and lemon wedges. Serve hot with additional soy sauce, if desired.

Per Serving:
calorie: 187 | fat: 10g | protein: 18g | carbs: 4g | sugars: 2g | fiber: 1g | sodium: 158mg

Porcupine Meatballs

Prep time: 20 minutes | Cook time: 15 minutes | Serves 8

1 pound ground sirloin or turkey
½ cup raw brown rice, parboiled
1 egg
¼ cup finely minced onion

1 or 2 cloves garlic, minced
¼ teaspoon dried basil and/or oregano, optional
10¾-ounce can reduced-fat condensed tomato soup
½ soup can of water

1. Mix all ingredients, except tomato soup and water, in a bowl to combine well. 2. Form into balls about 1½-inch in diameter. 3. Mix tomato soup and water in the inner pot of the Instant Pot, then add the meatballs. 4. Secure the lid and make sure the vent is turned to sealing. 5. Press the Meat button and set for 15 minutes on high pressure. 6. Allow the pressure to release naturally after cook time is up.

Per Serving:
calories: 141 | fat: 2g | protein: 16g | carbs: 14g | sugars: 3g | fiber: 1g | sodium: 176mg

Prep time: 5 minutes | Cook time: 4 minutes | Serves 11

8 ounces low-fat cream cheese
10-ounce box frozen spinach
½ cup no-sodium chicken broth
14-ounce can artichoke hearts, drained
½ cup low-fat sour cream

½ cup low-fat mayo
3 cloves of garlic, minced
1 teaspoon onion powder
16 ounces reduced-fat shredded Parmesan cheese
8 ounces reduced-fat shredded mozzarella

1. Put all ingredients in the inner pot of the Instant Pot, except the Parmesan cheese and the mozzarella cheese. 2. Secure the lid and set vent to sealing. Place on Manual high pressure for 4 minutes. 3. Do a quick release of steam. 4. Immediately stir in the cheeses.

Per Serving:

calories: 288 | fat: 18g | protein: 19g | carbs: 15g | sugars: 3g | fiber: 3g | sodium: 1007mg

Chapter 11 Vegetables and Sides

Caramelized Onions

Prep time: 10 minutes | Cook time: 35 minutes | Serves 8

4 tablespoons margarine
6 large Vidalia or other sweet onions, sliced into thin half

rings
10-ounce can chicken, or vegetable, broth

1. Press Sauté on the Instant Pot. Add in the margarine and let melt. 2. Once the margarine is melted, stir in the onions and sauté for about 5 minutes. Pour in the broth and then press Cancel. 3. Secure the lid and make sure vent is set to sealing. Press Manual and set time for 20 minutes. 4. When cook time is up, release the pressure manually. Remove the lid and press Sauté. Stir the onion mixture for about 10 more minutes, allowing extra liquid to cook off.

Per Serving:
calorie: 123 | fat: 6g | protein: 2g | carbs: 15g | sugars: 10g | fiber: 3g | sodium: 325mg

Golden Lemony Wax Beans

Prep time: 5 minutes | Cook time: 15 minutes | Serves 4

2 pounds wax beans
2 tablespoons extra-virgin olive oil

Sea salt
Freshly ground black pepper
Juice of ½ lemon

1. Preheat the oven to 400°F. 2. Line a baking sheet with aluminum foil. 3. In a large bowl, toss the beans and olive oil. Season lightly with salt and pepper. 4. Transfer the beans to the baking sheet and spread them out. 5. Roast the beans until caramelized and tender, about 10 to 12 minutes. 6. Transfer the beans to a serving platter and sprinkle with the lemon juice.

Per Serving:
calories: 99 | fat: 3.52g | protein: 4.21g | carbs: 16.32g | sugars: 7.55g | fiber: 6.2g | sodium: 219mg

Spinach and Sweet Pepper Poppers

Prep time: 10 minutes | Cook time: 8 minutes |
Makes 16 poppers

4 ounces (113 g) cream cheese, softened
1 cup chopped fresh spinach leaves

½ teaspoon garlic powder
8 mini sweet bell peppers, tops removed, seeded, and halved lengthwise

1. In a medium bowl, mix cream cheese, spinach, and garlic powder. Place 1 tablespoon mixture into each sweet pepper half and press down to smooth. 2. Place poppers into ungreased air fryer basket. Adjust the temperature to 400°F (204°C) and air fry for 8

minutes. Poppers will be done when cheese is browned on top and peppers are tender-crisp. Serve warm.

Per Serving:
calories: 31 | fat: 2g | protein: 1g | carbs: 3g | fiber: 0g | sodium: 34mg

Charred Sesame Broccoli

Prep time: 5 minutes | Cook time: 15 minutes | Serves 4

1 tablespoon extra-virgin olive oil
1 tablespoon low-sodium soy sauce

½ tablespoon sesame oil
1 head broccoli
1 tablespoon toasted sesame seeds

1. Preheat the oven to 450°F. Line a baking sheet with parchment paper. 2. In a medium bowl, whisk together the extra-virgin olive oil, soy sauce, and sesame oil. Add the broccoli and toss to evenly coat it. 3. Spread the coated broccoli on the prepared baking sheet and bake for 10 minutes, until tender. 4. Remove the sheet from the oven, flip the broccoli over, and return it to the oven for an additional 5 to 10 minutes. 5. Serve the broccoli with toasted sesame seeds on top. 6. Store any leftovers in an airtight container in the refrigerator for up to 4 days.

Per Serving:
calories: 174 | fat: 7.3g | protein: 10.25g | carbs: 23.31g | sugars: 5.81g | fiber: 9.2g | sodium: 252mg

Broccoli Salad

Prep time: 5 minutes | Cook time: 7 minutes | Serves 4

2 cups fresh broccoli florets, chopped
1 tablespoon olive oil
¼ teaspoon salt
⅛ teaspoon ground black

pepper
¼ cup lemon juice, divided
¼ cup shredded Parmesan cheese
¼ cup sliced roasted almonds

1. In a large bowl, toss broccoli and olive oil together. Sprinkle with salt and pepper, then drizzle with 2 tablespoons lemon juice. 2. Place broccoli into ungreased air fryer basket. Adjust the temperature to 350°F (177°C) and set the timer for 7 minutes, shaking the basket halfway through cooking. Broccoli will be golden on the edges when done. 3. Place broccoli into a large serving bowl and drizzle with remaining lemon juice. Sprinkle with Parmesan and almonds. Serve warm.

Per Serving:
calories: 76 | fat: 5g | protein: 3g | carbs: 5g | fiber: 1g | sodium: 273mg

Cauliflower "Mashed Potatoes"

Prep time: 5 minutes | Cook time: 0 minutes | Serves 2

2 cups cooked cauliflower florets
1 tablespoon plain nonfat Greek yogurt
½ teaspoon extra-virgin olive

oil
Salt, to season
Freshly ground black pepper, to season

1. To a food processor, add the cauliflower, yogurt, and olive oil. Process until smooth. 2. Season with salt and pepper before serving.

Per Serving:
calories: 50 | fat: 1.8g | protein: 3.93g | carbs: 6.37g | sugars: 3.07g | fiber: 3.1g | sodium: 606mg

Asparagus with Cashews

Prep time: 10 minutes | Cook time: 20 minutes | Serves 4

1 tablespoon extra-virgin olive oil
Sea salt

Freshly ground black pepper
½ cup chopped cashews
Zest and juice of 1 lime

1. Preheat the oven to 400°F and line a baking sheet with aluminum foil. 2. In a large bowl, toss the asparagus with the oil and lightly season with salt and pepper. 3. Transfer the asparagus to the baking sheet and bake until tender and lightly browned, 15 to 20 minutes. 4. Transfer the asparagus to a serving bowl and toss them with the chopped cashews, lime zest, and lime juice.

Per Serving:
calories: 123 | fat: 11g | protein: 3g | carbs: 6g | sugars: 1g | fiber: 1g | sodium: 148mg

Parmesan Cauliflower Mash

Prep time: 7 minutes | Cook time: 5 minutes | Serves 4

1 head cauliflower, cored and cut into large florets
½ teaspoon kosher salt
½ teaspoon garlic pepper
2 tablespoons plain Greek yogurt

¾ cup freshly grated Parmesan cheese
1 tablespoon unsalted butter or ghee (optional)
Chopped fresh chives

1. Pour 1 cup of water into the electric pressure cooker and insert a steamer basket or wire rack. 2. Place the cauliflower in the basket. 3. Close and lock the lid of the pressure cooker. Set the valve to sealing. 4. Cook on high pressure for 5 minutes. 5. When the cooking is complete, hit Cancel and quick release the pressure. 6. Once the pin drops, unlock and remove the lid. 7. Remove the cauliflower from the pot and pour out the water. Return the cauliflower to the pot and add the salt, garlic pepper, yogurt, and cheese. Use an immersion blender or potato masher to purée or mash the cauliflower in the pot. 8. Spoon into a serving bowl, and garnish with butter (if using) and chives.

Per Serving:
calories: 141 | fat: 6g | protein: 12g | carbs: 12g | sugars: 9g | fiber: 4g | sodium: 592mg

Roasted Delicata Squash

Prep time: 10 minutes | Cook time: 20 minutes | Serves 4

1 (1- to 1½-pound) delicata squash, halved, seeded, cut into ½-inch-thick strips
1 tablespoon extra-virgin olive oil

½ teaspoon dried thyme
¼ teaspoon salt
¼ teaspoon freshly ground black pepper

1. Preheat the oven to 400°F. Line a baking sheet with parchment paper. 2. In a large mixing bowl, toss the squash strips with the olive oil, thyme, salt, and pepper. Arrange on the prepared baking sheet in a single layer. 3. Roast for 10 minutes, flip, and continue to roast for 10 more minutes until tender and lightly browned.

Per Serving:
calories: 79 | fat: 4g | protein: 1g | carbs: 12g | sugars: 3g | fiber: 2g | sodium: 123mg

Italian Roasted Vegetables

Prep time: 15 minutes | Cook time: 20 minutes | Serves 4

2 tablespoons extra-virgin olive oil
2 teaspoons chopped fresh oregano
1 teaspoon chopped fresh basil
1 teaspoon minced garlic
½ pound whole cremini

mushrooms
2 cups cauliflower florets
1 zucchini, cut into 1-inch chunks
2 cups cherry tomatoes
Sea salt
Freshly ground black pepper

1. Preheat the oven to 400°F. Line a baking sheet with aluminum foil. 2. In a large bowl, stir together the oil, oregano, basil, and garlic. 3. Add the mushrooms, cauliflower, zucchini, and cherry tomatoes and toss to coat. 4. Transfer the vegetables to the baking sheet and roast until they are tender and lightly browned, about 20 minutes. 5. Season with salt and pepper and serve.

Per Serving:
calories: 297 | fat: 7.79g | protein: 8.18g | carbs: 58.58g | sugars: 12.81g | fiber: 9.9g | sodium: 182mg

Teriyaki Chickpeas

Prep time: 5 minutes | Cook time: 20 to 25 minutes |
Serves 7

2 cans (15 ounces each) chickpeas, rinsed and drained
1½ tablespoons tamari
1 tablespoon pure maple syrup

1 tablespoon lemon juice
½–¾ teaspoon garlic powder
½ teaspoon ground ginger
½ teaspoon blackstrap molasses

1. Preheat the oven to 450°F. Line a baking sheet with parchment paper. 2. In a large mixing bowl, combine the chickpeas, tamari, syrup, lemon juice, garlic powder, ginger, and molasses. Toss to combine. Spread evenly on the prepared baking sheet and bake for 20 to 25 minutes, or until the marinade is absorbed. Serve warm, or refrigerate to enjoy later.

Per Serving:
calorie: 120 | fat: 2 | protein: 6g | carbs: 20g | sugars: 5g | fiber: 5g | sodium: 382mg

Broiled Spinach

Prep time: 5 minutes | Cook time: 4 minutes | Serves 4

8 cups spinach, thoroughly washed and spun dry
1 tablespoon extra-virgin olive oil
¼ teaspoon ground cumin
Sea salt
Freshly ground black pepper

1. Preheat the broiler. Put an oven rack in the upper third of the oven. 2. Set a wire rack on a large baking sheet. 3. In a large bowl, massage the spinach, oil, and cumin together until all the leaves are well coated. 4. Spread half the spinach out on the rack, with as little overlap as possible. Season the greens lightly with salt and pepper. 5. Broil the spinach until the edges are crispy, about 2 minutes. 6. Remove the baking sheet from the oven and transfer the spinach to a large serving bowl. 7. Repeat with the remaining spinach. 8. Serve immediately.

Per Serving:
calories: 44 | fat: 3.64g | protein: 1.75g | carbs: 2.33g | sugars: 0.26g | fiber: 1.4g | sodium: 193mg

Sautéed Spinach with Parmesan and Almonds

Prep time: 5 minutes | Cook time: 5 minutes | Serves 2

2 teaspoons extra-virgin olive oil
2 tablespoons sliced almonds
2 garlic cloves, minced
2 (5-ounce) bags prewashed spinach
2 teaspoons balsamic vinegar
⅛ teaspoon salt
2 tablespoons soy Parmesan cheese
Freshly ground black pepper, to season

1. In a large nonstick skillet or Dutch oven set over medium-high heat, heat the olive oil. 2. Add the almonds and garlic. Cook for 30 seconds, stirring, or until fragrant. 3. Add the spinach. Cook for about 2 minutes, stirring, until just wilted. Remove the pan from the heat. 4. Stir in the balsamic vinegar and salt. 5. Sprinkle with the soy Parmesan cheese. Season with pepper and serve immediately.

Per Serving:
calories: 84 | fat: 6.62g | protein: 2.55g | carbs: 4.26g | sugars: 0.96g | fiber: 0.9g | sodium: 262mg

Broccoli with Pine Nuts

Prep time: 10 minutes | Cook time: 5 minutes | Serves 2

1 bunch broccoli rabe
4 cups water
1 cup broccoli florets
1 tablespoon extra-virgin olive oil
2 medium garlic cloves, minced
1 tablespoon freshly squeezed lemon juice
Salt, to season
Freshly ground black pepper, to season
2 tablespoons pine nuts

1. Rinse the broccoli rabe well in cold water to remove any dirt particles. Tear into stalks. Set aside. 2. In a saucepan set over high heat, bring the water to a boil. 3. Place a colander in the sink. Add the broccoli rabe pieces and broccoli florets. Pour the boiling water over them to scald. Drain well. Set aside. 4. In a sauté pan or skillet set over medium heat, heat the olive oil. 5. Add the garlic. Sauté for 1 minute, or until browned. 6. Add the broccoli rabe and broccoli florets. Toss to coat with the garlic. Cook for about 3 minutes, or until heated through. 7. Drizzle the vegetables with the lemon juice. Season with salt and pepper. 8. Top with the pine nuts and serve.

Per Serving:
calories: 152 | fat: 8.18g | protein: 9.78g | carbs: 10.95g | sugars: 1.59g | fiber: 6.5g | sodium: 724mg

Roasted Peppers and Eggplant

Prep time: 5 minutes | Cook time: 20 minutes | Serves 2

Extra-virgin olive oil cooking spray
1 small eggplant, halved and sliced
1 red bell pepper, cut into thick strips
1 yellow bell pepper, cut into thick strips
1 red onion, sliced
2 garlic cloves, quartered
1 tablespoon extra-virgin olive oil
Salt, to season
Freshly ground black pepper, to season
½ cup chopped fresh basil

1. Preheat the oven to 350°F. 2. Coat a nonstick baking dish with cooking spray. 3. To the prepared dish, add the eggplant, red bell pepper, yellow bell pepper, onion, and garlic. Drizzle with the olive oil. Toss to coat well. Spray any uncoated surfaces with cooking spray. 4. Place the dish in the preheated oven. Bake for 20 minutes, turning once halfway through cooking. 5. Transfer the vegetables to a serving dish. Season with salt and pepper. 6. Garnish with the basil and serve.

Per Serving:
calories: 185 | fat: 10.52g | protein: 3.88g | carbs: 22.17g | sugars: 12.42g | fiber: 10g | sodium: 651mg

Zucchini Noodles with Lime-Basil Pesto

Prep time: 20 minutes | Cook time: 0 minutes | Serves 4

2 cups packed fresh basil leaves
½ cup pine nuts
2 teaspoons minced garlic
Zest and juice of 1 lime
Pinch sea salt
Pinch freshly ground black
pepper
¼ cup extra-virgin olive oil
4 green or yellow zucchini, rinsed, dried, and julienned or spiralized
1 tomato, diced

1. Place the basil, pine nuts, garlic, lime zest, lime juice, salt, and pepper in a food processor or a blender and pulse until very finely chopped. 2. While the machine is running, add the olive oil in a thin stream until a thick paste forms. 3. In a large bowl, combine the zucchini noodles and tomato. Add the pesto by the tablespoonful until you have the desired flavor. Serve the zucchini pasta immediately. 4. Store any leftover pesto in a sealed container in the refrigerator for up to 2 weeks.

Per Serving:
calories: 247 | fat: 25.18g | protein: 3.17g | carbs: 5.39g | sugars: 1.62g | fiber: 1.3g | sodium: 148mg

Chunky Red Pepper and Tomato Sauce

Prep time: 5 minutes | Cook time: 40 minutes | Makes 2½ cups

3 large red bell peppers, halved lengthwise, seeded, pressed open to flatten
2 tablespoons extra-virgin olive oil, plus additional for brushing the peppers
1 medium onion, minced
1½ teaspoons dried basil
1 teaspoon dried rosemary
½ teaspoon dried oregano
½ teaspoon salt
½ cup low-sodium vegetable broth
2 cups water
½ cup tomato purée
1 tablespoon tomato paste
2 teaspoons white wine vinegar
2 tablespoons chopped fresh basil leaves

1. Preheat the broiler to high. 2. Brush the red bell peppers with olive oil. Place them under the broiler, skin-side up. Cook for about 10 minutes, or until lightly charred. Transfer the peppers to a cutting board, stacking one on top of the other to create steam. Let sit for 10 minutes. Remove as much charred skin as possible. Slice into strips. 3. In a large skillet set over medium-high heat, heat the remaining 2 tablespoons of olive oil. 4. Add the red pepper strips, onion, basil, rosemary, oregano, and salt. Cook for 5 minutes, stirring. 5. Add the vegetable broth. Cook for about 15 minutes more, or until the mixture reduces to a sauce. 6. Add the water, tomato purée, and tomato paste. Reduce the heat to low. Simmer for 25 minutes. 7. Transfer the mixture to a food processor. Purée until smooth, but with some texture remaining. 8. Place the skillet back over low heat. Return the sauce to the skillet. Barely simmer for 1 to 2 minutes to rewarm. Stir in the white wine vinegar and basil. Serve warm. 9. Refrigerate any remaining sauce. Serve chilled or rewarmed, as desired.

Per Serving:
calories: 246 | fat: 14.67g | protein: 4.47g | carbs: 25.9g | sugars: 16.42g | fiber: 7.6g | sodium: 641mg

Summer Squash Casserole

Prep time: 15 minutes | Cook time: 30 minutes | Serves 8

1 tablespoon extra-virgin olive oil
6 yellow summer squash, thinly sliced
1 large portobello mushroom, thinly sliced
1 Vidalia onion, thinly sliced
1 cup shredded Parmesan
cheese, divided
1 cup shredded reduced-fat extra-sharp Cheddar cheese
½ cup whole-wheat bread crumbs
½ cup tri-color quinoa
1 tablespoon Creole seasoning

1. Preheat the oven to 350°F. 2. In a large cast iron pan, heat the oil over medium heat. 3. Add the squash, mushroom, and onion, and sauté for 7 to 10 minutes, or until softened. 4. Remove from the heat. Add ½ cup of Parmesan cheese and the Cheddar cheese and mix well. 5. In a small bowl, whisk the bread crumbs, quinoa, the remaining ½ cup of Parmesan, and the Creole seasoning together. Evenly distribute over the casserole. 6. Transfer the pan to the oven, and bake for 20 minutes, or until browned. Serve warm and enjoy.

Per Serving:
calories: 163 | fat: 7.2g | protein: 10.08g | carbs: 14.45g | sugars: 0.53g | fiber: 1.7g | sodium: 484mg

Fennel and Chickpeas

Prep time: 10 minutes | Cook time: 20 minutes | Serves 6

1 tablespoon extra-virgin olive oil
1 small fennel bulb, trimmed and cut into ¼-inch-thick slices
1 sweet onion, thinly sliced
1 (15½-ounce) can sodium-free chickpeas, rinsed and drained
1 cup low-sodium chicken
broth
2 teaspoons chopped fresh thyme
¼ teaspoon sea salt
¼ teaspoon freshly ground black pepper
1 tablespoon butter

1. Place a large saucepan over medium-high heat and add the oil. 2. Sauté the fennel and onion until tender and lightly browned, about 10 minutes. 3. Add the chickpeas, broth, thyme, salt, and pepper. 4. Cover and cook, stirring occasionally, for 10 minutes, until the liquid has reduced by about half. 5. Remove the pan from the heat and stir in the butter. 6. Serve hot.

Per Serving:
calories: 132 | fat: 5.59g | protein:4.75 g | carbs: 17.31g | sugars: 6.05g | fiber: 4.4g | sodium: 239mg

Soft-Baked Tamari Tofu

Prep time: 5 minutes | Cook time: 20 to 25 minutes | Serves 4

3 tablespoons tamari
1 package (16 ounces) medium-
firm tofu

1. Preheat the oven to 425°F. In an ovenproof dish just large enough to hold the tofu, add about half of the tamari. Use several paper towels to pat or squeeze some of the excess moisture from the tofu. Add the tofu to the dish, breaking it up slightly. Sprinkle the remaining tamari over the tofu. Bake for 20 to 25 minutes, or until the tofu is browned and drying in spots. Serve, spooning out tofu with some of the remaining tamari.

Per Serving:
calorie: 87 | fat: 5g | protein: 10g | carbs: 3g | sugars: 1g | fiber: 1g | sodium: 768mg

Sweet-and-Sour Cabbage Slaw

Prep time: 10 minutes | Cook time: 0 minutes | Serves 2

2 tablespoons apple cider vinegar
1 tablespoon granulated stevia
2 cups angel hair cabbage
1 tart apple, cored and diced
½ cup shredded carrot
2 medium scallions, sliced
2 tablespoons sliced almonds

1. In a medium bowl, stir together the vinegar and stevia. 2. In a large bowl, mix together the cabbage, apple, carrot, and scallions. 3. Pour the sweetened vinegar over the vegetable mixture. Toss to combine. 4. Garnish with the sliced almonds and serve.

Per Serving:
calories: 125 | fat: 0.99g | protein: 2.29g | carbs: 29.51g | sugars: 20.87g | fiber: 5.4g | sodium: 47mg

Chinese Asparagus

Prep time: 5 minutes | Cook time: 5 minutes | Serves 4

1 pound asparagus	2 teaspoons cornstarch
½ cup plus 1 tablespoon water, divided	1 tablespoon canola oil
1 tablespoon light soy sauce	2 teaspoons grated fresh ginger
1 tablespoon rice vinegar	1 scallion, minced

1. Trim the tough ends off the asparagus. Cut the stalks diagonally into 2-inch pieces. 2. In a small bowl, combine the ½ cup water, soy sauce, and rice vinegar. 3. In a measuring cup, combine the cornstarch and 1 tablespoon water. Set aside. 4. Heat the oil in a wok or skillet. Add the ginger and scallions, and stir-fry for 30 seconds. Add the asparagus and stir-fry for a few seconds more. Add the broth mixture, and bring to a boil. Cover, and simmer for 3–5 minutes, until the asparagus is just tender. 5. Add the cornstarch mixture, and cook until thickened. Serve.

Per Serving:

calories: 73 | fat: 4.37g | protein: 2.87g | carbs: 7.09g | sugars: 3.02g | fiber: 2.6g | sodium: 64mg

Avocado Slaw

Prep time: 15 minutes | Cook time: 0 minutes | Serves 4 to 6

1 avocado	4 cups packed shredded cabbage (red, green, or mixed)
⅓ cup water	2 cups shredded carrot
3 tablespoons apple cider vinegar	Kosher salt
1 tablespoon Dijon mustard	Freshly ground black pepper

1. Place the avocado, water, vinegar, and mustard in a blender and puree until smooth. Add water if needed until you've reached a thin consistency, making the dressing easy to toss with the shredded vegetables. 2. In a large bowl, toss the cabbage and carrot with the dressing. Season to taste with salt and pepper and serve. 3. Store any leftovers in an airtight container in the refrigerator for up to 3 days.

Per Serving:

calories: 137 | fat: 7.79g | protein: 2.29g | carbs: 16.81g | sugars: 6.43g | fiber: 7.1g | sodium: 400mg

Teriyaki Green Beans

Prep time: 15 minutes | Cook time: 20 minutes | Serves 4

10 oz (283 g) button mushrooms, thinly sliced	½ tsp smoked paprika
1 tbsp (15 ml) sesame oil, divided	2 cloves garlic, minced
2 tbsp (30 ml) low-sodium tamari, divided	1 lb (454 g) fresh green beans, trimmed and washed
	1 cup (165 g) finely chopped fresh pineapple

1. In a large bowl, combine the mushrooms with ½ tablespoon (8 ml) of the oil, 1½ tablespoons (23 ml) of the tamari, and the smoked paprika. Let the mushrooms rest for 10 minutes to allow them to absorb the marinade. 2. If you will be roasting the mushrooms, preheat the oven to 400°F (204°C) while the mushrooms marinate. Line a large baking sheet with parchment paper. 3. Spread out the mushrooms on the prepared baking sheet. Roast them for 20 minutes, or until they are very crispy. 4. Alternatively, if you will be stir-frying the mushrooms, heat a small skillet over medium heat. Add the mushrooms and stir-fry them for about 5 minutes, until they are tender. Note that this cooking method will yield mushrooms that are less crispy than roasting, but they will still be delicious. Meanwhile, heat the remaining ½ tablespoon (8 ml) of oil in a large skillet over medium-high heat. Add the garlic and cook it for 2 minutes, or until it is brown and fragrant. Add the green beans and pineapple. Cook the mixture for 10 minutes, until the green beans are bright green and starting to soften. Add the crispy mushrooms to the skillet. Stir to combine, then serve.

Per Serving:

calorie: 106 | fat: 3g | protein: 6g | carbs: 17g | sugars: 9g | fiber: 5g | sodium: 257mg

Lemon-Garlic Mushrooms

Prep time: 10 minutes | Cook time: 10 to 15 minutes | Serves 6

12 ounces (340 g) sliced mushrooms	1 teaspoon minced garlic
1 tablespoon avocado oil	1 teaspoon freshly squeezed lemon juice
Sea salt and freshly ground black pepper, to taste	½ teaspoon red pepper flakes
3 tablespoons unsalted butter	2 tablespoons chopped fresh parsley

1. Place the mushrooms in a medium bowl and toss with the oil. Season to taste with salt and pepper. 2. Place the mushrooms in a single layer in the air fryer basket. Set your air fryer to 375°F (191°C) and roast for 10 to 15 minutes, until the mushrooms are tender. 3. While the mushrooms cook, melt the butter in a small pot or skillet over medium-low heat. Stir in the garlic and cook for 30 seconds. Remove the pot from the heat and stir in the lemon juice and red pepper flakes. 4. Toss the mushrooms with the lemon-garlic butter and garnish with the parsley before serving.

Per Serving:

calories: 72| fat: 6g | protein: 2g | carbs: 3g | net carbs: 2g | fiber: 1g

"Honey" Mustard Sauce

Prep time: 5 minutes | Cook time: 0 minutes | Makes ½ cup

½ cup plain nonfat Greek yogurt	1 teaspoon dry mustard
1 tablespoon apple cider vinegar	¾ teaspoon garlic powder
	⅛ teaspoon paprika
	1 tablespoon granulated stevia

1. In a small bowl, whisk together the yogurt, apple cider vinegar, dry mustard, garlic powder, paprika, and stevia until smooth. 2. Refrigerate until needed.

Per Serving:

calories: 101 | fat: 0.48g | protein: 7.23g | carbs: 17.1g | sugars: 14.77g | fiber: 0.5g | sodium: 81mg

Garlic Roasted Radishes

Prep time: 5 minutes | Cook time: 15 minutes |

Serves 2 to 4

1 pound radishes, halved	4 garlic cloves, thinly sliced
1 tablespoon canola oil	¼ cup chopped fresh dill
Pinch kosher salt	

1. Preheat the oven to 425°F. Line a baking sheet with parchment paper. 2. In a medium bowl, toss the radishes with the canola oil and salt. Spread the vegetables on the prepared baking sheet and roast for 10 minutes. Remove the sheet from the oven, add the garlic, mix well, and return to the oven for 5 minutes. 3. Remove the radishes from the oven, adjust the seasoning as desired, and serve topped with dill on a serving plate or as a side dish. 4. Store any leftovers in an airtight container in the refrigerator for 3 to 4 days.

Per Serving:

calories: 75 | fat: 4.85g | protein: 1.19g | carbs: 7.57g | sugars: 3.82g | fiber: 2.5g | sodium: 420mg

Radish Chips

Prep time: 10 minutes | Cook time: 5 minutes | Serves 4

2 cups water	½ teaspoon garlic powder
1 pound (454 g) radishes	2 tablespoons coconut oil,
¼ teaspoon onion powder	melted
¼ teaspoon paprika	

1. Place water in a medium saucepan and bring to a boil on stovetop. 2. Remove the top and bottom from each radish, then use a mandoline to slice each radish thin and uniformly. You may also use the slicing blade in the food processor for this step. 3. Place the radish slices into the boiling water for 5 minutes or until translucent. Remove them from the water and place them into a clean kitchen towel to absorb excess moisture. 4. Toss the radish chips in a large bowl with remaining ingredients until fully coated in oil and seasoning. Place radish chips into the air fryer basket. 5. Adjust the temperature to 320ºF (160ºC) and air fry for 5 minutes. 6. Shake the basket two or three times during the cooking time. Serve warm.

Per Serving:

calories: 81 | fat: 7g | protein: 1g | carbs: 5g | fiber: 2g | sodium: 27mg

Green Bean and Radish Potato Salad

Prep time: 10 minutes | Cook time: 20 minutes |

Serves 6

Kosher salt	lemon juice
6 ounces fresh green beans, trimmed and cut into 1-inch pieces	1 tablespoon Dijon or whole-grain mustard
1½ pounds fingerling potatoes	1 shallot, minced
⅓ cup extra-virgin olive oil	8 radishes, thinly sliced
2 tablespoons freshly squeezed	¼ cup fresh dill, chopped
	Freshly ground black pepper

1. Place a small saucepan filled three-quarters full of water and a pinch of salt over high heat and bring it to a boil. Add the green beans and boil for 2 minutes, then transfer them with a slotted spoon to a colander. Run the beans under cold running water until cool and transfer to a medium bowl. 2. Place the potatoes in the same pot of boiling water, reduce the heat to low, and simmer until tender, about 12 minutes. 3. Meanwhile, combine the extra-virgin olive oil, lemon juice, mustard, and shallot in a jar. Seal with the lid and shake vigorously. If you don't have a jar with a fitted lid, you can also whisk the ingredients in a bowl. 4. Transfer the cooked potatoes to a colander and cool them under cold running water. When they're cool enough to handle, slice the potatoes into thin rounds. 5. Add the potatoes and dressing to the bowl with the green beans, along with the radishes and dill, and toss to combine. 6. Season with salt and pepper and serve. 7. Store any leftovers in an airtight container in the refrigerator for 3 to 4 days.

Per Serving:

calories: 206 | fat: 12.18g | protein: 2.86g | carbs: 22.67g | sugars: 1.3g | fiber: 3.3g | sodium: 202mg

Ginger Broccoli

Prep time: 10 minutes | Cook time: 10 minutes |

Serves 4

1 tablespoon extra-virgin olive oil	florets
½ sweet onion, thinly sliced	¼ cup low-sodium chicken broth
2 teaspoons grated fresh ginger	Sea salt
1 teaspoon minced fresh garlic	Freshly ground black pepper
2 heads broccoli, cut into small	

1. Place a large skillet over medium-high heat and add the oil. 2. Sauté the onion, ginger, and garlic until softened, about 3 minutes. 3. Add the broccoli florets and chicken broth, and sauté until the broccoli is tender, about 5 minutes. 4. Season with salt and pepper. 5. Serve immediately.

Per Serving:

calories: 240 | fat: 6g | protein: 17g | carbs: 41g | sugars: 12g | fiber: 15g | sodium: 341mg

Zucchini Sauté

Prep time: 5 minutes | Cook time: 10 minutes | Serves 4

1 tablespoon olive oil	thick rounds
1 medium red onion, finely chopped	¼ teaspoon dried oregano
3 medium zucchini (about 5–6 ounces each), cut into ¼-inch	⅛ teaspoon salt
	⅛ teaspoon freshly ground black pepper

1. In a large skillet over medium heat, heat the oil. Add the onion, and sauté until the onion is translucent but not browned. 2. Add the zucchini, cover, and simmer 3–4 minutes. Sprinkle with the oregano, salt, and pepper, and serve hot.

Per Serving:

calories: 43 | fat: 3.44g | protein: 0.54g | carbs: 2.94g | sugars: 1.17g | fiber: 0.6g | sodium: 79mg

Corn on the Cob

Prep time: 5 minutes | Cook time: 12 to 15 minutes | Serves 4

2 large ears fresh corn
Olive oil for misting

Salt, to taste (optional)

1. Shuck corn, remove silks, and wash. 2. Cut or break each ear in half crosswise. 3. Spray corn with olive oil. 4. Air fry at 390ºF (199ºC) for 12 to 15 minutes or until browned as much as you like. 5. Serve plain or with coarsely ground salt.

Per Serving:
calories: 67 | fat: 1g | protein: 2g | carbs: 14g | fiber: 2g | sodium: 156mg

Roasted Beets, Carrots, and Parsnips

Prep time: 10 minutes | Cook time: 30 minutes | Serves 4

1 pound beets, peeled and quartered
½ pound carrots, peeled and cut into chunks
½ pound parsnips, peeled and cut into chunks

1 tablespoon extra-virgin olive oil
1 teaspoon apple cider vinegar
Sea salt
Freshly ground black pepper

1. Preheat the oven to 375°F. Line a baking tray with aluminum foil. 2. In a large bowl, toss the beets, carrots, and parsnips with the oil and vinegar until everything is well coated. Spread them out on the baking sheet. 3. Roast until the vegetables are tender and lightly caramelized, about 30 minutes. 4. Transfer the vegetables to a serving bowl, season with salt and pepper, and serve warm.

Per Serving:
calories: 122 | fat: 3.84g | protein: 3.73g | carbs: 20.75g | sugars: 5.98g | fiber: 8.6g | sodium: 592mg

Lemony Brussels Sprouts with Poppy Seeds

Prep time: 10 minutes | Cook time: 2 minutes | Serves 4

1 pound (454 g) Brussels sprouts
2 tablespoons avocado oil, divided
1 cup vegetable broth or chicken bone broth

1 tablespoon minced garlic
½ teaspoon kosher salt
Freshly ground black pepper, to taste
½ medium lemon
½ tablespoon poppy seeds

1. Trim the Brussels sprouts by cutting off the stem ends and removing any loose outer leaves. Cut each in half lengthwise (through the stem). 2. Set the electric pressure cooker to the Sauté/More setting. When the pot is hot, pour in 1 tablespoon of the avocado oil. 3. Add half of the Brussels sprouts to the pot, cut-side down, and let them brown for 3 to 5 minutes without disturbing. Transfer to a bowl and add the remaining tablespoon of avocado oil and the remaining Brussels sprouts to the pot. Hit Cancel and return all of the Brussels sprouts to the pot. 4. Add the broth, garlic, salt, and a few grinds of pepper. Stir to distribute the seasonings. 5. Close and lock the lid of the pressure cooker. Set the valve to sealing. 6. Cook on high pressure for 2 minutes. 7. While the Brussels sprouts are cooking, zest the lemon, then cut it into quarters. 8. When the cooking is complete, hit Cancel and quick release the pressure. 9. Once the pin drops, unlock and remove the lid. 10. Using a slotted spoon, transfer the Brussels sprouts to a serving bowl. Toss with the lemon zest, a squeeze of lemon juice, and the poppy seeds. Serve immediately.

Per Serving:
calories: 125 | fat: 8g | protein: 4g | carbs: 13g | sugars: 3g | fiber: 5g | sodium: 504mg

Mushroom Cassoulets

Prep time: 5 minutes | Cook time: 30 minutes | Serves 6

1 pound mushrooms, sliced
½ cup lentils, cooked
1 medium onion, chopped
1 cup low-sodium chicken broth
1 sprig thyme
1 bay leaf

Leaves from 1 celery stalk
2 tablespoons lemon juice
⅛ teaspoon freshly ground black pepper
½ cup wheat germ
2 tablespoons extra-virgin olive oil

1. Preheat the oven to 350 degrees. 2. In a saucepan, combine the mushrooms, lentils, onion, and chicken broth. Tie together the thyme, bay leaf, and celery leaves and add to the mushrooms. 3. Add the lemon juice and pepper, and bring to a boil. Boil until the liquid is reduced, about 10 minutes. Remove the bundle of herbs. 4. Divide the mushroom mixture equally into small ramekins. Mix the wheat germ and oil together, and sprinkle on top of each casserole. 5. Bake at 350 degrees for 20 minutes or until the tops are golden brown. Remove from the oven, and let cool slightly before serving. Add salt if desired.

Per Serving:
calories: 114 | fat: 6.01g | protein: 6.19g | carbs: 11.63g | sugars: 2.49g | fiber: 2.5g | sodium: 21mg

Garlicky Cabbage and Collard Greens

Prep time: 10 minutes | Cook time: 10 minutes | Serves 8

2 tablespoons extra-virgin olive oil
1 collard greens bunch, stemmed and thinly sliced
½ small green cabbage, thinly

sliced
6 garlic cloves, minced
1 tablespoon low-sodium gluten-free soy sauce or tamari

1. In a large skillet, heat the oil over medium-high heat. 2. Add the collards to the pan, stirring to coat with oil. Sauté for 1 to 2 minutes until the greens begin to wilt. 3. Add the cabbage and stir to coat. Cover and reduce the heat to medium low. Continue to cook for 5 to 7 minutes, stirring once or twice, until the greens are tender. 4. Add the garlic and soy sauce and stir to incorporate. Cook until just fragrant, about 30 seconds longer. Serve warm and enjoy!

Per Serving:
calories: 72| fat: 4g | protein: 3g | carbs: 6g | sugars: 0g | fiber: 3g | sodium: 129mg

Sun-Dried Tomato Brussels Sprouts

Prep time: 15 minutes | Cook time: 20 minutes | Serves 4

1 pound Brussels sprouts, trimmed and halved	½ cup sun-dried tomatoes, chopped
1 tablespoon extra-virgin olive oil	2 tablespoons freshly squeezed lemon juice
Sea salt	1 teaspoon lemon zest
Freshly ground black pepper	

1. Preheat the oven to 400°F. Line a large baking sheet with aluminum foil. 2. In a large bowl, toss the Brussels sprouts with oil and season with salt and pepper. 3. Spread the Brussels sprouts on the baking sheet in a single layer. 4. Roast the sprouts until they are caramelized, about 20 minutes. 5. Transfer the sprouts to a serving bowl. Mix in the sun-dried tomatoes, lemon juice, and lemon zest. 6. Stir to combine, and serve.

Per Serving:

calories: 98 | fat: 3.94g | protein: 4.83g | carbs: 14.62g | sugars: 5.26g | fiber: 5.2g | sodium: 191mg

Wild Rice Salad with Cranberries and Almonds

Prep time: 10 minutes | Cook time: 25 minutes | Serves 18

For the rice	Juice of 1 medium orange (about ¼ cup)
2 cups wild rice blend, rinsed	1 teaspoon honey or pure maple syrup
1 teaspoon kosher salt	For the salad
2½ cups Vegetable Broth or Chicken Bone Broth	¾ cup unsweetened dried cranberries
For the dressing	½ cup sliced almonds, toasted
¼ cup extra-virgin olive oil	Freshly ground black pepper
¼ cup white wine vinegar	
1½ teaspoons grated orange zest	

Make the Rice 1. In the electric pressure cooker, combine the rice, salt, and broth. 2. Close and lock the lid. Set the valve to sealing. 3. Cook on high pressure for 25 minutes. 4. When the cooking is complete, hit Cancel and allow the pressure to release naturally for 15 minutes, then quick release any remaining pressure. 5. Once the pin drops, unlock and remove the lid. 6. Let the rice cool briefly, then fluff it with a fork. Make the Dressing 7. While the rice cooks, make the dressing: In a small jar with a screw-top lid, combine the olive oil, vinegar, zest, juice, and honey. (If you don't have a jar, whisk the ingredients together in a small bowl.) Shake to combine. Make the Salad 8. In a large bowl, combine the rice, cranberries, and almonds. 9. Add the dressing and season with pepper. 10. Serve warm or refrigerate.

Per Serving:

calories: 129 | fat: 4.25g | protein: 3.46g | carbs: 20.34g | sugars: 5.08g | fiber: 1.7g | sodium: 200mg

Simple Bibimbap

Prep time: 15 minutes | Cook time: 15 minutes | Serves 2

4 teaspoons canola oil, divided	sliced
2½ cups cauliflower rice	2 large eggs
2 cups fresh baby spinach	1 cup bean sprouts, rinsed
3 teaspoons low-sodium soy sauce or tamari, divided	1 cup kimchi
8 ounces mushrooms, thinly	½ cup shredded carrots

1. Heat 1 teaspoon of canola oil in a medium skillet and sauté the cauliflower rice, spinach, and 2 teaspoons of soy sauce until the greens are wilted, about 5 minutes. Put the vegetables in a small bowl and set aside. 2. Return the skillet to medium heat, add 2 teaspoons of vegetable oil and, when it's hot, add the mushrooms in a single layer and cook for 3 to 5 minutes, then stir and cook another 3 minutes or until mostly golden-brown in color. Put the mushrooms in a small bowl and toss them with the remaining 1 teaspoon of soy sauce. 3. Wipe out the skillet and heat the remaining 1 teaspoon of vegetable oil over low heat. Crack in the eggs and cook until the whites are set and the yolks begin to thicken but not harden, 4 to 5 minutes. 4. Assemble two bowls with cauliflower rice and spinach at the bottom. Then arrange each ingredient separately around the rim of the bowl: bean sprouts, mushrooms, kimchi, and shredded carrots, with the egg placed in the center, and serve.

Per Serving:

calories: 275 | fat: 15.83g | protein: 19.66g | carbs: 20.43g | sugars: 8.04g | fiber: 8.1g | sodium: 518mg

Curry Roasted Cauliflower

Prep time: 10 minutes | Cook time: 20 minutes | Serves 4

¼ cup olive oil	1 head cauliflower, cut into bite-size florets
2 teaspoons curry powder	½ red onion, sliced
½ teaspoon salt	2 tablespoons freshly chopped parsley, for garnish (optional)
¼ teaspoon freshly ground black pepper	

1. Preheat the air fryer to 400°F (204ºC). 2. In a large bowl, combine the olive oil, curry powder, salt, and pepper. Add the cauliflower and onion. Toss gently until the vegetables are completely coated with the oil mixture. Transfer the vegetables to the basket of the air fryer. 3. Pausing about halfway through the cooking time to shake the basket, air fry for 20 minutes until the cauliflower is tender and beginning to brown. Top with the parsley, if desired, before serving.

Per Serving:

calories: 141 | fat: 14g | protein: 2g | carbs: 4g | fiber: 2g | sodium: 312mg

Chapter 12 Vegetarian Mains

Spinach Salad with Eggs, Tempeh Bacon, and Strawberries

Prep time: 10 minutes | Cook time: 15 minutes | Serves 4

2 tablespoons soy sauce, tamari, or coconut aminos
1 tablespoon raw apple cider vinegar
1 tablespoon pure maple syrup
½ teaspoon smoked paprika
Freshly ground black pepper
One 8-ounce package tempeh, cut crosswise into ⅛-inch-thick slices
8 large eggs

3 tablespoons extra-virgin olive oil
1 shallot, minced
1 tablespoon red wine vinegar
1 tablespoon balsamic vinegar
1 teaspoon Dijon mustard
¼ teaspoon fine sea salt
One 6-ounce bag baby spinach
2 hearts romaine lettuce, torn into bite-size pieces
12 fresh strawberries, sliced

1. In a 1-quart ziplock plastic bag, combine the soy sauce, cider vinegar, maple syrup, paprika, and ½ teaspoon pepper and carefully agitate the bag to mix the ingredients to make a marinade. Add the tempeh, seal the bag, and turn the bag back and forth several times to coat the tempeh evenly with the marinade. Marinate in the refrigerator for at least 2 hours or up to 24 hours. 2. Pour 1 cup water into the Instant Pot and place the wire metal steam rack, an egg rack, or a steamer basket into the pot. Gently place the eggs on top of the rack or in the basket, taking care not to crack them. 3. Secure the lid and set the Pressure Release to Sealing. Select the Steam setting and set the cooking time for 3 minutes at high pressure. (The pot will take about 5 minutes to come up to pressure before the cooking program begins.) 4. While the eggs are cooking, prepare an ice bath. 5. When the cooking program ends, perform a quick pressure release by moving the Pressure Release to Venting. Open the pot and, using tongs, transfer the eggs to the ice bath to cool. 6. Remove the tempeh from the marinade and blot dry between layers of paper towels. Discard the marinade. In a large nonstick skillet over medium-high heat, warm 1 tablespoon of the oil for 2 minutes. Add the tempeh in a single layer and fry, turning once, for 2 to 3 minutes per side, until well browned. Transfer the tempeh to a plate and set aside. 7. Wipe out the skillet and set it over medium heat. Add the remaining 2 tablespoons oil and the shallot and sauté for about 2 minutes, until the shallot is golden brown. Turn off the heat and stir in the red wine vinegar, balsamic vinegar, mustard, salt, and ¼ teaspoon pepper to make a vinaigrette. 8. In a large bowl, combine the spinach and romaine. Pour in the vinaigrette and toss until all of the leaves are lightly coated. Divide the dressed greens evenly among four large serving plates or shallow bowls and arrange the strawberries and fried tempeh on top. Peel the eggs, cut them in half lengthwise, and place them on top of the salads. Top with a couple grinds of pepper and serve right away.

Per Serving:
calorie: 435 | fat: 25g | protein: 29g | carbs: 25g | sugars: 10g | fiber: 5g | sodium: 332mg

Tofu and Bean Chili

Prep time: 10 minutes | Cook time 30 minutes | Serves 4

1 (15-ounce) can low-sodium dark red kidney beans, drained and rinsed, divided
2 (15-ounce) cans no-salt-added diced tomatoes
1½ cups low-sodium vegetable broth

½ teaspoon chili powder
½ teaspoon ground cumin
½ teaspoon garlic powder
½ teaspoon dried oregano
¼ teaspoon onion powder
¼ teaspoon salt
8 ounces extra-firm tofu

1. In a small bowl, mash ⅓ of the beans with a fork. 2. Put the mashed beans, the remaining whole beans, and the diced tomatoes with their juices in a large stockpot. 3. Add the broth, chili powder, cumin, garlic powder, dried oregano, onion powder, and salt. Simmer over medium-high heat for 15 minutes. 4. Press the tofu between 3 or 4 layers of paper towels to squeeze out any excess moisture. 5. Crumble the tofu into the stockpot and stir. Simmer for another 10 to 15 minutes.

Per Serving:
calories: 207 | fat: 4.73g | protein: 14.71g | carbs: 31.18g | sugars: 10.97g | fiber: 11.6g | sodium: 376mg

Cheesy Zucchini Patties

Prep time: 10 minutes | Cook time: 20 minutes | Serves 2

1 cup grated zucchini
1 cup chopped fresh mushrooms
½ cup grated carrot
½ cup nonfat shredded mozzarella cheese
¼ cup finely ground flaxseed
1 large egg, beaten
1 garlic clove, minced

Salt, to season
Freshly ground black pepper, to season
1 tablespoon extra-virgin olive oil
4 cup mixed baby greens, divided

1. In a medium bowl, stir together the zucchini, mushrooms, carrot, mozzarella cheese, flaxseed, egg, and garlic. Season with salt and pepper. Stir again to combine. 2. In a large skillet set over medium-high heat, heat the olive oil. 3. Drop 1 tablespoon of the zucchini mixture into the skillet. Continue dropping tablespoon-size portions in the pan until it is full, but not crowded. Cook for 2 to 3 minutes on each side, or until golden. Transfer to a serving plate. Repeat with the remaining mixture. 4. Place 2 cups of greens on each serving plate. Top each with zucchini patties. 5. Enjoy!

Per Serving:
calories: 252 | fat: 14.61g | protein: 18.96g | carbs: 14.36g | sugars: 3.67g | fiber: 8.6g | sodium: 644mg

Parmesan Artichokes

Prep time: 10 minutes | Cook time: 10 minutes | Serves 4

2 medium artichokes, trimmed and quartered, center removed
2 tablespoons coconut oil
1 large egg, beaten
½ cup grated vegetarian

Parmesan cheese
¼ cup blanched finely ground almond flour
½ teaspoon crushed red pepper flakes

1. In a large bowl, toss artichokes in coconut oil and then dip each piece into the egg. 2. Mix the Parmesan and almond flour in a large bowl. Add artichoke pieces and toss to cover as completely as possible, sprinkle with pepper flakes. Place into the air fryer basket. 3. Adjust the temperature to 400°F (204°C) and air fry for 10 minutes. 4. Toss the basket two times during cooking. Serve warm.

Per Serving:
calories: 207 | fat: 13g | protein: 10g | carbs: 15g | fiber: 5g | sodium: 211mg

Stuffed Portobellos

Prep time: 10 minutes | Cook time: 8 minutes | Serves 4

3 ounces (85 g) cream cheese, softened
½ medium zucchini, trimmed and chopped
¼ cup seeded and chopped red bell pepper
1½ cups chopped fresh spinach

leaves
4 large portobello mushrooms, stems removed
2 tablespoons coconut oil, melted
½ teaspoon salt

1. In a medium bowl, mix cream cheese, zucchini, pepper, and spinach. 2. Drizzle mushrooms with coconut oil and sprinkle with salt. Scoop ¼ zucchini mixture into each mushroom. 3. Place mushrooms into ungreased air fryer basket. Adjust the temperature to 400°F (204°C) and air fry for 8 minutes. Portobellos will be tender and tops will be browned when done. Serve warm.

Per Serving:
calories: 151 | fat: 13g | protein: 4g | carbs: 6g | fiber: 2g | sodium: 427mg

No-Tuna Lettuce Wraps

Prep time: 10 minutes | Cook time: 0 minutes | Serves 4

1 (15-ounce) can low-sodium chickpeas, drained and rinsed
1 celery stalk, thinly sliced
3 tablespoons honey mustard
2 tablespoons finely chopped

red onion
2 tablespoons unsalted tahini
1 tablespoon capers, undrained
12 butter lettuce leaves

1. In a large bowl, mash the chickpeas. 2. Add the celery, honey mustard, onion, tahini, and capers, and mix well. 3. For each serving, place three lettuce leaves on a plate so they overlap, top with one-fourth of the chickpea filling, and roll up into a wrap. Repeat with the remaining lettuce leaves and filling.

Per Serving:
calories: 163 | fat: 8.42g | protein: 6.47g | carbs: 17.06g | sugars: 3.51g | fiber: 5.9g | sodium: 333mg

Quinoa–White Bean Loaf

Prep time: 15 minutes | Cook time: 1 hour | Serves 2

Extra-virgin olive oil cooking spray
2 teaspoons extra-virgin olive oil
2 garlic cloves, minced
½ cup sliced fresh button mushrooms
6 ounces extra-firm tofu, crumbled
Salt, to season

Freshly ground black pepper, to season
1 (8-ounce) can cannellini beans, drained and rinsed
2 tablespoons coconut flour
1 tablespoon chia seeds
⅓ cup water
½ cup cooked quinoa
¼ cup chopped red onion
¼ cup chopped fresh parsley

1. Preheat the oven to 350°F. 2. Lightly coat 2 mini loaf pans with cooking spray. Set aside. 3. In a large skillet set over medium-high heat, heat the olive oil. 4. Add the garlic, mushrooms, and tofu. Season with salt and pepper. 5. Cook for 6 to 8 minutes, stirring occasionally, until the mushrooms and tofu are golden brown. 6. In a food processor, combine the cannellini beans, coconut flour, chia seeds, and water. Pulse until almost smooth. 7. In a large bowl, mix together the mushroom and tofu mixture, cannellini bean mixture, quinoa, red onion, and parsley. Season with salt and pepper. 8. Evenly divide the mixture between the 2 prepared loaf pans, gently pressing down and mounding the mixture in the middle. 9. Place the pans in the preheated oven. Bake for about 1 hour, or until firm and golden brown. Remove from the oven. Let rest for 10 minutes. 10. Slice and serve.

Per Serving:
calories: 193 | fat: 8.42g | protein: 12.26g | carbs: 20.3g | sugars: 4.02g | fiber: 4g | sodium: 366mg

Veggie Fajitas

Prep time: 10 minutes | Cook time: 15 minutes | Serves 4

For The Guacamole
2 small avocados pitted and peeled
1 teaspoon freshly squeezed lime juice
¼ teaspoon salt
9 cherry tomatoes, halved
For The Fajitas
1 red bell pepper

1 green bell pepper
1 small white onion
Avocado oil cooking spray
1 cup canned low-sodium black beans, drained and rinsed
½ teaspoon ground cumin
¼ teaspoon chili powder
¼ teaspoon garlic powder
4 (6-inch) yellow corn tortillas

To Make The Guacamole 1. In a medium bowl, use a fork to mash the avocados with the lime juice and salt. 2. Gently stir in the cherry tomatoes. To Make The Fajitas 1. Cut the red bell pepper, green bell pepper, and onion into ½-inch slices. 2. Heat a large skillet over medium heat. When hot, coat the cooking surface with cooking spray. Put the peppers, onion, and beans into the skillet. 3. Add the cumin, chili powder, and garlic powder, and stir. 4. Cover and cook for 15 minutes, stirring halfway through. 5. Divide the fajita mixture equally between the tortillas, and top with guacamole and any preferred garnishes.

Per Serving:
calories: 269 | fat: 15g | protein: 8g | carbs: 30g | sugars: 5g | fiber: 11g | sodium: 175mg

Caprese Eggplant Stacks

Prep time: 5 minutes | Cook time: 12 minutes | Serves 4

1 medium eggplant, cut into ¼-inch slices	Mozzarella, cut into ½-ounce / 14-g slices
2 large tomatoes, cut into ¼-inch slices	2 tablespoons olive oil
4 ounces (113 g) fresh	¼ cup fresh basil, sliced

1. In a baking dish, place four slices of eggplant on the bottom. Place a slice of tomato on top of each eggplant round, then Mozzarella, then eggplant. Repeat as necessary. 2. Drizzle with olive oil. Cover dish with foil and place dish into the air fryer basket. 3. Adjust the temperature to 350°F (177°C) and bake for 12 minutes. 4. When done, eggplant will be tender. Garnish with fresh basil to serve.

Per Serving:

calories: 97 | fat: 7g | protein: 2g | carbs: 8g | fiber: 4g | sodium: 11mg

Mushroom and Cauliflower Rice Risotto

Prep time: 5 minutes | Cook time: 10 minutes | Serves 4

1 teaspoon extra-virgin olive oil	broth
½ cup chopped portobello mushrooms	½ cup half-and-half
4 cups cauliflower rice	1 cup shredded Parmesan cheese
¼ cup low-sodium vegetable	

1. Heat the oil in a medium skillet over medium-low heat. When hot, put the mushrooms in the skillet and cook for 3 minutes, stirring once. 2. Add the cauliflower rice, broth, and half-and-half. Stir and cover. Increase to high heat and boil for 5 minutes. 3. Add the cheese. Stir to incorporate. Cook for 3 more minutes.

Per Serving:

calories: 159 | fat: 8.23g | protein: 10.29g | carbs: 12.43g | sugars: 4.23g | fiber: 2.4g | sodium: 531mg

Crispy Eggplant Rounds

Prep time: 15 minutes | Cook time: 10 minutes | Serves 4

1 large eggplant, ends trimmed, cut into ½-inch slices	cheese crisps, finely ground
½ teaspoon salt	½ teaspoon paprika
2 ounces (57 g) Parmesan 100%	¼ teaspoon garlic powder
	1 large egg

1. Sprinkle eggplant rounds with salt. Place rounds on a kitchen towel for 30 minutes to draw out excess water. Pat rounds dry. 2. In a medium bowl, mix cheese crisps, paprika, and garlic powder. In a separate medium bowl, whisk egg. Dip each eggplant round in egg, then gently press into cheese crisps to coat both sides. 3. Place eggplant rounds into ungreased air fryer basket. Adjust the temperature to 400°F (204°C) and air fry for 10 minutes, turning rounds halfway through cooking. Eggplant will be golden and crispy when done. Serve warm.

Per Serving:

calories: 113 | fat: 5g | protein: 7g | carbs: 10g | fiber: 4g | sodium: 567mg

Italian Zucchini Boats

Prep time: 5 minutes | Cook time: 15 minutes | Serves 4

1 cup canned low-sodium chickpeas, drained and rinsed	2 zucchini
1 cup no-sugar-added spaghetti sauce	¼ cup shredded Parmesan cheese

1. Preheat the oven to 425°F. 2. In a medium bowl, mix the chickpeas and spaghetti sauce together. 3. Cut the zucchini in half lengthwise, and scrape a spoon gently down the length of each half to remove the seeds. 4. Fill each zucchini half with the chickpea sauce, and top with one-quarter of the Parmesan cheese. 5. Place the zucchini halves on a baking sheet and roast in the oven for 15 minutes.

Per Serving:

calories: 120 | fat: 4.48g | protein: 6.69g | carbs: 13.56g | sugars: 4.79g | fiber: 3.8g | sodium: 441mg

Edamame Falafel with Roasted Vegetables

Prep time: 10 minutes | Cook time: 55 minutes | Serves 2

For the roasted vegetables	1 small onion, chopped
1 cup broccoli florets	1 garlic clove, chopped
1 medium zucchini, sliced	1 tablespoon freshly squeezed lemon juice
½ cup cherry tomatoes, halved	
1½ teaspoons extra-virgin olive oil	2 tablespoons hemp hearts
Salt, to season	1 teaspoon ground cumin
Freshly ground black pepper, to season	2 tablespoons oat flour
	¼ teaspoon salt
Extra-virgin olive oil cooking spray	Pinch freshly ground black pepper
For the falafel	2 tablespoons extra-virgin olive oil, divided
1 cup frozen shelled edamame, thawed	Prepared hummus, for serving (optional)

To make the roasted vegetables 1. Preheat the oven to 425°F. 2. In a large bowl, toss together the broccoli, zucchini, tomatoes, and olive oil to coat. Season with salt and pepper. 3. Spray a baking sheet with cooking spray. 4. Spread the vegetables evenly atop the sheet. Place the sheet in the preheated oven. Roast for 35 to 40 minutes, stirring every 15 minutes, or until the vegetables are soft and cooked through. 5. Remove from the oven. Set aside. To make the falafel 1. In a food processor, pulse the edamame until coarsely ground. 2. Add the onion, garlic, lemon juice, and hemp hearts. Process until finely ground. Transfer the mixture to a medium bowl. 3. By hand, mix in the cumin, oat flour, salt, and pepper. 4. Roll the dough into 1-inch balls. Flatten slightly. You should have about 12 silver dollar–size patties. 5. In a large skillet set over medium heat, heat 1 tablespoon of olive oil. 6. Add 4 falafel patties to the pan at a time (or as many as will fit without crowding), and cook for about 3 minutes on each side, or until lightly browned. Remove from the pan. Repeat with the remaining 1 tablespoon of olive oil and falafel patties. 7. Serve immediately with the roasted vegetables and hummus (if using) and enjoy!

Per Serving:

calories: 316 | fat: 22.48g | protein: 11.78g | carbs: 20.68g | sugars: 3.73g | fiber: 5.8g | sodium: 649mg

Grilled Vegetables on White Bean Mash

Prep time: 15 minutes | Cook time: 30 minutes | Serves 2

2 medium zucchini, sliced
1 red bell pepper, seeded and quartered
2 portobello mushroom caps, quartered
3 teaspoons extra-virgin olive oil, divided
1 (8-ounce) can cannellini beans, drained and rinsed
1 garlic clove, minced

½ cup low-sodium vegetable broth
4 cups baby spinach, divided
Salt, to season
Freshly ground black pepper, to season
1 tablespoon chopped fresh parsley
2 lemon wedges, divided, for garnish

1. Preheat the grill. Use a stove-top grill pan or broiler if a grill is not available. 2. Lightly brush the zucchini, red bell pepper, and mushrooms with 1½ teaspoons of olive oil. Arrange them in a barbecue grill pan. Place the pan on the preheated grill. Cook the vegetables for 5 to 8 minutes, or until lightly browned. Turn the vegetables. Brush with the remaining 1½ teaspoons of olive oil. Cook for 5 to 8 minutes more, or until tender. 3. To a small pan set over high heat, add the cannellini beans, garlic, and vegetable broth. Bring to a boil. Reduce the heat to low. Simmer for 10 minutes, uncovered. Using a potato masher, roughly mash the beans, adding a little more broth if they seem too dry. 4. Place 2 cups of spinach on each serving plate. 5. Top each with half of the bean mash and half of the grilled vegetables. Season with salt and pepper. Garnish with parsley. 6. Place 1 lemon wedge on each plate and serve.

Per Serving:

calories: 289.5 | fat: 8.55g | protein: 11.3g | carbs:28.91 g | sugars: 7.88g | fiber: 4.4g | sodium: 398mg

Chile Relleno Casserole with Salsa Salad

Prep time: 10 minutes | Cook time: 55 minutes | Serves 4

Casserole
½ cup gluten-free flour (such as King Arthur or Cup4Cup brand)
1 teaspoon baking powder
6 large eggs
½ cup nondairy milk or whole milk
Three 4-ounce cans fire-roasted diced green chiles, drained
1 cup nondairy cheese shreds or shredded mozzarella cheese
Salad
1 head green leaf lettuce, shredded

2 Roma tomatoes, seeded and diced
1 green bell pepper, seeded and diced
½ small yellow onion, diced
1 jalapeño chile, seeded and diced (optional)
2 tablespoons chopped fresh cilantro
4 teaspoons extra-virgin olive oil
4 teaspoons fresh lime juice
⅛ teaspoon fine sea salt

1. To make the casserole: Pour 1 cup water into the Instant Pot. Butter a 7-cup round heatproof glass dish or coat with nonstick cooking spray and place the dish on a long-handled silicone steam rack. (If you don't have the long-handled rack, use the wire metal steam rack and a homemade sling) 2. In a medium bowl, whisk together the flour and baking powder. Add the eggs and milk and whisk until well blended, forming a batter. Stir in the chiles and ¾ cup of the cheese. 3. Pour the batter into the prepared dish and cover tightly with aluminum foil. Holding the handles of the steam

rack, lower the dish into the Instant Pot. 4. Secure the lid and set the Pressure Release to Sealing. Select the Pressure Cook or Manual setting and set the cooking time for 40 minutes at high pressure. (The pot will take about 10 minutes to come up to pressure before the cooking program begins.) 5. When the cooking program ends, let the pressure release naturally for at least 10 minutes, then move the Pressure Release to Venting to release any remaining steam. Open the pot and, wearing heat-resistant mitts, grasp the handles of the steam rack and lift it out of the pot. Uncover the dish, taking care not to get burned by the steam or to drip condensation onto the casserole. While the casserole is still piping hot, sprinkle the remaining ¼ cup cheese evenly on top. Let the cheese melt for 5 minutes. 6. To make the salad: While the cheese is melting, in a large bowl, combine the lettuce, tomatoes, bell pepper, onion, jalapeño (if using), cilantro, oil, lime juice, and salt. Toss until evenly combined. 7. Cut the casserole into wedges. Serve warm, with the salad on the side.

Per Serving:

calorie: 361 | fat: 22g | protein: 21g | carbs: 23g | sugars: 8g | fiber: 3g | sodium: 421mg

Chickpea Coconut Curry

Prep time: 5 minutes | Cook time: 15 minutes | Serves 4

3 cups fresh or frozen cauliflower florets
2 cups unsweetened almond milk
1 (15-ounce) can coconut milk
1 (15-ounce) can low-sodium

chickpeas, drained and rinsed
1 tablespoon curry powder
¼ teaspoon ground ginger
¼ teaspoon garlic powder
⅛ teaspoon onion powder
¼ teaspoon salt

1. In a large stockpot, combine the cauliflower, almond milk, coconut milk, chickpeas, curry, ginger, garlic powder, and onion powder. Stir and cover. 2. Cook over medium-high heat for 10 minutes. 3. Reduce the heat to low, stir, and cook for 5 minutes more, uncovered. Season with up to ¼ teaspoon salt.

Per Serving:

calories: 225 | fat: 6.9g | protein: 12.46g | carbs: 30.99g | sugars: 14.27g | fiber: 9.3g | sodium: 489mg

Black-Eyed Pea Sauté with Garlic and Olives

Prep time: 5 minutes | Cook time: 5 minutes | Serves 2

2 teaspoons extra-virgin olive oil
1 garlic clove, minced
½ red onion, chopped
1 cup cooked black-eyed peas; if canned, drain and rinse
½ teaspoon dried thyme

¼ cup water
¼ teaspoon salt
¼ teaspoon freshly ground black pepper
6 Kalamata olives, pitted and halved

1. In a medium saucepan set over medium heat, stir together the olive oil, garlic, and red onion. Cook for 2 minutes, continuing to stir. 2. Add the black-eyed peas and thyme. Cook for 1 minute. 3. Stir in the water, salt, pepper, and olives. Cook for 2 minutes more, or until heated through.

Per Serving:

calories: 140 | fat: 6.13g | protein: 4.65g | carbs: 18.02g | sugars: 7.75g | fiber: 4.6g | sodium: 426mg

Stuffed Portobello Mushrooms

Prep time: 5 minutes | Cook time: 20 minutes | Serves 4

8 large portobello mushrooms	4 cups fresh spinach
3 teaspoons extra-virgin olive oil, divided	1 medium red bell pepper, diced
	¼ cup crumbled feta

1. Preheat the oven to 450°F. 2. Remove the stems from the mushrooms, and gently scoop out the gills and discard. Coat the mushrooms with 2 teaspoons of olive oil. 3. On a baking sheet, place the mushrooms cap-side down, and roast for 20 minutes. 4. Meanwhile, heat the remaining 1 teaspoon of olive oil in a medium skillet over medium heat. When hot, sauté the spinach and red bell pepper for 8 to 10 minutes, stirring occasionally. 5. Remove the mushrooms from the oven. Drain, if necessary. Spoon the spinach and pepper mix into the mushrooms, and top with feta.

Per Serving:
calories: 91 | fat: 4.24g | protein: 6.04g | carbs: 9.77g | sugars: 5.96g | fiber: 3.5g | sodium: 155mg

Chickpea and Tofu Bolognese

Prep time: 5 minutes | Cook time: 25 minutes |

Serves 4

1 (3- to 4-pound) spaghetti squash	sauce
½ teaspoon ground cumin	1 (15-ounce) can low-sodium chickpeas, drained and rinsed
1 cup no-sugar-added spaghetti	6 ounces extra-firm tofu

1. Preheat the oven to 400°F. 2. Cut the squash in half lengthwise. Scoop out the seeds and discard. 3. Season both halves of the squash with the cumin, and place them on a baking sheet cut-side down. Roast for 25 minutes. 4. Meanwhile, heat a medium saucepan over low heat, and pour in the spaghetti sauce and chickpeas. 5. Press the tofu between two layers of paper towels, and gently squeeze out any excess water. 6. Crumble the tofu into the sauce and cook for 15 minutes. 7. Remove the squash from the oven, and comb through the flesh of each half with a fork to make thin strands. 8. Divide the "spaghetti" into four portions, and top each portion with one-quarter of the sauce.

Per Serving:
calories: 221 | fat: 6.39g | protein: 12.46g | carbs: 31.8g | sugars: 6.36g | fiber: 7.8g | sodium: 405mg

Seitan Curry

Prep time: 10 minutes | Cook time: 15 minutes | Serves 2

1 tablespoon extra-virgin olive oil	1 cup diced tomatoes
½ cup chopped onion	⅓ cup unsweetened light canned coconut milk
2 garlic cloves, chopped	¼ cup water
1 cup cauliflower florets	Salt, to season
½ cup diced carrots	Freshly ground black pepper, to season
6 ounces seitan (wheat gluten), finely chopped	2 tablespoons chopped cashews, for garnish
2 teaspoons garam masala	

1. In a large wok or skillet set over high heat, heat the olive oil. 2. Add the onion and garlic. Sauté for 3 minutes. 3. Add the cauliflower, carrots, seitan, and garam masala. Mix well. Reduce the heat to medium-high. 4. Stir in the tomatoes, coconut milk, and water. Cover and bring to a simmer. Cook for about 10 minutes, covered, or until the cauliflower and carrots are tender. 5. Season with salt and pepper. Garnish with the cashews. 6. Serve and enjoy!

Per Serving:
calories: 617 | fat: 28.29g | protein:5.32 g | carbs: 43g | sugars: 8.31g | fiber: 5.7g | sodium: 434.3mg

Orange Tofu

Prep time: 10 minutes | Cook time: 20 minutes | Serves 4

⅓ cup freshly squeezed orange juice (zest orange first; see orange zest ingredient below)	ginger
	1 large clove garlic, grated
	½–1 teaspoon orange zest
1 tablespoon tamari	¼ teaspoon sea salt
1 tablespoon tahini	Few pinches of crushed red-pepper flakes (optional)
½ tablespoon coconut nectar or pure maple syrup	1 package (12 ounces) extra-firm tofu, sliced into ¼"–½" thick squares and patted to remove excess moisture
2 tablespoons apple cider vinegar	
½ tablespoon freshly grated	

1. Preheat the oven to 400°F. 2. In a small bowl, combine the orange juice, tamari, tahini, nectar or syrup, vinegar, ginger, garlic, orange zest, salt, and red-pepper flakes (if using). Whisk until well combined. Pour the sauce into an 8" x 12" baking dish. Add the tofu and turn to coat both sides. Bake for 20 minutes. Add salt to taste.

Per Serving:
calorie: 122 | fat: 7g | protein: 10g | carbs: 7g | sugars: 4g | fiber: 1g | sodium: 410mg

Farro Bowl

Prep time: 5 minutes | Cook time: 25 minutes | Serves 4

3 cups water	black pepper
1 cup uncooked farro	4 hardboiled eggs, sliced
1 tablespoon extra-virgin olive oil	1 avocado, sliced
1 teaspoon ground cumin	⅓ cup plain low-fat Greek yogurt
½ teaspoon salt	4 lemon wedges
½ teaspoon freshly ground	

1. In a medium saucepan, bring the water to a boil over high heat. 2. Pour the farro into the boiling water, and stir to submerge the grains. Reduce the heat to medium and cook for 20 minutes. Drain and set aside. 3. Heat a medium skillet over medium-low heat. When hot, pour in the oil, then add the cooked farro, cumin, salt, and pepper. Cook for 3 to 5 minutes, stirring occasionally. 4. Divide the farro into four equal portions, and top each with one-quarter of the eggs, avocado, and yogurt. Add a squeeze of lemon over the top of each portion.

Per Serving:
calories: 330 | fat: 14.66g | protein: 14.24g | carbs: 40.3g | sugars: 6.11g | fiber: 8.3g | sodium: 409mg

Chickpea-Spinach Curry

Prep time: 5 minutes | Cook time: 10 minutes | Serves 2

1 cup frozen chopped spinach, thawed	chopped tomatoes, undrained
1 cup canned chickpeas, drained and rinsed	1 tablespoon curry powder
½ cup frozen green beans	1 tablespoon granulated garlic
½ cup frozen broccoli florets	Salt, to season
½ cup no-salt-added canned	Freshly ground black pepper, to season
	½ cup chopped fresh parsley

1. In a medium saucepan set over high heat, stir together the spinach, chickpeas, green beans, broccoli, tomatoes and their juice, curry powder, and garlic. Season with salt and pepper. Bring to a fast boil. Reduce the heat to low. Cover and simmer for 10 minutes, or until heated through. 2. Top with the parsley, serve, and enjoy!

Per Serving:
calories: 203 | fat: 3.42g | protein: 12.63g | carbs: 34.72g | sugars: 6.94g | fiber: 13g | sodium: 375mg

Roasted Veggie Bowl

Prep time: 10 minutes | Cook time: 15 minutes | Serves 2

1 cup broccoli florets	½ medium green bell pepper, seeded and sliced ¼ inch thick
1 cup quartered Brussels sprouts	1 tablespoon coconut oil
½ cup cauliflower florets	2 teaspoons chili powder
¼ medium white onion, peeled and sliced ¼ inch thick	½ teaspoon garlic powder
	½ teaspoon cumin

1. Toss all ingredients together in a large bowl until vegetables are fully coated with oil and seasoning. 2. Pour vegetables into the air fryer basket. 3. Adjust the temperature to 360ºF (182ºC) and roast for 15 minutes. 4. Shake two or three times during cooking. Serve warm.

Per Serving:
calories: 112 | fat: 7.68g | protein: 3.64g | carbs: 10.67g | sugars: 3.08g | fiber: 4.6g | sodium: 106mg

Asparagus, Sun-Dried Tomato, and Green Pea Sauté

Prep time: 10 minutes | Cook time: 10 minutes | Serves 2

6 packaged sun-dried tomatoes (not packed in oil)	mushrooms
½ cup boiling water	¼ cup reduced-sodium vegetable broth
1 tablespoon extra-virgin olive oil	2 tablespoons sliced almonds
2 garlic cloves, minced	1 large tomato, diced (about 1 cup)
¾ pound fresh asparagus, trimmed and cut into 2-inch pieces	1½ teaspoons dried tarragon
¼ cup chopped red bell pepper	½ cup frozen peas
½ cup sliced fresh button	Freshly ground black pepper, to season

1. In a small heatproof bowl, place the sun-dried tomatoes. Cover with the boiling water. Set aside. 2. In a large skillet or wok set over high heat, heat the olive oil. 3. Add the garlic. Swirl in the oil for a few seconds. 4. Toss in the asparagus, red bell pepper, and mushrooms. Stir-fry for 30 seconds. 5. Add the vegetable broth and almonds. Cover and steam for about 2 minutes. Uncover the skillet. 6. Add the tomato and tarragon. Cook for 2 to 3 minutes to reduce the liquid. 7. Drain and chop the sun-dried tomatoes. Add them and the peas to the skillet. Stir-fry for 3 to 4 minutes, or until the vegetables are crisp-tender and the liquid is reduced to a sauce. 8. Season with pepper and serve immediately.

Per Serving:
calories: 165 | fat: 8.22g | protein: 7.51g | carbs: 20g | sugars: 9.15g | fiber: 7.3g | sodium: 46mg

Palak Tofu

Prep time: 5 minutes | Cook time: 40 minutes | Serves 4

One 14-ounce package extra-firm tofu, drained	¼ teaspoon cayenne pepper
5 tablespoons cold-pressed avocado oil	One 16-ounce bag frozen chopped spinach
1 yellow onion, diced	⅓ cup water
1-inch piece fresh ginger, peeled and minced	One 14½-ounce can fire-roasted diced tomatoes and their liquid
3 garlic cloves, minced	¼ cup coconut milk
1 teaspoon fine sea salt	2 teaspoons garam masala
½ teaspoon freshly ground black pepper	Cooked brown rice or cauliflower "rice" or whole-grain flatbread for serving

1. Cut the tofu crosswise into eight ½-inch-thick slices. Sandwich the slices between double layers of paper towels or a folded kitchen towel and press firmly to wick away as much moisture as possible. Cut the slices into ½-inch cubes. 2. Select the Sauté setting on the Instant Pot and and heat 4 tablespoons of the oil for 2 minutes. Add the onion and sauté for about 10 minutes, until it begins to brown. 3. While the onion is cooking in the Instant Pot, in a large nonstick skillet over medium-high heat, warm the remaining 1 tablespoon oil. Add the tofu in a single layer and cook without stirring for about 3 minutes, until lightly browned. 4. Using a spatula, turn the cubes over and cook for about 3 minutes more, until browned on the other side. Remove from the heat and set aside. 5. Add the ginger and garlic to the onion in the Instant Pot and sauté for about 2 minutes, until the garlic is bubbling but not browned. Add the sautéed tofu, salt, black pepper, and cayenne and stir gently to combine, taking care not to break up the tofu. Add the spinach and stir gently. Pour in the water and then pour the tomatoes and their liquid over the top in an even layer. Do not stir them in. 6. Secure the lid and set the Pressure Release to Sealing. Press the Cancel button to reset the cooking program, then select the Manual or Pressure Cook setting and set the cooking time for 10 minutes at low pressure. (The pot will take about 15 minutes to come up to pressure before the cooking program begins.) 7. When the cooking program ends, let the pressure release naturally for 10 minutes, then move the Pressure Release to Venting to release any remaining steam. Open the pot, add the coconut milk and garam masala, and stir to combine. 8. Ladle the tofu onto plates or into bowls. Serve piping hot, with the "rice" alongside.

Per Serving:
calories: 345 | fat: 24g | protein: 14g | carbs: 18g | sugars: 5g | fiber: 6g | sodium: 777mg

Pra Ram Vegetables and Peanut Sauce with Seared Tofu

Prep time: 5 minutes | Cook time: 20 minutes | Serves 4

Peanut Sauce
2 tablespoons cold-pressed avocado oil
2 garlic cloves, minced
½ cup creamy natural peanut butter
½ cup coconut milk
2 tablespoons brown rice syrup
1 tablespoon plus 1 teaspoon soy sauce, tamari, or coconut aminos
¼ cup water
Vegetables
2 carrots, sliced on the diagonal ¼ inch thick

8 ounces zucchini, julienned ¼ inch thick
1 pound broccoli florets
½ small head green cabbage, cut into 1-inch-thick wedges (with core intact so wedges hold together)
Tofu
One 14-ounce package extra-firm tofu, drained
¼ teaspoon fine sea salt
¼ teaspoon freshly ground black pepper
1 tablespoon cornstarch
2 tablespoons coconut oil

1. To make the peanut sauce: In a small saucepan over medium heat, warm the oil and garlic for about 2 minutes, until the garlic is bubbling but not browned. Add the peanut butter, coconut milk, brown rice syrup, soy sauce, and water; stir to combine; and bring to a simmer (this will take about 3 minutes). As soon as the mixture is fully combined and at a simmer, remove from the heat and keep warm. The peanut sauce will keep in an airtight container in the refrigerator for up to 5 days. 2. To make the vegetables: Pour 1 cup water into the Instant Pot and place a steamer basket into the pot. In order, layer the carrots, zucchini, broccoli, and cabbage in the steamer basket, finishing with the cabbage. 3. Secure the lid and set the Pressure Release to Sealing. Select the Steam setting and set the cooking time for 0 (zero) minutes at low pressure. (The pot will take about 15 minutes to come up to pressure before the cooking program begins.) 4. To prepare the tofu: While the vegetables are steaming, cut the tofu crosswise into eight ½-inch-thick slices. Cut each of the slices in half crosswise, creating squares. Sandwich the squares between double layers of paper towels or a folded kitchen towel and press firmly to wick away as much moisture as possible. Sprinkle the tofu squares on both sides with the salt and pepper, then sprinkle them on both sides with the cornstarch. Using your fingers, spread the cornstarch on the top and bottom of each square to coat evenly. 5. In a large nonstick skillet over medium-high heat, warm the oil for about 3 minutes, until shimmering. Add the tofu and sear, turning once, for about 6 minutes per side, until crispy and golden. Divide the tofu evenly among four plates. 6. When the cooking program ends, perform a quick pressure release by moving the Pressure Release to Venting. Open the pot and, wearing heat-resistant mitts, grasp the handles of the steamer basket and lift it out of the pot. 7. Divide the vegetables among the plates, arranging them around the tofu. Spoon the peanut sauce over the tofu and serve.

Per Serving:
calories: 380 | fat: 22g | protein: 18g | carbs: 30g | sugars: 9g | fiber: 10g | sodium: 381mg

Instant Pot Hoppin' John with Skillet Cauli "Rice"

Prep time: 0 minutes | Cook time: 30 minutes | Serves 6

Hoppin' John
1 pound dried black-eyed peas (about 2¼ cups)
8⅔ cups water
1½ teaspoons fine sea salt
2 tablespoons extra-virgin olive oil
2 garlic cloves, minced
8 ounces shiitake mushrooms, stemmed and chopped, or cremini mushrooms, chopped
1 small yellow onion, diced
1 green bell pepper, seeded and diced
2 celery stalks, diced
2 jalapeño chiles, seeded and

diced
½ teaspoon smoked paprika
½ teaspoon dried thyme
½ teaspoon dried sage
¼ teaspoon cayenne pepper
2 cups low-sodium vegetable broth
Cauli "Rice"
1 tablespoon vegan buttery spread or unsalted butter
1 pound riced cauliflower
½ teaspoon fine sea salt
2 green onions, white and green parts, sliced
Hot sauce (such as Tabasco or Crystal) for serving

1. To make the Hoppin' John: In a large bowl, combine the black-eyed peas, 8 cups of the water, and 1 teaspoon of the salt and stir to dissolve the salt. Let soak for at least 8 hours or up to overnight. 2. Select the Sauté setting on the Instant Pot and heat the oil and garlic for 3 minutes, until the garlic is bubbling but not browned. Add the mushrooms and the remaining ½ teaspoon salt and sauté for 5 minutes, until the mushrooms have wilted and begun to give up their liquid. Add the onion, bell pepper, celery, and jalapeños and sauté for 4 minutes, until the onion is softened. Add the paprika, thyme, sage, and cayenne and sauté for 1 minute. 3. Drain the black-eyed peas and add them to the pot along with the broth and remaining ⅔ cup water. The liquid should just barely cover the beans. (Add an additional splash of water if needed.) 4. Secure the lid and set the Pressure Release to Sealing. Press the Cancel button to reset the cooking program, then select the Bean/Chili, Pressure Cook, or Manual setting and set the cooking time for 5 minutes at high pressure. (The pot will take about 10 minutes to come up to pressure before the cooking program begins.) 5. When the cooking program ends, let the pressure release naturally for 10 minutes, then move the Pressure Release to Venting to release any remaining steam. 6. To make the cauli "rice": While the pressure is releasing, in a large skillet over medium heat, melt the buttery spread. Add the cauliflower and salt and sauté for 3 to 5 minutes, until cooked through and piping hot. (If using frozen riced cauliflower, this may take another 2 minutes or so.) 7. Spoon the cauli "rice" onto individual plates. Open the pot and spoon the black-eyed peas on top of the cauli "rice". Sprinkle with the green onions and serve right away, with the hot sauce on the side.

Per Serving:
calories: 287 | fat: 7g | protein: 23g | carbs: 56g | sugars: 8g | fiber: 24g | sodium: 894mg

Gingered Tofu and Greens

Prep time: 15 minutes | Cook time: 20 minutes | Serves 2

For the marinade
2 tablespoons low-sodium soy sauce
¼ cup rice vinegar
⅓ cup water
1 tablespoon grated fresh ginger
1 tablespoon coconut flour
1 teaspoon granulated stevia
1 garlic clove, minced
For the tofu and greens

8 ounces extra-firm tofu, drained, cut into 1-inch cubes
3 teaspoons extra-virgin olive oil, divided
1 tablespoon grated fresh ginger
2 cups coarsely shredded bok choy
2 cups coarsely shredded kale, thoroughly washed
½ cup fresh, or frozen, chopped green beans
1 tablespoon freshly squeezed lime juice
1 tablespoon chopped fresh cilantro
2 tablespoons hemp hearts

To make the marinade 1. In a small bowl, whisk together the soy sauce, rice vinegar, water, ginger, coconut flour, stevia, and garlic until well combined. 2. Place a small saucepan set over high heat. Add the marinade. Bring to a boil. Cook for 1 minute. Remove from the heat. To make the tofu and greens 1. In a medium ovenproof pan, place the tofu in a single layer. Pour the marinade over. Drizzle with 1½ teaspoons of olive oil. Let sit for 5 minutes. 2. Preheat the broiler to high. 3. Place the pan under the broiler. Broil the tofu for 7 to 8 minutes, or until lightly browned. Using a spatula, turn the tofu over. Continue to broil for 7 to 8 minutes more, or until browned on this side. 4. In a large wok or skillet set over high heat, heat the remaining 1½ teaspoons of olive oil. 5. Stir in the ginger. 6. Add the bok choy, kale, and green beans. Cook for 2 to 3 minutes, stirring constantly, until the greens wilt. 7. Add the lime juice and cilantro. Remove from the heat. 8. Add the browned tofu with any remaining marinade in the pan to the bok choy, kale, and green beans. Toss gently to combine. 9. Top with the hemp hearts and serve immediately.

Per Serving:
calories: 252 | fat: 13.79g | protein: 15.05g | carbs: 19.62g | sugars: 3.87g | fiber: 2.7g | sodium: 679mg

Cashew-Kale and Chickpeas

Prep time: 15 minutes | Cook time: 15 minutes | Serves 2

For the cashew sauce
½ cup unsalted cashews soaked in ½ cup hot water for at least 20 minutes
1 cup reduced-sodium vegetable broth
1 garlic clove, minced
For the kale
1 medium red bell pepper, diced
1 medium carrot, julienned
½ cup sliced fresh mushrooms

1 cup canned chickpeas, drained and rinsed
1 bunch kale, thoroughly washed, central stems removed, leaves thinly sliced (about 2½ cups)
2 to 3 tablespoons water
1 teaspoon red pepper flakes
½ teaspoon salt
Freshly ground black pepper, to season
¼ cup minced fresh cilantro

To make the cashew sauce 1. Drain the cashews. 2. In a blender or food processor, blend together the cashews, vegetable broth, and garlic until completely smooth. Set aside. To make the kale 1. In a large nonstick skillet or Dutch oven set over medium-low heat, stir together the red bell pepper, carrot, and mushrooms. Cook for 5 to 7 minutes, or until softened. 2. Stir in the chickpeas. Increase the heat to high. 3. Add the kale and the water. Stir to combine. Cover and cook for 5 minutes, or until the kale is tender. 4. Stir in the cashew sauce, red pepper flakes, and salt. Season with pepper. Cook for 2 to 3 minutes more, uncovered, or until the sauce thickens. 5. Garnish with the cilantro before serving. 6. Enjoy!

Per Serving:
calories: 480 | fat: 19.73g | protein: 20.16g | carbs: 62.12g | sugars: 17g | fiber: 15.3g | sodium: 843mg

Chapter 13 Stews and Soups

Cauliflower Chili

Prep time: 10 minutes | Cook time: 35 minutes | Serves 5

2 cups thickly sliced carrot
½ large or 1 full small head cauliflower
4 or 5 cloves garlic, minced
1 tablespoon balsamic vinegar
1½ cups diced onion
1 teaspoon sea salt
1½ tablespoons mild chili powder
1 tablespoon cocoa powder
2 teaspoons ground cumin
2 teaspoons dried oregano
⅛ teaspoon allspice
¼ teaspoon crushed red-pepper flakes (or to taste)
1 can (28 ounces) crushed tomatoes
1 can (15 ounces) pinto beans, rinsed and drained
1 can (15 ounces) kidney beans or black beans, rinsed and drained
½ cup water
Lime wedges

1. In a food processor, combine the carrot, cauliflower, and garlic, and pulse until finely minced. (Alternatively, you could mince by hand.) In a large pot over medium heat, combine the vinegar, onion, salt, chili powder, cocoa, cumin, oregano, allspice, and red-pepper flakes. Cook for 3 to 4 minutes, stirring occasionally. Add the minced carrot, cauliflower, and garlic, and cook for 5 to 6 minutes, stirring occasionally. Add the tomatoes, pinto and kidney beans, and water, and stir to combine. Increase the heat to high to bring to a boil. Reduce the heat to low, cover, and simmer for 25 minutes. Taste, and season as desired. Serve with lime wedges.

Per Serving:
calorie: 237 | fat: 3g | protein: 13g | carbs: 45g | sugars: 13g | fiber: 15g | sodium: 1036mg

Thai Corn and Sweet Potato Stew

Prep time: 10 minutes | Cook time: 20 minutes | Serves 4

1 small can (5.5 ounces) light coconut milk
1 cup chopped onion
½ cup chopped celery
2 cups cubed sweet potato (can use frozen)
¾–1 teaspoon sea salt
2 cups water
1½ tablespoons Thai yellow or red curry paste
1½ cups frozen corn kernels
1½ cups chopped red bell
pepper
1 package (12–14 ounces) tofu, cut into cubes, or 1 can (14 ounces) black beans, rinsed and drained
2½ tablespoons freshly squeezed lime juice
4–5 cups baby spinach leaves
⅓–½ cup fresh cilantro or Thai basil, chopped
Lime wedges (optional)

1. In a soup pot over high heat, warm 2 tablespoons of the coconut milk. Add the onion, celery, sweet potato, and ¾ teaspoon of the salt, and sauté for 4 to 5 minutes. Add the water, Thai paste, and remaining coconut milk. Increase the heat to high to bring to a boil. Cover and reduce the heat to medium-low, and let the mixture simmer for 8 to 10 minutes, or until the sweet potato has softened. Turn off the heat, and use an immersion blender to puree the soup base. Add the corn, bell pepper, and tofu or beans, and turn the heat to medium-low. Cover and cook for 3 to 4 minutes to heat through. Add the lime juice, spinach, and cilantro or basil, and stir until the spinach has just wilted. Taste, and season with the remaining ¼ teaspoon salt, if desired. Serve with the lime wedges (if using).

Per Serving:
calorie: 223 | fat: 7g | protein: 10g | carbs: 36g | sugars: 11g | fiber: 6g | sodium: 723mg

Cream of Carrot Soup

Prep time: 5 minutes | Cook time: 15 minutes | Serves 4

1 cup plus 2 tablespoons low-sodium chicken broth, divided
3 tablespoons finely chopped shallots or onions
2 tablespoons flour
2 cups fat-free milk, scalded and hot
1 teaspoon cinnamon
1 cup cooked, pureed carrots
Freshly ground black pepper

1. In a stockpot, heat 2 tablespoons of the broth over medium heat. Add the shallots and cook until limp. Sprinkle the shallots with the flour and cook 2–3 minutes. 2. Pour in the hot milk and cook until the mixture thickens. Add the remaining ingredients. Bring almost to a boil, stirring often, and cook for approximately 5 minutes. Add pepper to taste.

Per Serving:
calories: 77 | fat: 0.68g | protein: 6.06g | carbs: 12.22g | sugars: 6.81g | fiber: 1.1g | sodium: 89mg

Slow Cooker Chicken and Vegetable Soup

Prep time: 10 minutes | Cook time: 4 hours | Serves 4

1 medium potato, peeled and chopped into 1-inch pieces
3 celery stalks, chopped into 1-inch pieces
2 cups chopped baby carrots
1 cup chopped white onion
2 cups chopped green beans
2 cups low-sodium chicken broth
2 tablespoons tomato paste
2 tablespoons Italian seasoning
1 pound boneless, skinless chicken breasts, chopped
Freshly ground black pepper

1. Put the potato, celery, carrots, onion, green beans, broth, tomato paste, Italian seasoning, and chicken into a slow cooker and cook on high for 4 hours. 2. Season with freshly ground black pepper.

Per Serving:
calories: 256 | fat: 1.84g | protein: 25.68g | carbs: 36.11g | sugars: 7.14g | fiber: 6.8g | sodium: 980mg

Golden Chicken Soup

Prep time: 10 minutes | Cook time: 20 minutes | Serves 4 to 6

1 tablespoon extra-virgin olive oil
1 yellow onion, chopped
2 teaspoons garlic powder
1 tablespoon ginger powder
2 teaspoons turmeric
½ teaspoon freshly ground black pepper
6 cups low-sodium chicken broth
3 (5- to 6-ounce) boneless, skinless chicken breasts
4 celery stalks, cut into ¼-inch-thick slices
1 fennel bulb, thinly sliced

1. Heat the extra-virgin olive oil in a large stockpot over medium heat. Sauté the onion until translucent, about 3 minutes. Add the garlic powder, ginger powder, turmeric, black pepper, and chicken broth. 2. Bring to a boil, then carefully add the chicken, celery, and fennel. Reduce the heat to medium-low, cover, and simmer until the internal temperature of the chicken is 160°F, 5 to 10 minutes. 3. Remove the chicken breasts and allow them to cool for 5 minutes while the soup keeps simmering. 4. Shred the chicken using two forks and return it to the stockpot. Heat the soup for about 1 minute and adjust the seasonings as desired. 5. Store the cooled soup in an airtight container in the refrigerator for 3 to 5 days.

Per Serving:
calories: 107 | fat: 4.25g | protein: 9.79g | carbs: 9.5g | sugars: 2.76g | fiber: 2g | sodium: 370mg

Creamy Sweet Potato Soup

Prep time: 15 minutes | Cook time: 10 minutes | Serves 6

2 tablespoons avocado oil
1 small onion, chopped
2 celery stalks, chopped
2 teaspoons minced garlic
1 teaspoon kosher salt
½ teaspoon freshly ground black pepper
1 teaspoon ground turmeric
½ teaspoon ground cinnamon
2 pounds sweet potatoes, peeled
and cut into 1-inch cubes
3 cups Vegetable Broth or Chicken Bone Broth
Plain Greek yogurt, to garnish (optional)
Chopped fresh parsley, to garnish (optional)
Pumpkin seeds (pepitas), to garnish (optional)

1. Set the electric pressure cooker to the Sauté setting. When the pot is hot, pour in the avocado oil. 2. Sauté the onion and celery for 3 to 5 minutes or until the vegetables begin to soften. 3. Stir in the garlic, salt, pepper, turmeric, and cinnamon. Hit Cancel. 4. Stir in the sweet potatoes and broth. 5. Close and lock the lid of the pressure cooker. Set the valve to sealing. 6. Cook on high pressure for 10 minutes. 7. When the cooking is complete, hit Cancel and allow the pressure to release naturally. 8. Once the pin drops, unlock and remove the lid. 9. Use an immersion blender to purée the soup right in the pot. If you don't have an immersion blender, transfer the soup to a blender or food processor and purée. (Follow the instructions that came with your machine for blending hot foods.) 10. Spoon into bowls and serve topped with Greek yogurt, parsley, and/or pumpkin seeds (if using).

Per Serving:
calories: 175 | fat: 5.26g | protein: 4.69g | carbs: 28.87g | sugars: 3.99g | fiber: 3.5g | sodium: 706mg

Down South Corn Soup

Prep time: 10 minutes | Cook time: 35 minutes | Serves 8 to 10

1 tablespoon extra-virgin olive oil
½ Vidalia onion, minced
2 garlic cloves, minced
3 cups chopped cabbage
1 small cauliflower, broken into florets or 1 (10-ounce) bag frozen cauliflower
1 (10-ounce) bag frozen corn
1 cup store-bought low-sodium vegetable broth
1 teaspoon smoked paprika
1 teaspoon ground cumin
1 teaspoon dried dill
½ teaspoon freshly ground black pepper
1 cup plain unsweetened cashew milk

1. In a large stockpot, heat the oil over medium heat. 2. Add the onion and garlic, and sauté, stirring to prevent the garlic from scorching, for 3 to 5 minutes, or until translucent. 3. Add the cabbage and a splash of water, cover, and cook for 5 minutes, or until tender. 4. Add the cauliflower, corn, broth, paprika, cumin, dill, and pepper. Cover and cook for 20 minutes, or until tender. 5. Add the cashew milk and stir well. Cover and cook for 5 minutes, letting the flavors come together. 6. Serve with a heaping plate of greens and seafood of your choice.

Per Serving:
calories: 98 | fat: 3.41g | protein: 3.52g | carbs: 14.83g | sugars: 6.17g | fiber: 2.5g | sodium: 53mg

Minted Sweet Pea Soup

Prep time: 10 minutes | Cook time: 10 minutes | Serves 2 to 4

2 tablespoons extra-virgin olive oil
1 small yellow onion, minced
Pinch kosher salt
Pinch freshly ground black pepper
2 garlic cloves, minced
1 zucchini, diced
4 cups low-sodium vegetable
broth
3 cups frozen peas
Juice of 1 lemon
½ cup plain Greek yogurt (optional)
½ cup thinly sliced fresh mint
2 tablespoons chopped pistachios (optional)

1. Heat the extra-virgin olive oil in a medium stockpot over medium heat. Add the onion, salt, and pepper and sauté until translucent. 2. Add the garlic and zucchini and sauté until tender, about 3 minutes. 3. Transfer the vegetables to a blender and puree them with the vegetable broth, peas, and lemon juice. 4. Adjust the seasonings as desired and serve the soup warmed in a saucepan over medium heat or cooled in the refrigerator. To cool it in an ice bath, transfer the soup to a medium bowl and nestle that in a large bowl filled with ice water. 5. Serve with a dollop of optional Greek yogurt (if using) and topped with mint and pistachios (if using). 6. Store the cooled soup in an airtight container in the refrigerator for up to 5 days, with garnishes kept separately.

Per Serving:
calories: 181 | fat: 5.91g | protein: 8.32g | carbs: 26.74g | sugars: 12.52g | fiber: 5.7g | sodium: 442mg

Chicken Rice Soup

Prep time: 10 minutes | Cook time: 10 minutes | Serves 8

1 teaspoon vegetable oil
2 ribs celery, chopped in ½"-thick pieces
1 medium onion, chopped
1 cup wild rice, uncooked
½ cup long-grain rice, uncooked
1 pound boneless skinless

chicken breasts, cut into ¾" cubes
5¼ cups fat-free, low-sodium chicken broth
2 teaspoons dried thyme leaves
¼ teaspoon red pepper flakes

1. Using the Sauté function on the Instant Pot, heat the teaspoon of vegetable oil. Sauté the celery and onion until the onions are slightly translucent (3–5 minutes). Once cooked, press Cancel. 2. Add the remaining ingredients to the inner pot. 3. Secure the lid and make sure the vent is set to sealing. Using the Manual function, set the time to 10 minutes. 4. When cook time is over, let the pressure release naturally for 10 minutes, then perform a quick release.

Per Serving:

calories: 160 | fat: 2g | protein: 16g | carbs: 18g | sugars: 2g | fiber: 1g | sodium: 375mg

Hearty Hamburger and Lentil Stew

Prep time: 0 minutes | Cook time: 55 minutes | Serves 8

2 tablespoons cold-pressed avocado oil
2 garlic cloves, chopped
1 large yellow onion, diced
2 carrots, diced
2 celery stalks, diced
2 pounds 95 percent lean ground beef
½ cup small green lentils
2 cups low-sodium roasted beef bone broth or vegetable broth

1-tablespoon Italian seasoning
1 tablespoon paprika
1½ teaspoons fine sea salt
1 extra-large russet potato, diced
1 cup frozen green peas
1 cup frozen corn
One 14½-ounce can no-salt petite diced tomatoes and their liquid
¼ cup tomato paste

1. Select the Sauté setting on the Instant Pot and heat the oil and garlic for 3 minutes, until the garlic is bubbling but not browned. Add the onion, carrots, and celery and sauté for 5 minutes, until the onion begins to soften. Add the beef and sauté, using a wooden spoon or spatula to break up the meat as it cooks, for 6 minutes, until cooked through and no streaks of pink remain. 2. Stir in the lentils, broth, Italian seasoning, paprika, and salt. Add the potato, peas, corn, and tomatoes and their liquid in layers on top of the lentils and beef, then add the tomato paste in a dollop on top. Do not stir in the vegetables and tomato paste. 3. Secure the lid and set the Pressure Release to Sealing. Press the Cancel button to reset the cooking program, then select the Pressure Cook or Manual setting and set the cooking time for 20 minutes at high pressure. (The pot will take about 20 minutes to come up to pressure before the cooking program begins.) 4. When the cooking program ends, let the pressure release naturally for at least 15 minutes, then move the Pressure Release to Venting to release any remaining steam. Open the pot and stir the stew to mix all of the ingredients. 5. Ladle the stew into bowls and serve hot.

Per Serving:

calories: 334 | fat: 8g | protein: 34g | carbs: 30g | sugars: 6g | fiber: 7g | sodium: 902mg

Hodgepodge Stew

Prep time: 10 minutes | Cook time: 25 minutes | Serves 4

3 tablespoons water
2 cups roughly chopped onion
2–2½ cups cauliflower florets
1½ cups thickly sliced carrots
1 teaspoon dried thyme leaves
1 teaspoon dried savory or rosemary leaves (or ½ teaspoon each)
1 teaspoon mustard seeds
½ teaspoon dill seed (optional)
¼ teaspoon sea salt
3 tablespoons spelt or other

flour
2 cups vegetable stock
3 cups cubed potatoes (can substitute sweet potatoes)
1 can (15 ounces) kidney beans, drained and rinsed
1½ cups low-fat nondairy milk
1 cup chopped green beans or frozen green peas
2 tablespoons nutritional yeast (optional)

1. In a large pot over medium-high heat, combine the water, onion, cauliflower, carrots, thyme, savory or rosemary, mustard seeds, dill (if using), and salt. Cook for 3 to 4 minutes, stirring a few times. Add the flour and stir frequently for another few minutes, to help cook out the raw flavor of the flour. Add a splash of the vegetable stock if needed to prevent sticking. Add the remainder of the stock gradually, starting with ¼ to ½ cup and stirring it into the flour steadily, allowing the flour and stock to thicken together. Let the mixture bubble, and then continue adding the stock. Add the potatoes and beans, and let the mixture come to a boil. Reduce the heat to medium-low, cover the pot, and cook for 15 minutes, or until the potatoes are tender when pierced. Add the milk, green beans or peas, and yeast (if using). Heat through for 4 to 5 minutes, then serve.

Per Serving:

calorie: 250 | fat: 2g | protein: 10g | carbs: 51g | sugars: 11g | fiber: 9g | sodium: 558mg

Asparagus Soup

Prep time: 5 minutes | Cook time: 10 minutes | Serves 2

1 pound asparagus, woody ends removed, sliced into 1-inch pieces
1 (8-ounce) can cannellini beans, drained and rinsed
2 cups reduced-sodium vegetable broth
1 medium shallot, thinly sliced

1 garlic clove, thinly sliced
½ teaspoon dried thyme
½ teaspoon dried marjoram leaves
⅛ teaspoon salt
Freshly ground black pepper, to season

1. In a large saucepan set over high heat, stir together the asparagus, cannellini beans, vegetable broth, shallot, garlic, thyme, marjoram, and salt. Bring to a boil. Reduce the heat to medium-low. Cover and simmer for about 5 minutes, or until the asparagus is tender. 2. In a large blender or food processor, purée the soup until smooth, scraping down the sides, if necessary. Season with pepper. 3. Serve immediately and enjoy!

Per Serving:

calories: 83 | fat: 0.69g | protein: 6.22g | carbs: 17.22g | sugars: 7.28g | fiber: 6.8g | sodium: 712mg

Spanish Black Bean Soup

Prep time: 5 minutes | Cook time: 1 hour 10 minutes | Serves 6

1 ½ cups plus 2 teaspoons low-sodium chicken broth, divided	1 teaspoon cumin
1 teaspoon extra-virgin olive oil	1 teaspoon chili powder or ½ teaspoon cayenne pepper
3 garlic cloves, minced	1 red bell pepper, chopped
1 yellow onion, minced	1 carrot, coarsely chopped
1 teaspoon minced fresh oregano	3 cups cooked black beans
	½ cup dry red wine

1. In a large pot, heat 2 teaspoons of the chicken broth and the olive oil. Add the garlic and onion, and sauté for 3 minutes. Add the oregano, cumin, and chili powder; stir for another minute. Add the red pepper and carrot. 2. Puree 1½ cups of the black beans in a blender or food processor. Add the pureed beans, the remaining 1½ cups of whole black beans, the remaining 1½ cups of chicken broth, and the red wine to the stockpot. Simmer 1 hour. 3. Taste before serving; add additional spices if you like.

Per Serving:

calories: 160 | fat: 2.91g | protein: 9.4g | carbs: 24.58g | sugars: 1.44g | fiber: 8.4g | sodium: 48mg

Manhattan Clam Chowder

Prep time: 10 minutes | Cook time: 1 hour 30 minutes | Serves 8

3 medium carrots, peeled and coarsely chopped	2½ cups minced clams, drained
3 large white or russet potatoes, peeled and coarsely chopped	2 cups canned tomatoes, slightly crushed
4 celery stalks, coarsely chopped	½ teaspoon dried thyme or 1 teaspoon minced fresh thyme
	Freshly ground black pepper

1. Add all the ingredients to a large stockpot. Cover and let simmer for 1½ hours. Taste and add a dash of salt if needed. Serve hot.

Per Serving:

calories: 164 | fat: 0.42g | protein: 4.05g | carbs: 37.36g | sugars: 5.54g | fiber: 3.4g | sodium: 305mg

Tasty Tomato Soup

Prep time: 10 minutes | Cook time: 1 hour 25 minutes | Serves 2

3 cups chopped tomatoes	1 medium onion, chopped
1 red bell pepper, cut into chunks	1 garlic clove, minced
2 tablespoons extra-virgin olive oil, divided	2 cups low-sodium vegetable broth
Salt, to season	1 cup sliced fresh button mushrooms
Freshly ground black pepper, to season	½ cup fresh chopped basil

1. Preheat the oven to 400°F. 2. On a baking sheet, spread out the tomatoes and red bell pepper. 3. Drizzle with 1 tablespoon of olive oil. Toss to coat. Season with salt and pepper. Place the sheet in the preheated oven. Roast for 45 minutes. 4. In a large stockpot set over medium heat, heat the remaining 1 tablespoon of olive oil. 5. Add the onion. Cook for 2 to 3 minutes, or until tender. 6. Stir in the garlic. Cook for 2 minutes more. 7. Add the vegetable broth, mushrooms, and basil. 8. Stir in the roasted tomatoes and peppers. Reduce the heat to medium-low. Cook for 30 minutes. 9. To a blender or food processor, carefully transfer the soup in batches, blending until smooth. Return the processed soup to the pot. Simmer for 5 minutes. 10. Serve warm and enjoy!

Per Serving:

calories: 255 | fat: 15.09g | protein: 5.97g | carbs: 28.64g | sugars: 17.95g | fiber: 6.6g | sodium: 738mg

Spicy Turkey Chili

Prep time: 10 minutes | Cook time: 50 minutes | Serves 6

2 onions, chopped	kidney or pinto beans
2 garlic cloves, minced	2 cups canned tomatoes with liquid
½ cup chopped green bell pepper	1 cup low-sodium chicken broth
1 tablespoon extra-virgin olive oil	2 tablespoon chili powder
1 pound lean ground turkey breast meat	2 teaspoons cumin
2 cups cooked (not canned)	Freshly ground black pepper

1. In a large saucepan, sauté the onion, garlic, and green pepper in the oil for 10 minutes. Add the turkey, and sauté until the turkey is cooked, about 5–10 minutes. Drain any fat away. 2. Add the remaining ingredients, bring to a boil, lower the heat, and simmer uncovered for 30 minutes. Add additional chili powder if you like your chili extra spicy.

Per Serving:

calories: 214 | fat: 9.94g | protein: 20.55g | carbs: 11.57g | sugars: 4.11g | fiber: 2.2g | sodium: 363mg

Ham and Potato Chowder

Prep time: 25 minutes | Cook time: 8 hour s | Serves 5

5-ounce package scalloped potatoes	bouillon powder
Sauce mix from potato package	4 cups water
1 cup extra-lean, reduced-sodium, cooked ham, cut into narrow strips	1 cup chopped celery
4 teaspoons sodium-free	⅓ cup chopped onions
	Pepper to taste
	2 cups fat-free half-and-half
	⅓ cup flour

1. Combine potatoes, sauce mix, ham, bouillon powder, water, celery, onions, and pepper in the inner pot of the Instant Pot. 2. Secure the lid and cook using the Slow Cook function on low for 7 hours. 3. Combine half-and-half and flour. Remove the lid and gradually add to the inner pot, blending well. 4. Secure the lid once more and cook on the low Slow Cook function for up to 1 hour more, stirring occasionally until thickened.

Per Serving:

calories: 241 | fat: 3g | protein: 11g | carbs: 41g | sugars: 8g | fiber: 3g | sodium: 836mg

Thai Peanut, Carrot, and Shrimp Soup

Prep time: 10 minutes | Cook time: 10 minutes | Serves 4

1 tablespoon coconut oil	broth
1 tablespoon Thai red curry paste	½ cup unsweetened plain almond milk
½ onion, sliced	½ pound shrimp, peeled and deveined
3 garlic cloves, minced	
2 cups chopped carrots	Minced fresh cilantro, for garnish
½ cup whole unsalted peanuts	
4 cups low-sodium vegetable	

1. In a large pan, heat the oil over medium-high heat until shimmering. 2. Add the curry paste and cook, stirring constantly, for 1 minute. Add the onion, garlic, carrots, and peanuts to the pan, and continue to cook for 2 to 3 minutes until the onion begins to soften. 3. Add the broth and bring to a boil. Reduce the heat to low and simmer for 5 to 6 minutes until the carrots are tender. 4. Using an immersion blender or in a blender, purée the soup until smooth and return it to the pot. With the heat still on low, add the almond milk and stir to combine. Add the shrimp to the pot and cook for 2 to 3 minutes until cooked through. 5. Garnish with cilantro and serve.

Per Serving:

calories: 237 | fat: 14g | protein: 14g | carbs: 17g | sugars: 6g | fiber: 5g | sodium: 619mg

Minestrone with Parmigiano-Reggiano

Prep time: 25 minutes | Cook time: 3 to 8 hours | Serves 8

2 tablespoons extra-virgin olive oil	cabbage, cut into small pieces
3 cloves garlic, minced	8 ounces (227 g) green beans, ends snipped, cut into 1-inch pieces
1 cup coarsely chopped sweet onion	
1 cup coarsely chopped carrots	1 medium head cauliflower, cut into florets
1 cup coarsely chopped celery	Rind from Parmigiano-Reggiano cheese, cut into ½-inch pieces, plus ½ to 1 cup finely grated Parmigiano-Reggiano cheese, for garnish
1 tablespoon finely chopped fresh rosemary	
1 (14- to 15-ounce / 397- to 425-g) can plum tomatoes, with their juice	
¼ cup dry white wine	2 cups vegetable broth
2 medium zucchini, cut into ½-inch rounds	1 teaspoon salt
1 (14- to 15-ounce / 397- to 425-g) can small white beans, drained and rinsed	½ teaspoon freshly ground black pepper
	8 ounces (227 g) cooked small pasta (shells, ditalini, or other short tubular pasta)
1 head escarole or Savoy	

1. Heat the oil in a large skillet over medium-high heat. Add the garlic, onion, carrots, celery, and rosemary and sauté until the vegetables begin to soften, 4 to 5 minutes. 2. Add the tomatoes and wine and allow some of the liquid to evaporate in the pan. 3. Transfer the contents of the skillet to the insert of a 5- to 7-quart slow cooker. Add the zucchini, white beans, cabbage, green beans, cauliflower, Parmigiano-Reggiano rind, broth, salt, and pepper. 4. Cover the slow cooker and cook on high for 3 to 4 hours or on low for 6 to 8 hours. 5. Stir in the cooked pasta at the end of the cooking time, cover, and set on warm until ready to serve. Serve the soup garnished with the grated Parmigiano-Reggiano.

Per Serving:

calories: 224 | fat: 5g | protein: 9g | carbs: 40g | net carbs: 29g | sugars: 11g | fiber: g | sodium: 552mg | cholesterol: 0mg

Vegetarian Chili

Prep time: 25 minutes | Cook time: 10 minutes | Serves 6

2 teaspoons olive oil	1 jalapeño pepper, seeds removed, chopped
3 garlic cloves, minced	
2 onions, chopped	28-ounce can diced Italian tomatoes
1 green bell pepper, chopped	
1 cup textured vegetable protein (T.V.P.)	1 bay leaf
	1 tablespoon dried oregano
1-pound can beans of your choice, drained	½ teaspoons salt
	¼ teaspoons pepper

1. Set the Instant Pot to the Sauté function. As it's heating, add the olive oil, garlic, onions, and bell pepper. Stir constantly for about 5 minutes as it all cooks. Press Cancel. 2. Place all of the remaining ingredients into the inner pot of the Instant pot and stir. 3. Secure the lid and make sure vent is set to sealing. Cook on Manual mode for 10 minutes. 4. When cook time is up, let the steam release naturally for 5 minutes and then manually release the rest.

Per Serving:

calories: 242 | fat: 2g | protein: 17g | carbs: 36g | sugars: 9g | fiber: 12g | sodium: 489mg

Mexican Tortilla Soup

Prep time: 10 minutes | Cook time: 40 minutes | Serves 8

2 tablespoons extra-virgin olive oil	One 15-ounce can low-sodium whole tomatoes, drained and coarsely chopped
1 onion, chopped	
2 cloves garlic, minced	1 medium zucchini, sliced
¼ cup freshly chopped cilantro	1 medium yellow squash, sliced
1 tablespoon cumin	1 cup yellow corn
1 teaspoon cayenne pepper	Six 6-inch corn tortillas
1 quart low-sodium chicken broth	½ cup reduced-fat shredded cheddar cheese

1. Preheat the oven to 350 degrees. 2. In a large saucepan, heat the oil, and sauté the onion and garlic for 5 minutes. 3. Add the cilantro, cumin, and cayenne pepper; sauté for 3 more minutes. Add the remaining ingredients except the tortillas and cheese. Bring to a boil; cover and let simmer for 30 minutes. 4. Cut each tortilla into about 10 strips (use a pizza cutter to do this easily). Place the strips on a cookie sheet and bake for 5–6 minutes at 350 degrees until slightly browned and toasted. Remove from the oven. 5. To serve the soup, place strips of tortilla into each bowl. Ladle the soup on top of the tortilla strips. Top with cheese.

Per Serving:

calories: 193 | fat: 4.48g | protein: 9.22g | carbs: 31.23g | sugars: 3.25g | fiber: 3.4g | sodium: 172mg

Easy Southern Brunswick Stew

Prep time: 20 minutes | Cook time: 8 minutes | Serves 12

2 pounds pork butt, visible fat removed
17-ounce can white corn
1¼ cups ketchup
2 cups diced, cooked potatoes
10-ounce package frozen peas
2 10¾-ounce cans reduced-sodium tomato soup
Hot sauce to taste, optional

1. Place pork in the Instant Pot and secure the lid. 2. Press the Slow Cook setting and cook on low 6–8 hours. 3. When cook time is over, remove the meat from the bone and shred, removing and discarding all visible fat. 4. Combine all the meat and remaining ingredients (except the hot sauce) in the inner pot of the Instant Pot. 5. Secure the lid once more and cook in Slow Cook mode on low for 30 minutes more. Add hot sauce if you wish.

Per Serving:
calories: 213 | fat: 7g | protein: 13g | carbs: 27g | sugars: 9g | fiber: 3g | sodium: 584mg

Pumpkin Soup

Prep time: 15 minutes | Cook time: 30 minutes | Serves 6

2 cups store-bought low-sodium seafood broth, divided
1 bunch collard greens, stemmed and cut into ribbons
1 tomato, chopped
1 garlic clove, minced
1 butternut squash or other
winter squash, peeled and cut into 1-inch cubes
1 teaspoon paprika
1 teaspoon dried dill
2 (5-ounce) cans boneless, skinless salmon in water, rinsed

1. In a heavy-bottomed large stockpot, bring ½ cup of broth to a simmer over medium heat. 2. Add the collard greens, tomato, and garlic and cook for 5 minutes, or until the greens are wilted and the garlic is softened. 3. Add the squash, paprika, dill, and remaining 1½ cups of broth. Cover and cook for 20 minutes, or until the squash is tender. 4. Add the salmon and cook for 3 minutes, or just enough for the flavors to come together.

Per Serving:
calories: 161 | fat: 5.5g | protein: 23.92g | carbs: 4.51g | sugars: 1.18g | fiber: 1g | sodium: 579mg

Freshened-Up French Onion Soup

Prep time: 15 minutes | Cook time: 30 minutes | Serves 2

1 tablespoon extra-virgin olive oil
2 medium onions, sliced
2 cups low-sodium beef broth
1 (8-ounce) can chickpeas, drained and rinsed
½ teaspoon dried thyme
Salt
Freshly ground black pepper
4 slices nonfat Swiss deli-style cheese

1. In a medium soup pot set over medium-low heat, heat the olive oil. 2. Add the onions. Stir to coat them in oil. Cook for about 10 minutes, or until golden brown. 3. Add the beef broth, chickpeas, and thyme. Bring to a simmer. 4. Taste the broth. Season with salt and pepper. Cook for 10 minutes more. 5. Preheat the broiler to high. 6. Ladle the soup into 2 ovenproof soup bowls. 7. Top each with 2 slices of Swiss cheese. Place the bowls on a baking sheet. Carefully transfer the sheet to the preheated oven. Melt the cheese under the broiler for 2 minutes. Alternately, you can melt the cheese in the microwave (in microwave-safe bowls) on high in 30-second intervals until melted. 8. Enjoy immediately.

Per Serving:
calories: 278 | fat: 13.52g | protein: 15.39g | carbs: 28.6g | sugars: 3.04g | fiber: 1.8g | sodium: 804mg

Instantly Good Beef Stew

Prep time: 20 minutes | Cook time: 35 minutes | Serves 6

3 tablespoons olive oil, divided
2 pounds stewing beef, cubed
2 cloves garlic, minced
1 large onion, chopped
3 ribs celery, sliced
3 large potatoes, cubed
2–3 carrots, sliced
8 ounces no-salt-added tomato
sauce
10 ounces low-sodium beef broth
2 teaspoons Worcestershire sauce
¼ teaspoon pepper
1 bay leaf

1. Set the Instant Pot to the Sauté function, then add in 1 tablespoon of the oil. Add in ⅓ of the beef cubes and brown and sear all sides. Repeat this process twice more with the remaining oil and beef cubes. Set the beef aside. 2. Place the garlic, onion, and celery into the pot and sauté for a few minutes. Press Cancel. 3. Add the beef back in as well as all of the remaining ingredients. 4. Secure the lid and make sure the vent is set to sealing. Choose Manual for 35 minutes. 5. When cook time is up, let the pressure release naturally for 15 minutes, then release any remaining pressure manually. 6. Remove the lid, remove the bay leaf, then serve.

Per Serving:
calories: 401 | fat: 20g | protein: 35g | carbs: 19g | sugars: 5g | fiber: 3g | sodium: 157mg

White Bean Soup

Prep time: 15 minutes | Cook time: 20 minutes | Serves 2

1 teaspoon extra-virgin olive oil
⅓ cup chopped yellow onion
1 garlic clove, minced
1 teaspoon dried rosemary
½ cup sliced fresh mushrooms
½ cup jarred roasted red peppers, chopped
1 teaspoon freshly squeezed
lemon juice
1 teaspoon white wine vinegar
1 cup water
1 (15-ounce) can white beans, drained and rinsed
½ cup diced tomatoes, with juice
1½ cups fresh spinach

1. In a large pot set over medium heat, heat the olive oil. 2. Add the onion and garlic. Sauté for about 5 minutes, or until tender. 3. Add the rosemary, mushrooms, red peppers, lemon juice, white wine vinegar, and water. Cook for 5 minutes more, or until the mushrooms are soft. 4. Stir in the white beans, tomatoes, and spinach. Cook for 10 minutes more, or until the spinach is wilted. 5. Serve immediately and enjoy!

Per Serving:
calories: 96 | fat: 4.73g | protein: 3.19g | carbs: 12.65g | sugars: 4.41g | fiber: 4.4g | sodium: 28mg

Beef and Mushroom Barley Soup

Prep time: 10 minutes | Cook time: 1 hour 20 minutes | Serves 6

1 pound beef stew meat, cubed
¼ teaspoon salt
¼ teaspoon freshly ground black pepper
1 tablespoon extra-virgin olive oil
8 ounces sliced mushrooms
1 onion, chopped
2 carrots, chopped
3 celery stalks, chopped
6 garlic cloves, minced
½ teaspoon dried thyme
4 cups low-sodium beef broth
1 cup water
½ cup pearl barley

1. Season the meat with the salt and pepper. 2. In an Instant Pot, heat the oil over high heat. Add the meat and brown on all sides. Remove the meat from the pot and set aside. 3. Add the mushrooms to the pot and cook for 1 to 2 minutes, until they begin to soften. Remove the mushrooms and set aside with the meat. 4. Add the onion, carrots, and celery to the pot. Sauté for 3 to 4 minutes until the vegetables begin to soften. Add the garlic and continue to cook until fragrant, about 30 seconds longer. 5. Return the meat and mushrooms to the pot, then add the thyme, beef broth, and water. Set the pressure to high and cook for 15 minutes. Let the pressure release naturally. 6. Open the Instant Pot and add the barley. Use the slow cooker function on the Instant Pot, affix the lid (vent open), and continue to cook for 1 hour until the barley is cooked through and tender. Serve.

Per Serving:

calories: 245 | fat: 9g | protein: 21g | carbs: 19g | sugars: 3g | fiber: 4g | sodium: 516mg

Lentil Stew

Prep time: 10 minutes | Cook time: 30 minutes | Serves 2

½ cup dry lentils, picked through, debris removed, rinsed and drained
2½ cups water
1 bay leaf
2 teaspoons dried tarragon
2 teaspoons dried thyme
2 garlic cloves, minced
2 medium carrots, chopped
2 medium tomatoes, diced
1 celery stalk, chopped
1 tablespoon extra-virgin olive oil
1 medium onion, diced
1 cup frozen spinach
Salt, to season
Freshly ground black pepper, to season

1. In a soup pot set over high heat, stir together the lentils, water, bay leaf, tarragon, thyme, and garlic. 2. Add the carrots, tomatoes, and celery. Cover. Bring to a boil. Reduce the heat to low and stir the soup. Simmer for 15 to 20 minutes, covered, or until the lentils are tender. 3. While the vegetables simmer, place a skillet over medium heat. Add the olive oil and onion. Sauté for about 10 minutes, or until browned. Remove the skillet from the heat. 4. When the lentils are tender, remove and discard the bay leaf. Add the cooked onion and the spinach to the soup. Heat for 5 to 10 minutes more, or until the spinach is cooked. 5. Season with salt and pepper. 6. Enjoy immediately.

Per Serving:

calories: 214 | fat: 7.4g | protein: 9.84g | carbs: 31.38g | sugars: 9.94g | fiber: 10.9g | sodium: 871mg

Chicken Noodle Soup

Prep time: 15 minutes | Cook time: 20 minutes | Serves 12

2 tablespoons avocado oil
1 medium onion, chopped
3 celery stalks, chopped
1 teaspoon kosher salt
¼ teaspoon freshly ground black pepper
2 teaspoons minced garlic
5 large carrots, peeled and cut into ¼-inch-thick rounds
3 pounds bone-in chicken breasts (about 3)
4 cups Chicken Bone Broth or low-sodium store-bought chicken broth
4 cups water
2 tablespoons soy sauce
6 ounces whole grain wide egg noodles

1. Set the electric pressure cooker to the Sauté setting. When the pot is hot, pour in the avocado oil. 2. Sauté the onion, celery, salt, and pepper for 3 to 5 minutes or until the vegetables begin to soften. 3. Add the garlic and carrots, and stir to mix well. Hit Cancel. 4. Add the chicken to the pot, meat-side down. Add the broth, water, and soy sauce. Close and lock the lid of the pressure cooker. Set the valve to sealing. 5. Cook on high pressure for 20 minutes. 6. When the cooking is complete, hit Cancel and quick release the pressure. Unlock and remove the lid. 7. Using tongs, remove the chicken breasts to a cutting board. Hit Sauté/More and bring the soup to a boil. 8. Add the noodles and cook for 4 to 5 minutes or until the noodles are al dente. 9. While the noodles are cooking, use two forks to shred the chicken. Add the meat back to the pot and save the bones to make more bone broth. 10. Season with additional pepper, if desired, and serve.

Per Serving:

calories: 294 | fat: 13.92g | protein: 26.68g | carbs: 15.28g | sugars: 2.8g | fiber: 2.7g | sodium: 640mg

Pasta e Fagioli

Prep time: 10 minutes | Cook time: 25 minutes | Serves 12

1 tablespoon extra-virgin olive oil
1 large onion, chopped
3 cloves garlic, crushed
2 medium carrots, sliced
2 medium zucchini, sliced
2 tablespoons finely chopped fresh basil
2 teaspoons finely chopped
fresh oregano
Two 14.5-ounce cans unsalted tomatoes with liquid
Two 15-ounce cans low-sodium white cannellini or navy beans, drained and rinsed
¾ pound whole-wheat uncooked rigatoni or shell pasta

1. In a large saucepan, heat the oil and sauté the onion and garlic for 5 minutes. 2. Add the carrots, zucchini, basil, oregano, tomatoes with their liquid, and beans. Cook until the vegetables are just tender, about 15–17 minutes. 3. In a separate saucepan, cook the pasta according to package directions (without adding salt). Add the pasta to the soup, and mix thoroughly. Serve warm with crusty bread.

Per Serving:

calories: 84 | fat: 1.2g | protein: 3.81g | carbs: 15.64g | sugars: 1.16g | fiber: 3.1g | sodium: 68mg

Quick Moroccan-Inspired Chicken Stew

Prep time: 5 minutes | Cook time: 15 minutes | Serves 4 to 6

2 teaspoons ground cumin
1 teaspoon ground cinnamon
½ teaspoon turmeric
½ teaspoon paprika
1½ pounds boneless, skinless chicken, cut into strips
2 tablespoons extra-virgin olive oil

5 garlic cloves, smashed and coarsely chopped
2 onions, thinly sliced
1 tablespoon fresh lemon zest
½ cup coarsely chopped olives
2 cups low-sodium chicken broth
Cilantro, for garnish (optional)

1. In a medium bowl, mix together the cumin, cinnamon, turmeric, and paprika until well blended. Add the chicken, tossing to coat, and set aside. 2. Heat the extra-virgin olive oil in a large skillet or medium Dutch oven over medium-high heat. Add the chicken and garlic in one layer and cook, browning on all sides, about 2 minutes. 3. Add the onions, lemon zest, olives, and broth and bring the soup to a boil. Reduce the heat to medium low, cover, and simmer for 8 minutes. 4. Uncover the soup and let it simmer for another 2 to 3 minutes for the sauce to thicken slightly. Adjust the seasonings as desired and serve garnished with cilantro (if using). 5. Store the cooled soup in an airtight container in the refrigerator for up to 5 days.

Per Serving:

calories: 252 | fat: 10.35g | protein: 12.62g | carbs: 27.57g | sugars: 6.45g | fiber: 2.6g | sodium: 451mg

Chicken Tortilla Soup

Prep time: 10 minutes | Cook time: 35 minutes | Serves 4

1 tablespoon extra-virgin olive oil
1 onion, thinly sliced
1 garlic clove, minced
1 jalapeño pepper, diced
2 boneless, skinless chicken breasts
4 cups low-sodium chicken broth
1 roma tomato, diced

½ teaspoon salt
2 (6-inch) corn tortillas, cut into thin strips
Nonstick cooking spray
Juice of 1 lime
Minced fresh cilantro, for garnish
¼ cup shredded cheddar cheese, for garnish

1. In a medium pot, heat the oil over medium-high heat. Add the onion and cook for 3 to 5 minutes until it begins to soften. Add the garlic and jalapeño, and cook until fragrant, about 1 minute more. 2. Add the chicken, chicken broth, tomato, and salt to the pot and bring to a boil. Reduce the heat to medium and simmer gently for 20 to 25 minutes until the chicken breasts are cooked through. Remove the chicken from the pot and set aside. 3. Preheat a broiler to high. 4. Spray the tortilla strips with nonstick cooking spray and toss to coat. Spread in a single layer on a baking sheet and broil for 3 to 5 minutes, flipping once, until crisp. 5. When the chicken is cool enough to handle, shred it with two forks and return to the pot. 6. Season the soup with the lime juice. Serve hot, garnished with cilantro, cheese, and tortilla strips.

Per Serving:

calories: 191 | fat: 8g | protein: 19g | carbs: 13g | sugars: 2g | fiber: 2g | sodium: 482mg

Hot and Sour Soup

Prep time: 0 minutes | Cook time: 30 minutes | Serves 6

4 cups boiling water
1 ounce dried shiitake mushrooms
2 tablespoons cold-pressed avocado oil
3 garlic cloves, chopped
4 ounces cremini or button mushrooms, sliced
1 pound boneless pork loin, sirloin, or tip, thinly sliced against the grain into ¼-inch-thick, ½-inch-wide, 2-inch-long strips
1 teaspoon ground ginger
½ teaspoon ground white pepper

2 cups low-sodium chicken broth or vegetable broth
One 8-ounce can sliced bamboo shoots, drained and rinsed
2 tablespoons low-sodium soy sauce
1 tablespoon chile garlic sauce
1 teaspoon toasted sesame oil
2 teaspoons Lakanto Monkfruit Sweetener Classic
2 large eggs
¼ cup rice vinegar
2 tablespoons cornstarch
4 green onions, white and green parts, thinly sliced
¼ cup chopped fresh cilantro

1. In a large liquid measuring cup or heatproof bowl, pour the boiling water over the shiitake mushrooms. Cover and let soak for 30 minutes. Drain the mushrooms, reserving the soaking liquid. Remove and discard the stems and thinly slice the caps. 2. Select the Sauté setting on the Instant Pot and heat the avocado oil and garlic for 2 minutes, until the garlic is bubbling but not browned. Add the cremini and shiitake mushrooms and sauté for 3 minutes, until the mushrooms are beginning to wilt. Add the pork, ginger, and white pepper and sauté for about 5 minutes, until the pork is opaque and cooked through. 3. Pour the mushroom soaking liquid into the pot, being careful to leave behind any sediment at the bottom of the measuring cup or bowl. Using a wooden spoon, nudge any browned bits from the bottom of the pot. Stir in the broth, bamboo shoots, soy sauce, chile garlic sauce, sesame oil, and sweetener. 4. Secure the lid and set the Pressure Release to Sealing. Press the Cancel button to reset the cooking program, then select the Pressure Cook or Manual setting and set the cooking time for 5 minutes at high pressure. (The pot will take about 10 minutes to come up to pressure before the cooking program begins.) 5. While the soup is cooking, in a small bowl, beat the eggs until no streaks of yolk remain. 6. When the cooking program ends, let the pressure release naturally for at least 15 minutes, then move the Pressure Release to Venting to release any remaining steam. 7. In a small bowl, stir together the vinegar and cornstarch until the cornstarch dissolves. Open the pot and stir the vinegar mixture into the soup. Press the Cancel button to reset the cooking program, then select the Sauté setting. Bring the soup to a simmer and cook, stirring occasionally, for about 3 minutes, until slightly thickened. While stirring the soup constantly, pour in the beaten eggs in a thin stream. Press the Cancel button to turn off the pot and then stir in the green onions and cilantro. 8. Ladle the soup into bowls and serve hot.

Per Serving:

calories: 231 | fat: 13g | protein: 21g | carbs: 14g | sugars: 2g | fiber: 3g | sodium: 250mg

Butternut Squash Soup

Prep time: 30 minutes | Cook time: 15 minutes | Serves 4

2 tablespoons margarine
1 large onion, chopped
2 cloves garlic, minced
1 teaspoon thyme
½ teaspoon sage

Salt and pepper to taste
2 large butternut squash, peeled, seeded, and cubed (about 4 pounds)
4 cups low-sodium chicken stock

1. In the inner pot of the Instant Pot, melt the margarine using Sauté function. 2. Add onion and garlic and cook until soft, 3 to 5 minutes. 3. Add thyme and sage and cook another minute. Season with salt and pepper. 4. Stir in butternut squash and add chicken stock. 5. Secure the lid and make sure vent is at sealing. Using Manual setting, cook squash and seasonings 10 minutes, using high pressure. 6. When time is up, do a quick release of the pressure. 7. Puree the soup in a food processor or use immersion blender right in the inner pot. If soup is too thick, add more stock. Adjust salt and pepper as needed.

Per Serving:

calories: 279 | fat: 7g | protein: 6g | carbs: 56g | sugars: 10g | fiber: 9g | sodium: 144mg

Nancy's Vegetable Beef Soup

Prep time: 25 minutes | Cook time: 8 hours | Serves 8

2-pound roast, cubed, or 2 pounds stewing meat
15-ounce can corn
15-ounce can green beans
1-pound bag frozen peas

40-ounce can no-added-salt stewed tomatoes
5 teaspoons salt-free beef bouillon powder
Tabasco, to taste
½ teaspoons salt

1. Combine all ingredients in the Instant Pot. Do not drain vegetables. 2. Add water to fill inner pot only to the fill line. 3. Secure the lid, or use the glass lid and set the Instant Pot on Slow Cook mode, Low for 8 hours, or until meat is tender and vegetables are soft.

Per Serving:

calories: 229 | fat: 5g | protein: 23g | carbs: 24g | sugars: 10g | fiber: 6g | sodium: 545mg

Chapter 14 Pizzas, Wraps, and Sandwiches

Caesar Chicken Sandwiches

Prep time: 5 minutes | Cook time: 0 minutes | Serves 4

FOR THE DRESSING
4 tablespoons plain low-fat Greek yogurt
4 teaspoons Dijon mustard
4 teaspoons freshly squeezed lemon juice
4 teaspoons shredded Parmesan cheese
¼ teaspoon freshly ground black pepper
⅛ teaspoon garlic powder

FOR THE SANDWICHES
2 cups shredded rotisserie chicken
1½ cups chopped romaine lettuce
12 cherry tomatoes, halved
4 sandwich thins, 100% whole-wheat
¼ cup thinly sliced red onion (optional)

TO MAKE THE DRESSING 1. In a small bowl, whisk together the yogurt, mustard, lemon juice, Parmesan cheese, black pepper, and garlic powder. TO MAKE THE SANDWICHES 2. In a large bowl, combine the chicken, lettuce, and tomatoes. Add the dressing and stir until evenly coated. Divide the filling into four equal portions. 3. Slice the sandwich thins so there is a top and bottom half for each. Put one portion of filling on each of the bottom halves and cover with the top halves.

Tuna, Hummus, and Veggie Wraps

Prep time: 10 minutes | Cook time: 0 minutes | Serves 2

FOR THE HUMMUS
1 cup from 1 (15-ounce) can low-sodium chickpeas, drained and rinsed
2 tablespoons tahini
1 tablespoon extra-virgin olive oil
1 garlic clove
Juice of ½ lemon

¼ teaspoon salt
2 tablespoons water
FOR THE WRAPS
4 large lettuce leaves
1 (5-ounce) can chunk light tuna packed in water, drained
1 red bell pepper, seeded and cut into strips
1 cucumber, sliced

TO MAKE THE HUMMUS In a blender jar, combine the chickpeas, tahini, olive oil, garlic, lemon juice, salt, and water. Process until smooth. Taste and adjust with additional lemon juice or salt, as needed. TO MAKE THE WRAPS 1. On each lettuce leaf, spread 1 tablespoon of hummus, and divide the tuna among the leaves. Top each with several strips of red pepper and cucumber slices. 2. Roll up the lettuce leaves, folding in the two shorter sides and rolling away from you, like a burrito. Serve.
Per Serving:
calories: 191 | fat: 5g | protein: 26g | carbs: 15g | sugars: 6g | fiber: 4g | sodium: 357mg

Cauli-Lettuce Wraps

Prep time: 10 minutes | Cook time: 20 minutes | Serves 2 to 4

1½ tablespoons sesame oil
½ yellow onion, chopped
8 ounces mushrooms, thinly sliced
4 garlic cloves, minced
1½ tablespoons low-sodium soy sauce or tamari
4 teaspoons rice wine vinegar
5 ounces water chestnuts, drained and liquid reserved

2½ cups cauliflower rice
½ cup coarsely chopped cashews
4 large green leaf lettuce leaves
2 scallions, both white and green parts, thinly sliced (optional)
1 cup chopped cilantro (optional)

1. Heat the sesame oil in a large skillet over medium heat and sauté the onion until translucent, about 3 minutes. Add the mushrooms, garlic, tamari, vinegar, and water chestnuts to the skillet. Cover the skillet with a lid and cook until the mushrooms are softened, about 5 minutes. 2. Add the cauliflower and cashews and mix well. Cover the skillet and cook for 2 minutes. 3. Adjust the seasonings as desired and evenly divide the cauliflower mixture among the lettuce leaves. 4. Serve garnished with scallions (if using) and cilantro (if using). 5. Store any leftovers in an airtight container in the refrigerator for up to 2 days.

Grilled Nut Butter Sandwich

Prep time: 5 minutes | Cook time: 8 minutes | Serves 1

2–3 teaspoons almond or other nut butter (can substitute sunflower butter, Wowbutter, or tigernut butter)
2 slices sprouted grain bread

½ cup sliced ripe banana or apple
¼ teaspoon cinnamon
⅓ cup unsweetened applesauce

1. Place a nonstick skillet over medium-high heat. Spread about half of the nut butter on one slice of bread, then top with the banana or apple and cinnamon. Spread the remaining nut butter on the other slice of bread. Close up the sandwich, and place it in the skillet. Cook for 3 to 4 minutes, or until lightly browned. Flip and cook for another 3 to 4 minutes, or until lightly browned. Transfer to a cooling rack (so the underside doesn't soften) to cool slightly, then transfer to a plate and cut in half. Serve with the applesauce for dipping.
Per Serving:
calorie: 332 | fat: 8g | protein: 9g | carbs: 60g | sugars: 20g | fiber: 7g | sodium: 412mg

Turkey Pastrami and Pimento Cheese Sandwich

Prep time: 5 minutes | Cook time: 0 minutes | Serves 2

FOR THE PIMENTO
CHEESE (ENOUGH FOR 4
SANDWICHES)
6 ounces sharp cheddar cheese,
shredded
3 tablespoons cream cheese,
softened
1 tablespoon plain Greek yogurt
2 teaspoons diced pimentos

FOR THE TURKEY
PASTRAMI SANDWICH
4 ounces Pimento Cheese
4 slices marble rye bread
6 ounces low-sodium turkey
pastrami or peppered turkey
4 lettuce leaves
1 red bell pepper, cut into strips

TO MAKE THE PIMENTO CHEESE 1. In a medium bowl, cream together the cheddar, cream cheese, and yogurt using a spoon. 2. Add the pimentos and stir to combine. If it's too thick, add a bit of water or pimento juice. TO MAKE THE TURKEY PASTRAMI SANDWICH 3. Spread the pimento cheese on each slice of marble rye bread. Layer the turkey pastrami and lettuce on the cheese spread on two of the bread slices. Place the other two slices of bread, cheese-side down, on the fillings, creating the sandwich. 4. Serve the sandwiches accompanied by sliced red bell pepper.

Open-Faced Egg Salad Sandwiches

Prep time: 10 minutes | Cook time: 0 minutes | Serves 4

8 large hardboiled eggs
3 tablespoons plain low-fat
Greek yogurt
1 tablespoon mustard
½ teaspoon freshly ground
black pepper

1 teaspoon chopped fresh
chives
4 slices 100% whole-wheat
bread
2 cups fresh spinach, loosely
packed

1. Peel the eggs and cut them in half. 2. In a large bowl, mash the eggs with a fork, leaving chunks. 3. Add the yogurt, mustard, pepper, and chives, and mix. 4. For each portion, layer 1 slice of bread with one-quarter of the egg salad and spinach.

Roasted Tomato Tartine

Prep time: 5 minutes | Cook time: 15 minutes | Serves 2

3 tomatoes, cut into eighths
2 tablespoons extra-virgin olive
oil, divided
1 tablespoon balsamic vinegar
2 garlic cloves, minced
Pinch kosher salt
Pinch freshly ground black

pepper
½ cup ricotta cheese
2 slices whole-grain bread
2 tablespoons chopped fresh
basil
4 cups arugula

1. Preheat the oven to 450°F. Line a baking sheet with parchment paper. 2. In a medium-size bowl, toss the tomatoes with 1 tablespoon of extra-virgin olive oil, the vinegar, garlic, salt, and pepper. 3. Spread the tomatoes on the baking sheet and bake for 15 minutes. 4. Meanwhile, place the ricotta in the bowl of a food processor and, while it is running, add the remaining 1 tablespoon of extra-virgin olive oil in a thin stream. Pause to scrape down the sides if needed. Taste and adjust the seasonings as needed. If you do not have a food processor, whisk the ricotta and extra-virgin olive oil in a medium bowl. 5. Toast the bread and divide the ricotta between the slices, spreading it out evenly. Top the ricotta with the tomatoes and garnish with chopped basil. 6. Serve with the greens on the side.

Red Pepper, Goat Cheese, and Arugula Open-Faced Grilled Sandwich

Prep time: 5 minutes | Cook time: 15 minutes | Serves 1

½ red bell pepper, seeded
Nonstick cooking spray
1 slice whole-wheat thin-sliced
bread (I love Ezekiel sprouted
bread and Dave's Killer Bread)

2 tablespoons crumbled goat
cheese
Pinch dried thyme
½ cup arugula

1. Preheat the broiler to high. Line a baking sheet with parchment paper. 2. Cut the ½ bell pepper lengthwise into two pieces and arrange on the prepared baking sheet with the skin facing up. 3. Broil for 5 to 10 minutes until the skin is blackened. Transfer to a covered container to steam for 5 minutes, then remove the skin from the pepper using your fingers. Cut the pepper into strips. 4. Heat a small skillet over medium-high heat. Spray it with nonstick cooking spray and place the bread in the skillet. Top with the goat cheese and sprinkle with the thyme. Pile the arugula on top, followed by the roasted red pepper strips. Press down with a spatula to hold in place. 5. Cook for 2 to 3 minutes until the bread is crisp and browned and the cheese is warmed through. (If you prefer, you can make a half-closed sandwich instead: Cut the bread in half and place one half in the skillet. Top with the cheese, thyme, arugula, red pepper, and the other half slice of bread. Cook for 4 to 6 minutes, flipping once, until both sides are browned.)

Per Serving:

calories: 109 | fat: 2g | protein: 4g | carbs: 21g | sugars: 5g | fiber: 6g | sodium: 123mg

Miso, Tempeh, and Carrot Wraps

Prep time: 10 minutes | Cook time: 10 minutes | Serves 1

2 collard green leaves, washed
½ cup shredded carrots
1 teaspoon grated ginger
(optional)
½ tablespoon white or yellow
miso

½ tablespoon rice vinegar
½ tablespoon sesame oil
Nonstick cooking oil spray
4 ounces smoky tempeh, sliced
1 cup bean sprouts
4 radishes, thinly sliced

1. Fill a large saucepan three-quarters full of water and bring it to a boil over high heat. Blanch the collard greens for 3 minutes, remove them from the water, and cool immediately under cold running water. Allow to dry and blot with a towel to remove excess water. 2. In a medium bowl, combine the carrots, ginger (if using), miso, vinegar, and sesame oil until well mixed. 3. Lightly grease a large skillet with cooking spray and heat it over medium heat. Panfry the tempeh slices until crispy on each side, about 2 minutes per side. 4. Place the collard greens on a clean work surface and evenly divide the carrot mixture, tempeh, bean sprouts, and radishes between them. Fold over the end of each leaf, tuck one side under, and roll like a burrito. Serve. 5. Store any leftovers in an airtight container in the refrigerator for up to 2 days.

Chicken Salad Sandwiches

Prep time: 10 minutes | Cook time: 10 minutes | Serves 4

Avocado oil cooking spray
2 (4-ounce) boneless, skinless chicken breasts
⅛ teaspoon freshly ground black pepper
1½ tablespoons plain low-fat Greek yogurt

¼ cup halved purple seedless grapes
¼ cup chopped pecans
2 tablespoons chopped celery
4 sandwich thins, 100% whole-wheat

1. Heat a small skillet over medium-low heat. When hot, coat the cooking surface with cooking spray. 2. Season the chicken with the pepper. Place the chicken in the skillet and cook for 6 minutes. Flip and cook for 3 to 5 minutes more, or until cooked through. 3. Remove the chicken from the skillet and let cool for 5 minutes. 4. Chop or shred the chicken. 5. Combine the chicken, yogurt, grapes, pecans, and celery. 6. Cut the sandwich thins in half, so there is a top and bottom. 7. Divide the chicken salad into four equal portions, spoon one portion on each of the bottom halves of the sandwich thins, and cover with the top halves.

Thai-Style Chicken Roll-Ups

Prep time: 15 minutes | Cook time: 0 minutes | Serves 4

1½ cups shredded cooked chicken breast
1 cup bean sprouts
1 cup shredded green cabbage
½ cup shredded carrots
¼ cup chopped scallions, both white and green parts
¼ cup chopped fresh cilantro

2 tablespoons natural peanut butter
2 tablespoons water
1 tablespoon rice wine vinegar
1 garlic clove, minced
¼ teaspoon salt
4 (8-inch) low-carb whole-wheat tortillas

1. In a large mixing bowl, toss the chicken breast, bean sprouts, cabbage, carrots, scallions, and cilantro. 2. In a medium bowl, whisk together the peanut butter, water, rice vinegar, garlic, and salt. 3. Fill each tortilla with about 1 cup of the chicken and vegetable mixture, and spoon a tablespoon of sauce over the filling. 4. Fold in two opposite sides of the tortilla and roll up. Serve.

Per Serving:
calories: 210 | fat: 8g | protein: 21g | carbs: 17g | sugars: 3g | fiber: 10g | sodium: 360mg

Red Lentil Sloppy Joes with Roasted Asparagus

Prep time: 8 minutes | Cook time: 20 minutes | Serves 2

1 bunch asparagus, woody ends removed
1 tablespoon extra-virgin olive oil, divided
½ cup chopped onion
2 teaspoons chopped serrano pepper (optional)

2 garlic cloves, minced
1½ cups water
½ cup red lentils, rinsed
2 tablespoons ketchup
1 teaspoon paprika
1 sandwich thin or other bread option

1. Preheat the oven to 450°F. Line a baking sheet with parchment paper. 2. In a small bowl, toss the asparagus with 1½ teaspoons of extra-virgin olive oil until well coated, and spread the vegetables on the prepared baking sheet. Bake for 12 to 15 minutes. 3. Meanwhile, heat the remaining 1½ teaspoons of extra-virgin olive oil in a medium saucepan over medium heat and sauté the onion and pepper (if using) until soft and translucent, 2 to 3 minutes. Add the garlic and cook for 1 minute. 4. Add the water and lentils and bring to a boil. Reduce the heat to low and simmer, stirring occasionally, until the lentils are tender but not falling apart, about 10 minutes. 5. Add the ketchup and paprika. Adjust seasonings as desired and allow the mixture to thicken over the heat for a couple of minutes. 6. Serve on a sandwich thin or slice of bread with a side of roasted asparagus. 7. Store any leftover filling in an airtight container in the refrigerator for up to 5 days.

Smoked Salmon on Toast

Prep time: 10 minutes | Cook time: 0 minutes | Serves 4

FOR THE CREAM CHEESE SPREAD
4 ounces cream cheese
Juice of 1 lemon
1 teaspoon stone-ground mustard
FOR THE SANDWICH

4 slices whole-grain bread
8 ounces smoked salmon
4 radishes, thinly sliced
1 teaspoon capers, rinsed and dried (optional)
¼ cup chopped fresh dill
1 medium cucumber, sliced

TO MAKE THE CREAM CHEESE SPREAD 1. In a small bowl, combine the cream cheese, 1 teaspoon of lemon juice, and mustard. Cream together evenly and add more lemon juice if it's too thick. You should be able to spread it on a slice of bread easily. TO MAKE THE SANDWICH 2. Spread the cream cheese mixture on each slice of bread and top with the salmon, radish slices, capers (if using), and fresh dill. 3. Serve with cucumber slices on the side.

Open-Faced Chicken and Onion Grilled Cheese

Prep time: 10 minutes | Cook time: 15 minutes | Serves 4

1 small yellow onion
Avocado oil cooking spray
2 cups shredded rotisserie chicken
1½ tablespoons unsalted butter

4 slices 100% whole-wheat bread
3 slices provolone or Swiss cheese
2 cups fresh spinach

1. Cut the onion into ½-inch rounds. Leave them intact; do not separate. 2. Heat a medium or large skillet over medium-low heat. When hot, coat the cooking surface with cooking spray. Place the onions in the skillet. Cover and cook for 7 to 10 minutes, or until the onions are translucent. Remove from the skillet. 3. Meanwhile, shred the chicken, and butter one side of each slice of bread. Tear each slice of cheese into 3 strips. 4. Place 2 or 3 strips of cheese on the nonbuttered side of each piece of bread, then place the buttered side down on the skillet. 5. Layer one-quarter of the onion, spinach, and shredded chicken on top of each slice of bread. 6. Toast for 2 to 3 minutes over medium-low heat.

Prep time: 5 minutes | Cook time: 22 minutes | Serves 2

¼ pound ground bison
¼ pound ground beef
½ teaspoon garlic powder
½ teaspoon onion powder
½ teaspoon extra-virgin olive oil
1 small jicama, peeled
Juice of 1 lime

Chili powder (optional)
Bun (optional)
1 tomato, thinly sliced
4 lettuce leaves
OPTIONAL TOPPINGS
Other burger toppings (cheese, onions, mushrooms, etc.)

1. Preheat a grill to medium-high heat. 2. In a large bowl, combine the bison, beef, garlic powder, and onion powder until mixed well. Do not overhandle, squeeze, or compress the meat. 3. Divide the meat into two equal pieces and form each into a patty. 4. Lightly oil both sides of the burger to prevent sticking and grill on the first side for 5 to 6 minutes, or until juices start to come through. Turn once and grill on the other side for another 5 to 6 minutes, or until the internal temperature is 160°F. If you want to add cheese, layer on a slice during the last minute. 5. If you do not have a grill, heat a grill pan or cast-iron skillet with 1 tablespoon of oil over medium-high heat and cook the burgers, turning once, until they reach the correct internal temperature, about 14 minutes in total. 6. Let the burgers rest 5 to 10 minutes, so the juices settle, then add the desired toppings. 7. Meanwhile, slice the jicama into ¼-inch-thick slices, then into quarters. Put the jicama in a medium bowl and add the lime juice and chili powder (if using) to taste. 8. Serve the burgers on a bun, or wrapped in lettuce if you're watching carbs, with your favorite toppings and a side of jicama.

Chapter 15 Desserts

Baked Berry Cups with Crispy Cinnamon Wedges

Prep time: 25 minutes | Cook time: 30 minutes | Serves 4

2 teaspoons sugar
3⁄4 teaspoon ground cinnamon
Butter-flavor cooking spray
1 balanced carb whole wheat
tortilla (6 inch)
1⁄4 cup sugar
2 tablespoons white whole
wheat flour

1 teaspoon grated orange peel,
if desired
11⁄2 cups fresh blueberries
11⁄2 cups fresh raspberries
About 1 cup fat-free whipped
cream topping (from aerosol
can)

1 Heat oven to 375°F. In sandwich-size resealable food-storage plastic bag, combine 2 teaspoons sugar and 1⁄2 teaspoon of the cinnamon. Using cooking spray, spray both sides of tortilla, about 3 seconds per side; cut tortilla into 8 wedges. In bag with cinnamon-sugar, add wedges; seal bag. Shake to coat wedges evenly. 2 On ungreased cookie sheet, spread out wedges. Bake 7 to 9 minutes, turning once, until just beginning to crisp (wedges will continue to crisp while cooling). Cool about 15 minutes. 3 Meanwhile, spray 4 (6-oz) custard cups or ramekins with cooking spray; place cups on another cookie sheet. In small bowl, stir 1⁄4 cup sugar, the flour, orange peel and remaining 1⁄4 teaspoon cinnamon until blended. In medium bowl, gently toss berries with sugar mixture; divide evenly among custard cups. 4 Bake 15 minutes; stir gently. Bake 5 to 7 minutes longer or until liquid is bubbling around edges. Cool at least 15 minutes. 5 To serve, top each cup with about 1⁄4 cup whipped cream topping; serve tortilla wedges with berry cups. Serve warm.

Per Serving:
calorie: 180 | fat: 2g | protein: 3g | carbs: 37g | sugars: 25g | fiber: 7g | sodium: 60mg

Chipotle Black Bean Brownies

Prep time: 15 minutes | Cook time: 30 minutes | Serves 8

Nonstick cooking spray
1⁄2 cup dark chocolate chips,
divided
3⁄4 cup cooked calypso beans or
black beans
1⁄2 cup extra-virgin olive oil
2 large eggs
1⁄4 cup unsweetened dark
chocolate cocoa powder

1⁄3 cup honey
1 teaspoon vanilla extract
1⁄3 cup white wheat flour
1⁄2 teaspoon chipotle chili
powder
1⁄2 teaspoon ground cinnamon
1⁄2 teaspoon baking powder
1⁄2 teaspoon kosher salt

1. Spray a 7-inch Bundt pan with nonstick cooking spray. 2. Place half of the chocolate chips in a small bowl and microwave them for 30 seconds. Stir and repeat, if necessary, until the chips have completely melted. 3. In a food processor, blend the beans and oil together. Add the melted chocolate chips, eggs, cocoa powder, honey, and vanilla. Blend until the mixture is smooth. 4. In a large bowl, whisk together the flour, chili powder, cinnamon, baking powder, and salt. Pour the bean mixture from the food processor into the bowl and stir with a wooden spoon until well combined. Stir in the remaining chocolate chips. 5. Pour the batter into the prepared Bundt pan. Cover loosely with foil. 6. Pour 1 cup of water into the electric pressure cooker. 7. Place the Bundt pan onto the wire rack and lower it into the pressure cooker. 8. Close and lock the lid of the pressure cooker. Set the valve to sealing. 9. Cook on high pressure for 30 minutes. 10. When the cooking is complete, hit Cancel and quick release the pressure. 11. Once the pin drops, unlock and remove the lid. 12. Carefully transfer the pan to a cooling rack for about 10 minutes, then invert the cake onto the rack and let it cool completely. 13. Cut into slices and serve.

Per Serving:
(1 slice): calories: 296 | fat: 20g | protein: 5g | carbs: 29g | sugars: 16g | fiber: 4g | sodium: 224mg

Cream Cheese Swirl Brownies

Prep time: 10 minutes | Cook time: 20 minutes | Serves 12

2 eggs
1⁄4 cup unsweetened applesauce
1⁄4 cup coconut oil, melted
3 tablespoons pure maple syrup,
divided
1⁄4 cup unsweetened cocoa

powder
1⁄4 cup coconut flour
1⁄4 teaspoon salt
1 teaspoon baking powder
2 tablespoons low-fat cream
cheese

1. Preheat the oven to 350°F. Grease an 8-by-8-inch baking dish. 2. In a large mixing bowl, beat the eggs with the applesauce, coconut oil, and 2 tablespoons of maple syrup. 3. Stir in the cocoa powder and coconut flour, and mix well. Sprinkle the salt and baking powder evenly over the surface and mix well to incorporate. Transfer the mixture to the prepared baking dish. 4. In a small, microwave-safe bowl, microwave the cream cheese for 10 to 20 seconds until softened. Add the remaining 1 tablespoon of maple syrup and mix to combine. 5. Drop the cream cheese onto the batter, and use a toothpick or chopstick to swirl it on the surface. Bake for 20 minutes, until a toothpick inserted in the center comes out clean. Cool and cut into 12 squares. 6. Store refrigerated in a covered container for up to 5 days.

Per Serving:
calories: 84 | fat: 6g | protein: 2g | carbs: 6g | sugars: 4g | fiber: 2g | sodium: 93mg

Chocolate Chip Banana Cake

Prep time: 15 minutes | Cook time: 25 minutes | Serves 8

Nonstick cooking spray
3 ripe bananas
½ cup buttermilk
3 tablespoons honey
1 teaspoon vanilla extract
2 large eggs, lightly beaten
3 tablespoons extra-virgin olive oil

1½ cups whole wheat pastry flour
⅛ teaspoon ground nutmeg
1 teaspoon ground cinnamon
¼ teaspoon salt
1 teaspoon baking soda
⅓ cup dark chocolate chips

1. Spray a 7-inch Bundt pan with nonstick cooking spray. 2. In a large bowl, mash the bananas. Add the buttermilk, honey, vanilla, eggs, and olive oil, and mix well. 3. In a medium bowl, whisk together the flour, nutmeg, cinnamon, salt, and baking soda. 4. Add the flour mixture to the banana mixture and mix well. Stir in the chocolate chips. Pour the batter into the prepared Bundt pan. Cover the pan with foil. 5. Pour 1 cup of water into the electric pressure cooker. Place the pan on the wire rack and lower it into the pressure cooker. 6. Close and lock the lid of the pressure cooker. Set the valve to sealing. 7. Cook on high pressure for 25 minutes. 8. When the cooking is complete, hit Cancel and quick release the pressure. 9. Once the pin drops, unlock and remove the lid. 10. Carefully transfer the pan to a cooling rack, uncover, and let it cool for 10 minutes. 11. Invert the cake onto the rack and let it cool for about an hour. 12. Slice and serve the cake.

Per Serving:

(1 slice): calories: 261 | fat: 11g | protein: 6g | carbs: 39g | sugars: 16g | fiber: 4g | sodium: 239mg

Double-Ginger Cookies

Prep time: 45 minutes | Cook time: 8 to 10 minutes | Makes 5 dozen cookies

¾ cup sugar
¼ cup butter or margarine, softened
1 egg or ¼ cup fat-free egg product
¼ cup molasses
1¾ cups all-purpose flour
1 teaspoon baking soda

½ teaspoon ground cinnamon
½ teaspoon ground ginger
¼ teaspoon ground cloves
¼ teaspoon salt
¼ cup sugar
¼ cup orange marmalade
2 tablespoons finely chopped crystallized ginger

1 In medium bowl, beat ¾ cup sugar, the butter, egg and molasses with electric mixer on medium speed, or mix with spoon. Stir in flour, baking soda, cinnamon, ground ginger, cloves and salt. Cover and refrigerate at least 2 hours, until firm. 2 Heat oven to 350°F. Lightly spray cookie sheets with cooking spray. Place ¼ cup sugar in small bowl. Shape dough into ¾-inch balls; roll in sugar. Place balls about 2 inches apart on cookie sheet. Make indentation in center of each ball, using finger. Fill each indentation with slightly less than ¼ teaspoon of the marmalade. Sprinkle with crystallized ginger. 3 Bake 8 to 10 minutes or until set. Immediately transfer from cookie sheets to cooling racks. Cool completely, about 30 minutes.

Per Serving:

1 Cookie: calorie: 45 | fat: 1g | protein: 0g | carbs: 9g | sugars: 5g | fiber: 0g | sodium: 40mg

Chewy Chocolate-Oat Bars

Prep time: 20 minutes | Cook time: 30 minutes | Makes 16 bars

¾ cup semisweet chocolate chips
⅓ cup fat-free sweetened condensed milk (from 14-oz can)
1 cup whole wheat flour
½ cup quick-cooking oats
½ teaspoon baking powder
½ teaspoon baking soda
¼ teaspoon salt

¼ cup fat-free egg product or 1 egg
¾ cup packed brown sugar
¼ cup canola oil
1 teaspoon vanilla
2 tablespoons quick-cooking oats
2 teaspoons butter or margarine, softened

1 Heat oven to 350°F. Spray 8-inch or 9-inch square pan with cooking spray. 2 In 1-quart saucepan, heat chocolate chips and milk over low heat, stirring frequently, until chocolate is melted and mixture is smooth. Remove from heat. 3 In large bowl, mix flour, ½ cup oats, the baking powder, baking soda and salt; set aside. In medium bowl, stir egg product, brown sugar, oil and vanilla with fork until smooth. Stir into flour mixture until blended. Reserve ½ cup dough in small bowl for topping. 4 Pat remaining dough in pan (if dough is sticky, spray fingers with cooking spray or dust with flour). Spread chocolate mixture over dough. Add 2 tablespoons oats and the butter to reserved ½ cup dough; mix with pastry blender or fork until well mixed. Place small pieces of mixture evenly over chocolate mixture. 5 Bake 20 to 25 minutes or until top is golden and firm. Cool completely, about 1 hour 30 minutes. For bars, cut into 4 rows by 4 rows.

Per Serving:

1 Bar: calorie: 180 | fat: 7g | protein: 3g | carbs: 27g | sugars: 18g | fiber: 1g | sodium: 115mg

Fruit Dessert Topping

Prep time: 15 minutes | Cook time: 3hours 30 to 4 hours | Serves 40

3 tart apples, peeled and sliced
3 pears, peeled and sliced
1 tablespoon lemon juice
2 tablespoons brown sugar
Brown sugar substitute to equal 1 tablespoon sugar
2 tablespoons maple syrup

2 tablespoons light, soft tub margarine, melted
½ cup chopped pecans
¼ cup raisins
2 cinnamon sticks
1 tablespoon cornstarch
2 tablespoons cold water

1. Toss apples and pears in lemon juice in Instant Pot. 2. Combine brown sugar, brown sugar substitute, maple syrup, and margarine. Pour over fruit. 3. Stir in pecans, raisins, and cinnamon sticks. 4. Secure lid and press Slow Cook mode. Set on low 3–4 hours. 5. Combine cornstarch and water until smooth. Gradually stir into Instant Pot when cooking time is up. 6. Press Sauté and continue to cook until sauce is thickened, stirring frequently. 7. Discard cinnamon sticks.

Per Serving:

calories: 33 | fat: 1g | protein: 0g | carbs: 6g | sugars: 5g | fiber: 1g | sodium: 5mg

No-Added-Sugar Orange and Cream Slushy

Prep time: 5 minutes | Cook time: 0 minutes | Serves 2

½ cup (120 ml) unsweetened vanilla almond milk
½ cup (100 g) plain whole-milk yogurt
2 small oranges, peeled, seeds and pith removed, and frozen

1 small banana, frozen
1 tsp pure vanilla extract
2 tbsp (10 g) unsweetened coconut flakes
1 tbsp (12 g) chia seeds

1. In a high-power blender, combine the almond milk, yogurt, oranges, banana, vanilla, coconut flakes, and chia seeds. Blend the ingredients for 30 to 45 seconds, until a slushy consistency is reached.

Per Serving:

calorie: 203 | fat: 7g | protein: 8g | carbs: 29g | sugars: 17g | fiber: 7g | sodium: 67mg

Basic Pie Crust

Prep time: 10 minutes | Cook time: 40 minutes | Serves 9

¾ cup cake flour
½ teaspoon sugar
 teaspoon salt
3 tablespoons canola oil, frozen

for 15 minutes
½ teaspoon white vinegar
2 tablespoons ice water

1. In a medium bowl, combine the flour, sugar, and salt. Stir in the oil and mix until the mixture is the size of small peas. 2. Add the vinegar and ice water and mix with a fork until the dough starts to hold together. Gather into a ball, wrap, and refrigerate at least 30 minutes before rolling out. 3. Roll out the pie crust to fit an 8- or 9-inch pie dish. Lay the rolled dough in the pan without stretching it, and crimp the edges. 4. If the recipe requires a baked pie crust, preheat the oven to 425 degrees. Prick the crust with a fork, and lay a piece of parchment or wax paper in the pie shell. Pour in enough dried beans to cover the bottom (this prevents the crust from bubbling up while baking). Bake for 8 minutes or until golden brown.

Per Serving:

calories: 84 | fat: 5g | protein: 1g | carbs: 9g | sugars: 0g | fiber: 0g | sodium: 129mg

Cinnamon Spiced Baked Apples

Prep time: 10 minutes | Cook time: 15 minutes | Serves 4

2 apples, peeled, cored, and chopped
2 tablespoons pure maple syrup

½ teaspoon cinnamon
½ teaspoon ground ginger
¼ cup chopped pecans

1. Preheat the oven to 350°F. 2. In a bowl, mix the apples, syrup, cinnamon, and ginger. Pour the mixture into a 9-inch square baking dish. Sprinkle the pecans over the top. 3. Bake until the apples are tender, about 15 minutes.

Per Serving:

calories: 122 | fat: 5g | protein: 1g | carbs: 20g | sugars: 14g | fiber: 3g | sodium: 2mg

Crustless Peanut Butter Cheesecake

Prep time: 10 minutes | Cook time: 10 minutes | Serves 2

4 ounces (113 g) cream cheese, softened
2 tablespoons confectioners' erythritol

1 tablespoon all-natural, no-sugar-added peanut butter
½ teaspoon vanilla extract
1 large egg, whisked

1. In a medium bowl, mix cream cheese and erythritol until smooth. Add peanut butter and vanilla, mixing until smooth. Add egg and stir just until combined. 2. Spoon mixture into an ungreased springform pan and place into air fryer basket. Adjust the temperature to 300°F (149°C) and bake for 10 minutes. Edges will be firm, but center will be mostly set with only a small amount of jiggle when done. 3. Let pan cool at room temperature 30 minutes, cover with plastic wrap, then place into refrigerator at least 2 hours. Serve chilled.

Per Serving:

calories: 281 | fat: 26g | protein: 8g | carbs: 4g | net carbs: 4g | fiber: 0g

Crustless Key Lime Cheesecake

Prep time: 15 minutes | Cook time: 35 minutes | Serves 8

Nonstick cooking spray
16 ounces light cream cheese (Neufchâtel), softened
⅔ cup granulated erythritol sweetener
¼ cup unsweetened Key lime juice (I like Nellie & Joe's

Famous Key West Lime Juice)
½ teaspoon vanilla extract
¼ cup plain Greek yogurt
1 teaspoon grated lime zest
2 large eggs
Whipped cream, for garnish (optional)

1. Spray a 7-inch springform pan with nonstick cooking spray. Line the bottom and partway up the sides of the pan with foil. 2. Put the cream cheese in a large bowl. Use an electric mixer to whip the cream cheese until smooth, about 2 minutes. Add the erythritol, lime juice, vanilla, yogurt, and zest, and blend until smooth. Stop the mixer and scrape down the sides of the bowl with a rubber spatula. With the mixer on low speed, add the eggs, one at a time, blending until just mixed. (Don't overbeat the eggs.) 3. Pour the mixture into the prepared pan. Drape a paper towel over the top of the pan, not touching the cream cheese mixture, and tightly wrap the top of the pan in foil. (Your goal here is to keep out as much moisture as possible.) 4. Pour 1 cup of water into the electric pressure cooker. 5. Place the foil-covered pan onto the wire rack and carefully lower it into the pot. 6. Close and lock the lid of the pressure cooker. Set the valve to sealing. 7. Cook on high pressure for 35 minutes. 8. When the cooking is complete, hit Cancel. Allow the pressure to release naturally for 20 minutes, then quick release any remaining pressure. 9. Once the pin drops, unlock and remove the lid. 10. Using the handles of the wire rack, carefully transfer the pan to a cooling rack. Cool to room temperature, then refrigerate for at least 3 hours. 11. When ready to serve, run a thin rubber spatula around the rim of the cheesecake to loosen it, then remove the ring. 12. Slice into wedges and serve with whipped cream (if using).

Per Serving:

calories: 127 | fat: 2g | protein: 11g | carbs: 17g | sugars: 14g | fiber: 0g | sodium: 423mg

Blackberry Yogurt Ice Pops

Prep time: 10 minutes | Cook time: 0 minutes | Serves 4

12 ounces plain Greek yogurt
1 cup blackberries
Pinch nutmeg
¼ cup milk
2 (1-gram) packets stevia

1. In a blender, combine all of the ingredients. Blend until smooth.
2. Pour the mixture into 4 ice pop molds. Freeze for 6 hours before serving.

Per Serving:

calories: 71 | fat: 1g | protein: 10g | carbs: 8g | sugars: 5g | fiber: 2g | sodium: 37mg

Fried Apples

Prep time: 5 minutes | Cook time: 15 minutes | Serves 6 to 8

4 Pink Lady apples, quartered
¼ cup erythritol or other brown
sugar replacement

1. In a small mixing bowl, toss the apples in the erythritol. Working in batches, place in the basket of an air fryer. 2. Set the air fryer to 390°F, close, and cook for 15 minutes. 3. Once cooking is complete, transfer the apples to a plate. Repeat until no apples remain.

Per Serving:

calories: 50 | fat: 0g | protein: 0g | carbs: 13g | sugars: 9g | fiber: 2g | sodium: 5mg

Strawberry Cream Cheese Crepes

Prep time: 10 minutes | Cook time: 10 minutes | Serves 4

½ cup old-fashioned oats
1 cup unsweetened plain almond milk
1 egg
3 teaspoons honey, divided
Nonstick cooking spray
2 ounces low-fat cream cheese
¼ cup low-fat cottage cheese
2 cups sliced strawberries

1. In a blender jar, process the oats until they resemble flour. Add the almond milk, egg, and 1½ teaspoons honey, and process until smooth. 2. Heat a large skillet over medium heat. Spray with nonstick cooking spray to coat. 3. Add ¼ cup of oat batter to the pan and quickly swirl around to coat the bottom of the pan and let cook for 2 to 3 minutes. When the edges begin to turn brown, flip the crepe with a spatula and cook until lightly browned and firm, about 1 minute. Transfer to a plate. Continue with the remaining batter, spraying the skillet with nonstick cooking spray before adding more batter. Set the cooked crepes aside, loosely covered with aluminum foil, while you make the filling. 4. Clean the blender jar, then combine the cream cheese, cottage cheese, and remaining 1½ teaspoons honey, and process until smooth. 5. Fill each crepe with 2 tablespoons of the cream cheese mixture, topped with ¼ cup of strawberries. Serve.

Per Serving:

calories: 149 | fat: 6g | protein: 6g | carbs: 20g | sugars: 10g | fiber: 3g | sodium: 177mg

Blueberry Chocolate Clusters

Prep time: 5 minutes | Cook time: 5 minutes | Serves 10

1½ cups dark chocolate chips
1 tablespoon coconut oil, melted
½ cups chopped, toasted pecans
2 cups blueberries

1. Line a baking sheet with parchment paper. 2. Melt the chocolate in a microwave-safe bowl in 20- to 30-second intervals. 3. In a medium bowl, combine the melted chocolate with the coconut oil and pecans. 4. Spoon a small amount of chocolate mixture (about 1 teaspoon) on the prepared baking sheet. 5. Place a cluster of about 5 blueberries on top of the chocolate. You should get about 20 clusters in total. 6. Drizzle a small amount of chocolate over the berries. 7. Freeze until set, about 15 minutes. 8. Store in an airtight container in the refrigerator for up to 5 days or in the freezer for up to 1 month.

Per Serving:

calories: 224 | fat: 17g | protein: 3g | carbs: 17g | sugars: 9g | fiber: 4g | sodium: 6mg

Grilled Watermelon with Avocado Mousse

Prep time: 10 minutes | Cook time: 10 minutes | Serves 8

1 small, seedless watermelon, halved and cut into 1-inch rounds
2 ripe avocados, pitted and
peeled
½ cup fat-free plain yogurt
¼ teaspoon cayenne pepper

1. On a hot grill, grill the watermelon slices for 2 to 3 minutes on each side, or until you can see the grill marks. 2. To make the avocado mousse, in a blender, combine the avocados, yogurt, and cayenne and process until smooth. 3. To serve, cut each watermelon round in half. Top each with a generous dollop of avocado mousse.

Per Serving:

calories: 162 | fat: 8g | protein: 3g | carbs: 22g | sugars: 14g | fiber: 5g | sodium: 13mg

Raspberry Nice Cream

Prep time: 5 minutes | Cook time: 0 minutes | Serves 3

2 cups frozen, sliced, overripe bananas
2 cups frozen or fresh raspberries
Pinch of sea salt
1–2 tablespoons coconut nectar or 1–1½ tablespoons pure maple syrup

1. In a food processor or high-speed blender, combine the bananas, raspberries, salt, and 1 tablespoon of the nectar or syrup. Puree until smooth. Taste, and add the remaining nectar or syrup, if desired. Serve immediately, if you like a soft-serve consistency, or transfer to an airtight container and freeze for an hour or more, if you like a firmer texture.

Per Serving:

calorie: 193| fat: 1g | protein: 3g | carbs: 47g | sugars: 24g | fiber: 13g | sodium: 101mg

Banana Bread Nice Cream

Prep time: 5 minutes | Cook time: 0 minutes | Serves 3

½ cup (packed) pitted dates
¼–⅓ cup plain or vanilla low-fat nondairy milk
1 tablespoon raw cashew or raw almond butter

¼ teaspoon ground nutmeg
A couple pinches of sea salt
2 cups frozen, sliced, overripe bananas

1. In a blender, combine the dates with ¼ cup of the milk. (If you're using a high-speed blender, that should be enough milk, but if you're using a regular blender you may need to use ⅓ cup of the milk.) Blend until smooth. Add the nut butter, nutmeg, and salt, and blend. Add about half of the bananas and puree until the mixture is smooth, then add the remaining bananas and puree again until smooth. Transfer to a container and freeze for 1 to 2 hours (for soft serve) or 4 to 5 hours or overnight for a firmer-set ice cream.

Per Serving:
calorie: 198 | fat: 3g | protein: 3g | carbs: 44g | sugars: 29g | fiber: 5g | sodium: 205mg

Olive Oil Cake

Prep time: 10 minutes | Cook time: 30 minutes | Serves 8

2 cups blanched finely ground almond flour
5 large eggs, whisked
¾ cup extra-virgin olive oil

⅓ cup granular erythritol
1 teaspoon vanilla extract
1 teaspoon baking powder

1. In a large bowl, mix all ingredients. Pour batter into an ungreased round nonstick baking dish. 2. Place dish into air fryer basket. Adjust the temperature to 300ºF (149ºC) and bake for 30 minutes. The cake will be golden on top and firm in the center when done. 3. Let cake cool in dish 30 minutes before slicing and serving.

Per Serving:
calories: 363 | fat: 35g | protein: 9g | carbs: 6g | net carbs: 3g | fiber: 3g

Oatmeal Raisin Cookies

Prep time: 5 minutes | Cook time: 15 minutes | Serves 6

3 cups rolled oats
1 cup whole-wheat flour
1 teaspoon baking soda
2 teaspoons cinnamon
½ cup raisins

¼ cup unsweetened applesauce
¼ cup agave nectar
½ cup egg substitute
½ cup plain fat-free yogurt
1 teaspoon vanilla

1. Preheat the oven to 350 degrees. 2. In a medium bowl, combine the oats, flour, baking soda, cinnamon, and raisins. 3. In a large bowl, beat the applesauce, agave nectar, egg substitute, yogurt, and vanilla until creamy. Slowly add the dry ingredients, and mix together. 4. Spray cookie sheets with nonstick cooking spray, and drop by teaspoonfuls onto the cookie sheets. Bake for 12–15 minutes at 350 degrees; transfer to racks, and cool.

Per Serving:
calories: 274 | fat: 4g | protein: 14g | carbs: 64g | sugars: 16g | fiber: 10g | sodium: 56mg

Cherry Almond Cobbler

Prep time: 10 minutes | Cook time: 25 minutes | Serves 4

2 cups water-packed sour cherries
¼ teaspoon fresh lemon juice
⅛ teaspoon almond extract
½ cup almond flour, sifted
⅛ teaspoon salt
¼ cup flaxseeds

¾ teaspoon baking powder
1 tablespoon canola oil
¼ cup egg substitute
2 tablespoons fat-free milk
¼ cup granulated sugar substitute (such as stevia)

1. Preheat the oven to 425 degrees. Drain the cherries, reserving ⅔ cup of liquid, and place the cherries in a shallow 9-inch glass or porcelain cake pan. 2. In a small mixing bowl, combine the lemon juice, almond extract, and drained cherry liquid; mix well. Spoon over the cherries. 3. In a mixing bowl, combine the almond flour, flaxseeds, and baking powder. Mix thoroughly. Stir in the oil, egg substitute, milk, and sugar substitute, mixing well. 4. Spoon the mixture over the cherries, and bake at 425 degrees for 25–30 minutes or until the crust is golden brown.

Per Serving:
calories: 216 | fat: 14g | protein: 7g | carbs: 19g | sugars: 10g | fiber: 6g | sodium: 132mg

Lemon Dessert Shots

Prep time: 30 minutes | Cook time: 0 minutes | Serves 12

10 gingersnap cookies
2 oz ⅓-less-fat cream cheese (Neufchâtel), softened
½ cup marshmallow crème (from 7-oz jar)
1 container (6 oz) fat-free

Greek honey vanilla yogurt
½ cup lemon curd (from 10-oz jar)
36 fresh raspberries
½ cup frozen (thawed) lite whipped topping

1 In 1-quart resealable food-storage plastic bag, place cookies; seal bag. Crush with rolling pin or meat mallet; place in small bowl. 2 In medium bowl, beat cream cheese and marshmallow crème with electric mixer on low speed until smooth. Beat in yogurt until blended. Place mixture in 1-quart resealable food-storage plastic bag; seal bag. In 1-pint resealable food-storage plastic bag, place lemon curd; seal bag. Cut ⅛-inch opening diagonally across bottom corner of each bag. 3 In bottom of each of 12 (2-oz) shot glasses, place 1 raspberry. For each glass, pipe about 2 teaspoons yogurt mixture over raspberry. Pipe ¼-inch ring of lemon curd around edge of glass; sprinkle with about 1 teaspoon cookies. Repeat. 4 Garnish each dessert shot with dollop of about 2 teaspoons whipped topping and 1 raspberry. Place in 9-inch square pan. Refrigerate 30 minutes or until chilled but no longer than 3 hours.

Per Serving:
calorie: 110 | fat: 3g | protein: 2g | carbs: 18g | sugars: 14g | fiber: 0g | sodium: 70mg

Chewy Barley-Nut Cookies

Prep time: 45 minutes | Cook time: 10 to 14 minutes | Makes 2 dozen cookies

1/3 cup canola oil
1/2 cup granulated sugar
1/4 cup packed brown sugar
1/4 cup reduced-fat mayonnaise or salad dressing
1 teaspoon vanilla
1 egg
2 cups rolled barley flakes or 2 cups plus 2 tablespoons old-

fashioned oats
3/4 cup whole wheat flour
1/2 teaspoon baking soda
1/2 teaspoon salt
1/4 teaspoon ground cinnamon
1/3 cup "heart-healthy" mixed nuts (peanuts, almonds, pistachios, pecans, hazelnuts)

1 Heat oven to 350°F. Spray cookie sheet with cooking spray. 2 In medium bowl, mix oil, sugars, mayonnaise, vanilla and egg with spoon. Stir in barley, flour, baking soda, salt and cinnamon. Stir in nuts. 3 Drop dough by rounded tablespoonfuls 2 inches apart onto cookie sheet. 4 Bake 10 to 14 minutes or until edges are golden brown. Cool 2 minutes; transfer from cookie sheet to cooling rack.

Per Serving:
1 Cookie: calorie: 150 | fat: 5g | protein: 2g | carbs: 23g | sugars: 7g | fiber: 3g | sodium: 110mg

Mango Nice Cream

Prep time: 10 minutes | Cook time: 0 minutes | Serves 4

2 cups frozen mango chunks
1 cup frozen, sliced, overripe banana (can use room temperature, but must be overripe)
Pinch of sea salt

1/2 teaspoon pure vanilla extract
1/4 cup + 1–2 tablespoons low-fat nondairy milk
2–3 tablespoons coconut nectar or pure maple syrup (optional)

1. In a food processor or high-speed blender, combine the mango, banana, salt, vanilla, and 1/4 cup of the milk. Pulse to get things moving, and then puree, adding the remaining 1 to 2 tablespoons milk if needed. Taste, and add the nectar or syrup, if desired. Serve, or transfer to an airtight container and freeze for an hour or more to set more firmly before serving.

Per Serving:
calorie: 116 | fat: 0.5g | protein: 1g | carbs: 29g | sugars: 22g | fiber: 2g | sodium: 81mg

Oatmeal Cookies

Prep time: 5 minutes | Cook time: 15 minutes | Serves 16

3/4 cup almond flour
3/4 cup old-fashioned oats
1/4 cup shredded unsweetened coconut
1 teaspoon baking powder
1 teaspoon ground cinnamon

1/4 teaspoon salt
1/4 cup unsweetened applesauce
1 large egg
1 tablespoon pure maple syrup
2 tablespoons coconut oil, melted

1. Preheat the oven to 350°F. 2. In a medium mixing bowl, combine the almond flour, oats, coconut, baking powder, cinnamon, and salt, and mix well. 3. In another medium bowl, combine the applesauce, egg, maple syrup, and coconut oil, and mix. Stir the wet mixture

into the dry mixture. 4. Form the dough into balls a little bigger than a tablespoon and place on a baking sheet, leaving at least 1 inch between them. Bake for 12 minutes until the cookies are just browned. Remove from the oven and let cool for 5 minutes. 5. Using a spatula, remove the cookies and cool on a rack.

Per Serving:
calorie: 76 | fat: 6g | protein: 2g | carbs: 5g | sugars: 1g | fiber: 1g | sodium: 57mg

5-Ingredient Chunky Cherry and Peanut Butter Cookies

Prep time: 5 minutes | Cook time: 10 to 12 minutes | Makes 12 cookies

1 cup (240 g) all-natural peanut butter
1/4 cup (60 ml) pure maple syrup
1 large egg, beaten

1 cup (80 g) gluten-free rolled or quick oats
1/2 cup (80 g) dried cherries

1. Preheat the oven to 350°F (177°C). Line a large baking sheet with parchment paper. 2. In a large bowl, whisk together the peanut butter, maple syrup, and egg. Add the oats and cherries, and mix until the ingredients are combined. 3. Chill the dough for 10 to 15 minutes. 4. Use a cookie scoop to scoop balls of the dough onto the prepared baking sheet. 5. Using a fork, gently flatten the dough balls into your desired shape (the cookies will not change shape much during baking). Bake the cookies for 10 to 12 minutes, until they are lightly golden on top. 6. Remove the cookies from the oven and let them cool for 5 minutes before transferring them to a wire rack.

Per Serving:
calorie: 198 | fat: 12g | protein: 7g | carbs: 19g | sugars: 11g | fiber: 3g | sodium: 13mg

Mixed-Berry Snack Cake

Prep time: 15 minutes | Cook time: 28 to 33 minutes | Serves 8

1/4 cup low-fat granola
1/2 cup buttermilk
1/3 cup packed brown sugar
2 tablespoons canola oil
1 teaspoon vanilla
1 egg
1 cup whole wheat flour

1/2 teaspoon baking soda
1/2 teaspoon ground cinnamon
1/8 teaspoon salt
1 cup mixed fresh berries (such as blueberries, raspberries and blackberries)

1 Heat oven to 350°F. Spray 8- or 9-inch round pan with cooking spray. Place granola in resealable food-storage plastic bag; seal bag and slightly crush with rolling pin or meat mallet. Set aside. 2 In large bowl, stir buttermilk, brown sugar, oil, vanilla and egg until smooth. Stir in flour, baking soda, cinnamon and salt just until moistened. Gently fold in half of the berries. Spoon into pan. Sprinkle with remaining berries and the granola. 3 Bake 28 to 33 minutes or until golden brown and top springs back when touched in center. Cool in pan on cooling rack 10 minutes. Serve warm.

Per Serving:
calorie: 160 | fat: 5g | protein: 3g | carbs: 26g | sugars: 12g | fiber: 1g | sodium: 140mg

Chocolate Cupcakes

Prep time: 10 minutes | Cook time: 20 minutes | Serves 12

3 tablespoons canola oil
¼ cup agave nectar
¼ cup egg whites
1 teaspoon vanilla
1 teaspoon cold espresso or strong coffee
½ cup fat-free milk

1¼ cups quinoa flour
¼ cup ground walnuts
6 tablespoons cocoa powder
2 teaspoons baking powder
¼ teaspoon baking soda

1. Preheat the oven to 375 degrees. 2. In a medium bowl, beat the oil with the agave nectar, egg whites, vanilla, espresso, and milk. 3. In a separate bowl, combine the quinoa flour, walnuts, cocoa powder, baking powder, and baking soda. Add to the creamed mixture, and mix until smooth. 4. Spoon the batter into paper-lined muffin tins, and bake at 375 degrees for 20 minutes. Remove from the oven and let cool.

Per Serving:

calories: 113 | fat: 5g | protein: 3g | carbs: 15g | sugars: 4g | fiber: 2g | sodium: 43mg

Banana Pineapple Freeze

Prep time: 30 minutes | Cook time: 0 minutes | Serves 12

2 cups mashed ripe bananas
2 cups unsweetened orange juice
2 tablespoon fresh lemon juice

1 cup unsweetened crushed pineapple, undrained
½ teaspoon ground cinnamon

1. In a food processor, combine all ingredients, and process until smooth and creamy. 2. Pour the mixture into a 9-x-9-x-2-inch baking dish, and freeze overnight or until firm. Serve chilled.

Per Serving:

calories: 60 | fat: 0g | protein: 1g | carbs: 15g | sugars: 9g | fiber: 1g | sodium: 1mg

Appendix 1: Measurement Conversion Chart

MEASUREMENT CONVERSION CHART

VOLUME EQUIVALENTS(DRY)

US STANDARD	METRIC (APPROXIMATE)
1/8 teaspoon	0.5 mL
1/4 teaspoon	1 mL
1/2 teaspoon	2 mL
3/4 teaspoon	4 mL
1 teaspoon	5 mL
1 tablespoon	15 mL
1/4 cup	59 mL
1/2 cup	118 mL
3/4 cup	177 mL
1 cup	235 mL
2 cups	475 mL
3 cups	700 mL
4 cups	1 L

WEIGHT EQUIVALENTS

US STANDARD	METRIC (APPROXIMATE)
1 ounce	28 g
2 ounces	57 g
5 ounces	142 g
10 ounces	284 g
15 ounces	425 g
16 ounces (1 pound)	455 g
1.5 pounds	680 g
2 pounds	907 g

VOLUME EQUIVALENTS(LIQUID)

US STANDARD	US STANDARD (OUNCES)	METRIC (APPROXIMATE)
2 tablespoons	1 fl.oz.	30 mL
1/4 cup	2 fl.oz.	60 mL
1/2 cup	4 fl.oz.	120 mL
1 cup	8 fl.oz.	240 mL
1 1/2 cup	12 fl.oz.	355 mL
2 cups or 1 pint	16 fl.oz.	475 mL
4 cups or 1 quart	32 fl.oz.	1 L
1 gallon	128 fl.oz.	4 L

TEMPERATURES EQUIVALENTS

FAHRENHEIT(F)	CELSIUS(C) (APPROXIMATE)
225 °F	107 °C
250 °F	120 °C
275 °F	135 °C
300 °F	150 °C
325 °F	160 °C
350 °F	180 °C
375 °F	190 °C
400 °F	205 °C
425 °F	220 °C
450 °F	235 °C
475 °F	245 °C
500 °F	260 °C

Appendix 2: The Dirty Dozen and Clean Fifteen

The Dirty Dozen and Clean Fifteen

The Environmental Working Group (EWG) is a nonprofit, nonpartisan organization dedicated to protecting human health and the environment Its mission is to empower people to live healthier lives in a healthier environment. This organization publishes an annual list of the twelve kinds of produce, in sequence, that have the highest amount of pesticide residue-the Dirty Dozen-as well as a list of the fifteen kinds ofproduce that have the least amount of pesticide residue-the Clean Fifteen.

THE DIRTY DOZEN		THE CLEAN FIFTEEN	
• The 2016 Dirty Dozen includes the following produce. These are considered among the year's most important produce to buy organic:		• The least critical to buy organically are the Clean Fifteen list. The following are on the 2016 list:	
Strawberries	Spinach	Avocados	Papayas
Apples	Tomatoes	Corn	Kiw
Nectarines	Bell peppers	Pineapples	Eggplant
Peaches	Cherry tomatoes	Cabbage	Honeydew
Celery	Cucumbers	Sweet peas	Grapefruit
Grapes	Kale/collard greens	Onions	Cantaloupe
Cherries	Hot peppers	Asparagus	Cauliflower
		Mangos	
• *The Dirty Dozen list contains two additional itemskale/collard greens and hot peppers-because they tend to contain trace levels of highly hazardous pesticides.*		• *Some of the sweet corn sold in the United States are made from genetically engineered (GE) seedstock. Buy organic varieties of these crops to avoid GE produce.*	

Appendix 3 Recipes Index

V

W

Y

Z

Made in the USA
Las Vegas, NV
31 March 2023